Land Economics

Monograph Series

Number 3

a publication of

LAND ECONOMICS

a quarterly journal devoted to the study of
economic and social institutions

Land Reform in Latin America

Land Reform
in Latin America:
Issues and Cases

Edited by Peter Dorner

published by

Land Economics

for the Land Tenure Center

at the University of Wisconsin–Madison

1971

This book is dedicated to Professors
Kenneth H. Parsons
and
Raymond J. Penn

Contents

ACKNOWLEDGEMENTS

The several authors of the chapters in this book are deeply indebted to the many Latin American farmers, farm workers, and leaders of campesino organizations who gave freely of their time in providing economic and social information on their farming activities. Similar credit goes to the government officials, administrators, and technicians of various agencies who provided ideas and information for many of the research projects underlying this volume. We thank the many students and colleagues, in both Latin America and the United States, whose research made this volume possible. Although it is impossible to mention all of them by name, we wish to express our gratitude to all these individuals and to the institutions of which they are a part.

Many organizations and institutions have contributed to the research and training program of the Land Tenure Center. Some have provided professional help, others shared costs and cooperated with us in field research, and many sent students to the University of Wisconsin to work with faculty members associated with the Center. Most of the Center's research was carried out in Chile, Colombia, Bolivia, Brazil, Venezuela, Costa Rica, Guatemala and Nicaragua. In these countries we had the close cooperation of professionals from faculties of economics, sociology, law, and agronomy at several major universities. Likewise we have had the full cooperation and assistance of the agrarian reform agencies and institutes in these countries. We have had especially close working relationships and shared office facilities with the following: Instituto de Economía of the University of Chile; Departamento de Sociología, Universidad de Colombia; Centro Inter-americano de Reforma Agraria in Colombia; Servicio Nacional de Reforma Agraria in Bolivia; Centro Latino Americano de Pesquisas em Ciências Sociais in Brazil; Centro de Estudios de Desarrollo of the Central University in Venezuela; Consejo Superior Universitario Centroamericano, at the University of Costa Rica; Instituto de Investigaciones Económicas y Sociales of San Carlos University in Guatemala; and the Instituto Agrario Nacional in Nicaragua. In addition, we have had close professional ties and have cooperated with many professionals in international agencies: the Food and Agricultural Organization (FAO) of the United Nations; the Comité Inter-americano de Desarrollo Agrícola (CIDA) and the several agencies which are its sponsors—FAO, The United Nations Economic Commission for Latin America (ECLA), the Organization of American States (OAS), the Inter-American Institute for Agricultural Sciences (IICA), and the Inter-American Development Bank (IDB): and the Instituto de Capacitación e Investigación en Reforma Agraria in Santiago, Chile. To all the above named Faculties, institutes, and organizations—and to the many more that we cannot acknowledge individually—we express our sincere thanks and appreciation.

The Land Tenure Center could not function without the interest and cooperation of many on the Madison campus: the cooperating departments in which faculty hold appointments; the administration of the College of Agricultural and Life Sciences and of the University. We appreciate their interest and helpful cooperation over the past decade. We also thank all those who gave of their time and provided guidance to the Center's programs through their service on the Center's Advisory and Executive committees.

Three of our late colleagues were very active in formulating the Center's programs and guiding some of its research in the early years of its existence. We acknowledge the contributions of these three men: Jacob Beuscher, Professor of Law, Harlow Halvorson, Professor and Chairman of Agricultural Economics, and Mike Sund, CIDA Research Director in Venezuela.

Many of the ideas as well as the professional inspiration underlying the research discussed in this volume are attributable to the two men to whom it is dedicated: Kenneth H. Parsons and Raymond J. Penn, both Professors of Agricultural Economics. Professor Penn was Director of the Land Tenure Center during its first three years.

Professors Bryant A. Kearl and Robert L. Clodius not only contributed ideas to the Center's work, but also developed in the initial years the administrative flexibility necessary to make the Land Tenure Center a reality. Many social scientists, young and old, associated with the Center have been inspired and challenged by the ideas of Emeritus Professor of Philosophy, Carl Bögholt. Mrs. Julia Schwenn, Mr. Don Esser and Mrs. Teresa Anderson contributed significantly to the Center's work, managing program, office and library. In our field offices, Mrs. Silvia de Cabezas in Chile, Mrs. Olga de Muñoz in Colombia, and Mrs. Yolanda Kallmannsohn in Bolivia performed the many secretarial and office management functions contributing to effective operation. To all the above, and to the faithful work of the remainder of our Madison and other office staffs in the various Latin American countries over the years, we express our deep appreciation.

This book is therefore the result of wide cooperation and participation. On the Madison campus, the authors (with the exception of Ronald Clark who was in Latin America during this period) met frequently over a period of eighteen months to comment on and critically review various chapters as they were being written. Professor Harlan Davis, formerly with the University of Georgia, prepared a research report on United States aid to Latin America, the conclusions of which are incorporated in the final chapter. Research Associates Elsa Chaney and Rubens Medina met with the authors on numerous occasions to discuss manuscript drafts. But as everyone knows who has worked on an effort of this kind, there are innumerable tasks that need to be performed in the process of getting a manuscript to press. We wish to express our special thanks and appreciation to Mrs. Kenna Jarvis and Mr. John Bielefeldt for their skillful assistance. Mrs. Jarvis assembled reference materials, maintained files, and typed and re-typed draft manuscripts. Mr. Bielefeldt edited early drafts, consulted with authors on organization and style, and supervised the preparation of the manuscripts. Both also had the frustrating task of trying to keep the several authors on schedule in the preparation of their respective chapters. Finally, we wish to express our thanks for the financial assistance received from the United States Agency for International Development (AID). A number of other agencies and institutions also provided substantial financial support for both student and faculty salaries. Among these were the Ford and Rockefeller Foundations, the FAO, the Agricultural Development Council, the Midwest Universities Consortium on International Activities, the Ibero-American program of the University of Wisconsin, several United States AID field missions, and the University of Wisconsin. We gratefully acknowledge this assistance.

The views expressed in this book reflect the ideas of many individuals who have worked on these issues over the years. Present interpretations, however, are those of this book's authors and do not imply agreement by any of the supporting or cooperating individuals, agencies, or institutions.

FOREWORD

On May 11, 1962 the University of Wisconsin and the Agency for International Development entered into a contract to establish a Land Tenure Center. The goal was a research and training program integrated in such a way that training could be accomplished by performing research on land tenure and development issues in the rural areas of Latin American countries. Research projects were jointly formulated by the professionals of the host country, staff of the University of Wisconsin, and by both United States and Latin American students. Naturally it was hoped that analysis of the problems selected would prove valuable for policy decisions of the host country, of the United States government, of international agencies, and of other nations confronting similar problems.

Land Tenure Center research has involved the ideas and methods of many social science disciplines—most frequently, agricultural and general economics, rural and general sociology, agricultural journalism and mass communications, law, political science, and anthropology. Direct study and interviews carried out in rural communities have been the major source of research data. This emphasis was adopted since previously there had been so little policy oriented research which made use of primary data. Land tenure, land ownership, and resource control are critical and often overlooked problems. Tenure patterns obviously are related to the way in which resources are used and hence often affect development. Such patterns cannot be very well understood without looking at working rules at the local level and at who enforces those rules.

It is no accident that the University of Wisconsin should establish such a land tenure research and training center. From the beginnings of social science research there, studies have focused on problems in the field, observed the limitations of working rules, and experimented with or designed new rules to improve the situation.

One of Wisconsin's early economists, Richard T. Ely, held a continuing interest in the ownership of resources and how ownership affected land use. In 1914 he published his *Property and Contract*. Ely brought to Wisconsin persons such as John R. Commons who studied labor movements and labor organizations. When Professor Commons found a labor problem, he proposed policy changes to improve the situation. When labor safety was the issue, he worked out a system agreeable to both employees and employers. The result was what has come to be known as workmen's compensation insurance.

Ely, Commons, and their associates trained people to work in widely different areas. But whatever the field, their basic approach included acquisition of primary data on the problem, inter-disciplinary cooperation when necessary, and comprehension of the working rules or property interests involved. Professor B. H. Hibbard, a student and associate of Professor Ely, directed attention to land use problems, particularly those in rural areas. *A History of the Public Land Policies* by Hibbard is a scholarly source of information on the land policies of the United States. *Land Economics* by Professor Ely and Professor George Wehrwein was for many years the primary text for students interested in this field. In the late 1920s Hibbard was conducting research on land taxation, tax distribution, and tax delinquency. Professor Wehrwein was active in promoting the preparation of resource information and land use inventories. Professor Walter A. Rowlands was leading a "Land Use Planning" extension program in Wisconsin. As one result of these various efforts, more than one-third of the state's counties enacted zoning ordinances.

International land tenure problems were a part of regular seminars as early as the 1920s. Professors Ely, Hibbard, and later Wehrwein devoted every other year of their Land Tenure Problems seminar to the study of these issues in other countries. More recently, Professor Kenneth H. Parsons and his students developed further this work in land tenure.

In 1950, Hugh H. Bennett, the first chief of the Technical Cooperation Administration (TCA, predecessor of the present Agency for International Development) spoke to the annual Land Grant College Association meeting. Mr. Bennett asked what the universities could best do to improve United States foreign policy and to assist developing nations. Dean Rudolph Froker and Associate Director of the Experiment Station, Noble Clark, decided as a result of Wisconsin's long experience to attempt a new contribution in the field of land tenure. They asked Professors Raymond J. Penn of Agricultural Economics and William Sewell of Rural Sociology to initiate the preparation of a proposal on land tenure for submission to TCA. The proposal, prepared with major help from Professor Kenneth H. Parsons of Agricultural Economics, suggested a Wisconsin Conference on World Land Tenure Problems to be held in the Fall of 1951. The proposal was approved by the federal government, and three representatives from each of forty countries were invited to the conference. Insofar as possible, one representative was a senior academician, one a senior government administrator responsible for land programs, and one a junior person with promise in his country and ability to continue for a year of special training or graduate study. The conference met for six weeks in Madison and traveled one week through the midwest and southeast United States, ending in Washington, D.C. The conference financing allowed leading U.S. professionals to be invited to participate. The proceedings were published by the University of Wisconsin

Press in 1956 in a book entitled *Land Tenure*, edited by Professors Kenneth H. Parsons, Raymond J. Penn, and Philip Raup.

The 1951 conference had a specific bearing on the establishment of the Land Tenure Center. Conference representatives decided almost immediately on arrival in Madison to elect a steering committee. By deliberate choice this steering committee was to exclude representation from the University or from the U.S. government. It made many suggestions during the course of the conference and prepared a final report approved by the conference as a whole. A part of the steering committee's final report urged the University to establish a Land Tenure Center and a library:

It would be tragic to permit this stimulation and inspiration to die with the termination of this conference. To prevent this and to provide for the continuity of the work started at the conference the steering committee makes the following recommendations:

There should be established at the University of Wisconsin a permanent central committee with both resident and corresponding members. . . .

The trainee program . . . should involve not only the training of non-Americans in American universities; it should also involve the training of Americans in other countries of the world. . . .

. . . the University of Wisconsin [should] maintain an up-to-date and world-wide land tenure library with facilities for the lending of land tenure materials to interested . . . persons. . . .

A prime necessity is accelerated and broadened research in the land tenure field . . . . Comparative land tenure research criss-crossing national boundaries is called for. This can best be accomplished by collaborative arrangements between universities within the same or in two or more countries. . . .

Land tenure problems should be given considerations on the programs of international conferences dealing with natural resources lest the work done at this conference and by the central committee might remain confined to the purely academic sphere. [*Land Tenure*, pp. 693-695]

The idea and pattern of a Land Tenure Center were thus spelled out in considerable detail as early as 1951. University personnel later participated in land reform conferences in Latin America, the Middle East and the Far East. In 1961 when Congress permitted some of the Foreign Assistance appropriation to be used for research, the University immediately proposed a land tenure research and training program to be called the Land Tenure Center.

This book presents the results of some of the research of Land Tenure Center staff and students. Additionally, it draws widely from studies conducted by many other individuals and agencies carrying out research on land tenure and reform.

INTRODUCTION

In rural areas land ownership or other secure forms of tenure which assure the farmer of some control over the returns from his labor and the land he works is the real and practically the only means of participation in the political and economic life of the country. This *is* the access route to economic and political citizenship and to a share in the sovereign power of the nation state.

With the exception of several of the more industrialized nations, Latin American countries have 40 per cent or more of their population living and working in agriculture. In some countries this percentage ranges as high as 60-70 per cent and, given all historical experience, the absolute number of people dependent on agriculture for a living will continue to grow despite massive rural-to-urban migration.

High concentration of land ownership, increasing migration of rural people to the cities, a great but not fully realized productive capacity, the unfulfilled potential to provide employment for most rural people, a highly skewed income distribution, and a wide gulf between the mass of farm people and the upper classes in income, education, and culture characterize much of Latin American agriculture. The proportion of rural families without land, or with too little land to make a living, ranges from about 55 to 90 per cent. Although some of the land on large farms is operated in small units under sharecropping or other tenancy arrangement, many of the large farms continue to be managed and operated as units.

Latin America needs increased total agricultural output, increased employment, and increased productivity per worker. The combination of all three is unlikely to be achieved without expropriation and reorganization of many of these large farms. Modernization without reorganization may yield increases in the output of some crops and in labor productivity for a select group of skilled workers. However, it may reduce rural employment opportunities and throw the full burden of adjustment on the disadvantaged who join the ranks of the landless, become migrant workers, continue to crowd into existing small farm areas, move out to a rapidly shrinking frontier, or join the underemployed in the cities.

Land reform is a highly controversial political question and many Latin American governments have accomplished little to date. The conflicting interests of varying groups has resulted in a stand-off. Many continue to hope that programs designed to increase production will result in agricultural development without the need for reform. Yet experience over the past decade seems to indicate that the questions of increased agricultural production and a more equitable distribution of the fruits of that production must be viewed as parts of the same process. Policies designed to cope with one of these questions to the exclusion of the other have not been too successful.

Except for the revolutionary reforms of Mexico, Bolivia, and Cuba, the substantial though less massive reforms of Venezuela and Chile, and the recent efforts by Peru, very little expropriation and reorganization of the large farm sector has occurred. Not that massive redistribution alone offers a panacea: there are no simple solutions. The above cases illustrate well the fact that the task is far from finished once the land is reallocated. Agricultural policies must be reoriented to serve the reorganized system. Even with the widespread reforms in Mexico and Bolivia, agricultural policies have tended to favor the new commercial farming areas and to neglect the small farmers and those operating under cooperative or communal forms of tenure.

All factor market distortions are not removed by land reform. Special efforts are required to reorganize and reorient the marketing and service institutions to serve the reorganized agricultural production structures. Land redistribution and reorganization of the agricultural production structure seem to be necessary but not sufficient conditions for agricultural and general economic development—broadly conceived. The point is that without major land reforms and the redistribution of economic and political power inherent in such processes, it is difficult to achieve the necessary modification in related institutions and the basic goals of development—a reduction in mass poverty and a more equitable distribution of increased income earning opportunities. Land reform (a basic restructuring of the land tenure system) is no guarantee that these goals will be achieved, but it does create the possibilities for the enactment of policies which are more consistent with these requirements than the policies likely to be enacted in the absence of land reform.

In a region as diverse as Latin America, most generalizations concerning such complex policy issues are likely to be wrong in many particulars. This book does not pretend to cover in analytical detail all the issues related to land tenure and reform in Latin America, nor are studies presented for each country separately. The book, organized in five parts, deals with a number of general issues and several specific country studies.

Part I contains two chapters dealing with methodological and conceptual issues. Chapter one presents a methodological argument for expanding the concept of economic development to include the reduction of mass unemployment and poverty, and a more equal distribution of improved income earning opportunities. This chapter provides a rationale for the wide divergence in policy recommendations made by planners and analysts, and summarizes some of the basic premises underlying much of the research as well as the policy conclusions reported in this volume.

Chapter two details the social significance of land tenure systems and analyzes the differential roles of such systems in traditional, transitional and industrial societies. Latin America generally is viewed as passing through the transitional phase. The contrast between a traditional society and one moving toward modernization is seen as a contrast between a relatively stable technology and a stable social order in the former and a changing technology and a more fluid social order in the latter. A long evolutionary process (at times revolutionary upheavals) has stripped the developed nations' tenure system of social and political significance, and in these societies group conflicts run along lines other than those of land tenure.

Part II also contains two chapters, with the major focus on the relationship between land reform and development. Chapter three emphasizes the economic case for distributive reforms and the potential contribution of such reforms to accelerated economic development. Major contrasts between the large and the small farm subsectors are highlighted throughout the chapter since this dichotomy is a prominent characteristic of the present system. However, this is not intended to imply that land reform should split up these large farms and create a system of family farms. This is an area in which generalization is not warranted. Present conditions are too variable and too different from those in the United States and Europe when their family farm systems were established. A variety of new experiments with coopera-tive-collective ownership and operation are underway in Cuba, Chile, Peru and elsewhere. The main purpose of the evidence presented in chapter three is not to demonstrate that the small farms are the most efficient, but to dispose of the persistent myth and the corresponding propaganda that the large farms as presently organized have a great production advantage and therefore land reform is inconsistent with economic growth and development.

Chapter four deals with the interrelations between land reform, employment, and rural-urban migration. Special emphasis was given to this issue because of the increasing severity of the unemployment (and under-employment) problem throughout the region. Although a primary goal of agrarian reform must be to provide more secure opportunities on the land, this employment objective is too often ignored, and reforms are evaluated only in terms of possible or potential production consequences.

The four chapters in Part III present country case studies. There are several obvious omissions of countries which have had major land reforms—notably Mexico, Cuba, and Venezuela. The selection of countries for these specific case studies was based on several factors. The first and most compelling reason was the fact that much of the research sponsored by the Land Tenure Center was carried out in these countries. Each of the four authors lived and conducted research in the respective country for two or more years. However, the Center has sponsored considerable research in a number of other countries in Central and South America. A second reason for confining the case studies to the experiences in Chile, Bolivia, and Colombia is that these three countries provide a cross section of experience with land reform in Latin America—a massive revolutionary reform (Bolivia), a substantial but still quite modest evolutionary program of reform (Chile), and a reform effort that has concentrated, relatively speaking, on the peripheral issues of colonization, land titling, land reclamation and irrigation development, and has not yet come to grips with the tough political issues of transforming the tenure structure in the large farm subsector (Colombia).

Chapter five presents a detailed analysis of the agrarian reform legislation in Chile. It was concluded that a detailed analysis of the legislation in one country would be more useful than a survey of the laws in the several Latin American countries. The Chilean legislation is not being presented as a model for the other countries to follow. Yet a detailed discussion of this very comprehensive land reform law illustrates the basic issues that most countries will have to be concerned with if they are to carry out a land reform, and it highlights some of the essential legal requirements for effective implementation of a land reform program.

It should also be emphasized that Chile's land reform programs discussed in chapters five and six do not deal with the experience beyond the termination of the regime of President Frei. The policies and programs of President Allende's regime which took office in November 1970 are not included in these discussions. There was insufficient information available at the time these chapters were finalized to include an evaluation of such recent experiences. More generally, and with only a few exceptions, the empirical evidence presented in the various chapters does not extend beyond 1969-1970.

Part IV includes four chapters on supplementary reform measures with evidence and illustrations again drawn from a large number of countries. None of these, except strong peasant movements, is considered central to the basic political issue of restructuring the land tenure system in the large farm subsector of Latin American agriculture, although several of these can be of strategic importance in facilitating the reform process and in providing necessary supplementary measures for its successful completion.

Chapter nine presents several theories regarding peasant organizations along with information on the functions they have performed in the land reform programs of several countries. Chapter ten analyzes the experience of various directed and spontaneous land colonization efforts throughout Latin America. In chapter eleven, the importance of improving land tenure security through better cadastral and titling systems is discussed. Finally, chapter twelve evaluates a number of private efforts at reform such as inheritance, private land sales and subdivision, and profit sharing.

Part V consists of a concluding chapter. Based in part on the analysis in the preceding chapters, some policy implications for national governments and international agencies are summarized.

PART I
CONCEPTUAL FRAMEWORK

CHAPTER 1

Needed Redirections in Economic Analysis
for Agricultural Development Policy

PETER DORNER

Professor of Agricultural Economics,
Director of the Land Tenure Center
at the University of Wisconsin–Madison

CHAPTER 1

Needed Redirections in Economic Analysis for Agricultural Development Policy*

PETER DORNER

Economic literature identifies development with average rates of increase in real output per capita. Little research has focused on interrelations between productivity increases and other indicators of development such as the reduction of mass poverty, unemployment, and inequality. Such omissions may be a function of the way agricultural economics developed in the United States. Here a positive correlation between increased production, employment, and income-earning opportunities was assumed inherent in the family farm system and the relative labor-scarce conditions. Problems emerging in recent years throw considerable doubt on the appropriateness of these assumptions.

Influence of Institutions on Economic Concepts

Within the past several decades, especially the one just ended, agricultural economists have become increasingly concerned with agricultural *development* policies. I underline development since this is a new emphasis.[1] Agricultural economics and the related rural social sciences emerged as academic disciplines at about the turn of this century, after U.S. agriculture was far along the road to modernization. Initially, agricultural economists were concerned with problems of farm management and tenancy. Later, problems of marketing, credit, price and income protection, resource conservation, and aggregative characteristics of demand and supply became subfields of specialized interest and research. Since the discipline "grew up" after the basic economic, social, and political institutions of production and distribution were established, policy issues of concern to researchers were essentially those dealing with imperfections of the system—obstacles and barriers (to the free flow of information and resources) inhibiting the most efficient use and combination of *given* resources. [24, pp. 725-729; 35, p. 83]

* From *American Journal of Agricultural Economics* 53 (February 1971) 8-16, with some modifications. Reprinted with permission.

1 Development is here viewed in the broad sense of expanding opportunities and the human capacities needed to exploit them, along with a general reduction of mass poverty, unemployment, and inequality. [36, 31]

A look at the "growth of government in agriculture" [41, 1, 39] reveals a fairly close correspondence between policy issues in U.S. agriculture and the development of specialized areas of research.[2] The shape of agricultural economics as a discipline reflects the range of issues that arise in agricultural policy. Organized systems of thought are the result of man's efforts to cope with experienced difficulties. The configuration of such a system of thought will be different if establishment of basic institutions is a key issue, in contrast to the system of thought that emerges from inquiry into policy issues that arise *within* an established and accepted institutional framework. [14, p. 4]

At the time of United States' independence, economics was just emerging as a recognizable, separate branch of moral philosophy. A major policy issue in the late eighteenth and early nineteenth century was the nature of economic organization to establish in agriculture. The resulting system of family farms was rationalized more in terms of political theory (a major reaction to European feudalism) than economic theory. [16]

The system of economic, social, and political organization was firmly established by the time problems of agricultural policy attracted the attention of professional economists. Had our earlier policies fostered a feudal heirarchy or communal ownership of land instead of fee simple ownership and family farms; had our social organization developed around the extended family or the tribe instead of the nuclear family living in relative isolation on its farmstead; had our political system been one of centralized control and management of the economy with all transactions involving land, labor, capital, and commodities regulated by central political authority instead of the free private enterprise of individuals in their economic activities; much of our theory of the firm, of markets, of pricing, and of equilibrium would be irrelevant. In fact, we most likely would not have them. *They could be developed and perfected only within a particular political and institutional context.* They provide no analytical insight into a system whose institutions are different.[3]

Thus, there is little reason to believe that the concepts and hypotheses derived from our theories are entirely relevant to all of our country's

[2] Note also current policy issues (poverty, resource and environmental management, population, urban congestion, agricultural development, etc.) and the corresponding growing interest and research specialization (including new institutes and professional journals) in all of these areas.

[3] N. Georgescu-Roegen has observed: "As soon as we realize that for economic theory an economic system is characterized exclusively by institutional traits, it becomes obvious that neither Marxist nor Standard theory is valid as a whole for the analysis of a non-capitalist economy, i.e., of the economy of a society in which part or all of the capitalist institutions are absent. A proposition of either theory may eventually be valid for a non-capitalist economy, but its validity must be established *de novo* in each case.... Even the analytical concepts developed by these theories cannot be used indiscriminately in the description of other economies. Among the few that are of general applicability there is the concept of a production function together with all its derived notions. But this is due to the purely physical nature of the concept. Most economic concepts, on the contrary, are hard to transplant...." [13, pp. 147-148]

6

currently recognized problems; they are even less relevant to problems facing the poor, agricultural countries. The need, it would seem, is to understand institutional systems and the nature of public policy issues.

On some problems our theories and professional economic analyses are serving reasonably well in the United States and in other industrialized countries. The relevant questions are being asked and the data needed for analyses are being generated. But the categories in our census and other statistical series are not accidental.[4] They too are products of the policy issues and the theoretical formulations developed through the interaction of problems and ideas.

On other important policy questions, however, present theories provide little insight even on U.S. issues: environmental quality, poverty, race relations, a more acceptable distribution of economic and political power, congested cities, rural development, automation, and basic changes in the structure of resource ownership. Present theories do not seem to encompass these issues; they do not help us to formulate the right questions; hence, appropriate data are not available, and fundamental policy questions tend to fall outside the boundaries of traditional academic disciplines.[5]

Social Science and Policy Formulation

A basic question is whether economics, or any other social science, has anything significant to say on matters of development policy. More fundamentally, are the social sciences capable of generating guidelines for public policy that are in some sense "better" than those formulated by other means and criteria? Or are the value questions of public policy subject only to political compromise or the dictates of dogma, coercion, and personal tastes?

This depends, it seems, on one's view of the role of theory, how it is developed, and the manner in which it is tested. If one assumes that economic theory develops in some pure form independent of policy issues existing within a specific institutional matrix, it follows that theory can have an "independent career" and be set apart in a separate domain.[6] This view may

4 Seers has noted that "lack of data on poverty, unemployment and inequality reflects the priorities of statistical offices rather than the difficulties of data collection. The conceptual problems of these measures do not seem to be more formidable than those of the national income. We have just grown accustomed to ignoring [them]." [36, p.3]

5 "No where," says John Gardner, "can the operation of vested interests be more clearly seen than in the functioning of university departments. . . . [the department] assesses the significance of intellectual questions by the extent to which they can be answered without going outside the sacred territory." [12, p.98]

6 "To accept the distinction between 'pure' and 'applied' economics as generally valid and fundamental is not only to accept the view that 'theory' in its pure form can have an independent career but that it can be validated in some way other than by 'application'. . . . The crux of the issue is simply this: that the only alternative which we have to the validation of inquiry by problem solving is a reliance either upon self evidence of fact or principle as the foundations of knowledge—or upon revelation. Both of the latter alternatives are incompatible with a genuinely scientific viewpoint." [30, pp. 664 and 674; See also 6]

not be too harmful with respect to those aspects referred to by Kuhn as "normal science" or the "mop-up work" growing out of established theory.[7]

Another position, taken in this paper, is that as major changes occur in society the existing body of theory (developed through the study and eventual resolution of major policy issues) becomes inadequate and fails to comprehend the new policy issues that confront society. The major breakthroughs and theoretical syntheses in economics have come about from attempts to deal with major policy crises. Smith, Ricardo, Marx, and Keynes were deeply immersed in the policy issues of their time, and their theoretical advances resulted from their inquiry into the possible resolution of questions central to economic policy.[8] Advances in theory have always been constructed on the basis of detailed and specific research into the very issues that could not be forced "into the preformed and relatively inflexible" boxes available from existing theory. [22, p. 24]

Emphasizing the need for research on policy issues does not mean that the goals of policy are set by politicians, bureaucrats, or pressure groups and that the role of research is merely to seek the most efficient means of arriving at such predetermined goals. Rather, it means that the investigator must be concerned with both ends and means. "Since development is far from being achieved at present, the need is not, as is generally assumed, to accelerate economic growth—which could even be dangerous—but to change the nature of the development process." [36, p. 3]

This view holds certain dangers. For example, it raises the question of objectivity in research.[9] This is perhaps why many social scientists deny that they are working on policy questions and maintain that—as scientists—their only concern is establishing value-neutral relationships. This latter function is

---

[7] "Mopping-up operations are what engage most scientists throughout their careers. They constitute what I am here calling normal science. Closely examined, whether historically or in the contemporary laboratory that enterprise seems to attempt to force nature into the preformed and relatively inflexible box that the paradigm supplies. No part of the aim of normal science is to call forth new sets of phenomena; indeed those that will not fit the box are often not seen at all. Nor do scientists normally aim to invent new theories, and they are often intolerant of those invented by others.* Instead, normal scientific research is directed to the articulation of those phenomena and theories that the paradigm already supplies." [22, p.24]
* Here Kuhn cites Bernard Barber, "Resistance by Scientists to Scientific Discovery," Science 134:596-602, 1961.

[8] "One of the results of any survey of the development of economic doctrines is to show that in large measure the important departures of economic theory have been intellectual responses to changing current problems." [25, p.13]

[9] The problem-solving approach to inquiry "...easily and naturally frays out into a mere servicing of practical judgements. In fact, it requires strenuous intellectual effort to avoid this very outcome. Under such circumstances we gradually drift into an acceptance of the 'problems' as formulated by our constituency. The next step is simply that of making 'investigators' the mere tools of various interests.... Yet the issue must be faced. The argument seems inexorable, that there is no other alternative in genuinely scientific inquiry to having both the roots of inquiry and the final tests of validity in practical problem solving." [30, pp. 675-676]

of great social significance, and most social scientists will be engaged only in such studies. Indeed, new theoretical breakthroughs are impossible without them. [22] But without direct attention to relationships not prescribed by present theories, some of the most pressing public policy questions are ignored.

It may be helpful at this point to note a fundamental difference between the physical and the social sciences. Both physical and social scientists can carry on much of their normal science under laboratory conditions, but social scientists will always conduct some of their research within the context of human society. When a crisis in policy emerges, when accepted theories fail to offer insights into phenomena readily observed, when these anomalies become so obvious that they can no longer be ignored, a new theory cannot be validated except as it is tested in practice. In physical science this can still frequently be done under laboratory conditions; but in economics it requires new directions in policy. Its measured consequences must then serve as the experimental test.

The Keynesian reformulation of the 1930s is perhaps the best and most recent example in the field of economics. Today, many economists are indeed engaged in the normal science that is not directly concerned with ends or values. But this is made possible by the new Keynesian paradigm which has once again (for the industrialized, capitalist countries) relegated many evaluative or "normative" issues to the level of assumption, removing them for the time being from the immediate field of inquiry. This makes possible the common practice of reading prescriptions for public policy directly from the refined Keynesian models (a practice which Keynes himself did not recommend).10 But such prescriptions could not command the respect they do if the new theoretical constructions had not been tested—in the only meaningful terms possible—through their practical influence in shaping public policy and resulting in measured and anticipated consequences.

In the United States we have begun to accept as a measure of progress the number of people lifted from the misfortune of being poor. There is a growing recognition that development problems are not confined to some far-off "less-developed country," and people are beginning to realize that development is more than capital, investment, and markets. It is a complicated process of institutional change, redistribution of political power, human development, and concerted, deliberate public policy efforts for redistributing the gains and losses inherent in economic growth. [7, p. 291]

Despite such recognition, these issues are still often treated as "fringe problems," outside the mainstream of economic policy. And development economics, so far as I can determine, does not incorporate these issues into its

10 "The object of our analysis is, not to provide a machine, or method of blind manipulation, which will furnish an infallible answer, but to provide ourselves with an organized and orderly method of thinking out particular problems; and, after we have reached a provisional conclusion by isolating the complicating factors one by one, we then have to go back on ourselves and allow, as well as we can, for the probable interactions of the factors amongst themselves. This is the nature of economic thinking." [21, p.297]

analysis. As a result, the relevancy of development economics to development is being questioned. [36, 4] In viewing the core economic theory requirements at major Ph.D.-granting universities and the content of preliminary examinations, one would hardly suspect that such problems exist or that theory has any bearing on research related thereto.[11] While development questions in the United States are becoming more critical, they are at the heart of public policy issues in non-industrialized countries. Yet U.S. universities are presuming to educate and confer Ph.D. degrees on candidates from these countries.[12]

There is, it would appear, a crisis situation developing in economics (and perhaps in the social sciences generally) in the sense defined by Kuhn—"Crisis and the Emergence of Scientific Theories." [22, pp. 66-76] Unless some key development issues, presently ignored, are directly addressed in research, this crisis may challenge the very legitimacy of economics. As Boulding reminds us:

> The teaching of every profession produces a certain amount of what Veblen called "trained incapacity" and we should certainly look with a critical eye at economics to see if we are not doing this. If the training of the economist leads to his neglecting certain important aspects of the world about him, once he is in a position to give advice and to have his advice taken, disasters might easily ensue. . . . When one is giving advice, therefore, about a system that involves the total society, it is extremely dangerous to be overtrained in a certain abstract element of the total process. If we run into enough of this we may find indeed a widespread reaction against economics and a withdrawal of legitimacy from it. It is my own view frankly, at this point, that we must move toward a more integrated and perhaps even a rearranged social science, that the existing departmental and disciplinary lines often mask real problems. . . . [2, pp. 306-307]

Analytical Redirections

Given the rapid population growth in most of the developing countries, the large proportion in agriculture, and the continuing growth of absolute numbers dependent upon agriculture [9], it is surprising to see how little analytical attention has been given to the need for creating employment and improved income-earning opportunities in rural areas. There is a vague hope that programs designed to increase production will result in agricultural development irrespective of the short-run employment and distributional consequences of such programs. However, experience over the past decade

[11] "Workshop on Core Economics," sponsored by the Agricultural Development Council, October 10-11, 1967, held at ADC offices in New York.
[12] "If a student's formal course training is limited to two years of graduate study and he expects to work on development problems, he is, I'm afraid, in danger of finding that he has acquired a lot of mental luggage of dubious utility while he has not been expected to think very deeply on questions basic to an effective attack on the problems of development. It is not really an answer to say that you are giving him his analytical tools and that his thinking can come later. If he has not been made aware of the basic issues in his university training, he may well pass through life unaware of their very existence." [4, p.20]

indicates that the questions of increased agricultural production and a more equitable distribution of the fruits of that production must be viewed as parts of the same process. Policies designed to cope with one of these to the exclusion of the other have not succeeded.

These two aspects of development (increased production and a more equitable distribution) are sometimes viewed as being totally independent.[3] The first is seen as the key to development while the second is considered a peripheral problem of welfare or social justice. Some even assume that economists have the analytical tools that permit them to make policy recommendations for increased efficiency in production, but that the problem of a more equitable distribution is a political or cultural matter.[17]

In most of the non-industrialized countries a majority of the people depend on the land for employment; jobs in manufacturing are growing much less rapidly than manufacturing output; and the number of people dependent on farming for a livelihood is increasing. To achieve the benefits that may accrue from what Owen has called "farm-financed social welfare" requires that opportunities—even subsistence opportunities—be provided.[27, p. 61; 28]

Policies that emphasize modernization and increased production from the commercial farm sector without explicit attention to the creation of employment opportunities will yield increased output of certain farm commodities and growing labor productivity for a part of the farm labor force. But they tend to widen the income disparities and throw the burden of adjustment on the disadvantaged who join the ranks of the landless, become migrant seasonal workers, continue to crowd into the existing small farm areas, move out to rapidly shrinking frontiers, or join the underemployed in the cities. There is no evidence that the increased volume of commodities moving through commercial channels as a result of increased production creates sufficient jobs for workers displaced by modernization or for the growing numbers in the rural labor force.

Poverty (the massive poverty among the majority of people in the less-developed countries) is not only or primarily a welfare and humanitarian problem. It is a problem that has direct and important implications for increased productivity. Supply *does not* create its own demand under conditions of a highly skewed income distribution. To focus primarily on production widens the income gap between rich and poor. It is impossible in many circumstances of development to separate the issues of production and distribution, since distributional measures may be the key to achieving increases in production. And the trickle-down theory of distribution has never worked, especially under conditions of concentrated economic and political power.[13]

13 *The Economist* makes the following comments on FAO's "Indicative World Plan": "As long as incomes are so unevenly distributed within the developing countries themselves, and so little inroad is made with their traumatic unemployment problems, the people who are starving will not have the money to buy the food, even if it is there. This is where the planners of Asia, Africa and South America would like FAO guidance, but so far they only get alarming figures and some general advice." [15, p.75]

Why are policies not formulated to accommodate both of these requirements—increased production and increased employment with a more equitable distribution? The distributional questions, of course, raise many tough issues. Accordingly, and regretfully, policy recommendations of professional analysts using highly sophisticated models usually ignore employment and distributional aspects. Recommendations are too often based on private or project decision-making criteria rather than those appropriate to the interests of the entire nation. Some redirections in economic analysis are required. Three concepts in such a redirection (and examples of assumptions that frequently preclude their explicit inclusion in analyses) are highlighted in the following sections.

1. Creation of Secure Opportunities on the Land. The "war on hunger" position tends to assume that if there are hungry people, food should be produced by the cheapest, most efficient means possible. Yet frequently, and especially when viewed from the private interest of an individual firm, this course of action includes displacing people with machines. And professional analysts, viewing the problem with decision-making criteria appropriate to the private firm while ignoring the possible lack of correspondence between private and social costs and benefits, can reach conclusions such as the following: "One reason for the high cost [of corn in Guatemala] is the amount of hand labor required. Hence, my desire to try out the corn picker." [29, p. 716] However, this may not be a solution at all once the need for employment creation is taken into account. Even if means could be found to tax away or otherwise confiscate the increased production "... a nation cannot put most of itself on the dole, even if money and food are available for distribution." [26, p. 224]

Land must be viewed as a vehicle for human development as well as a resource for food production. As Raup has put it: "Wherever there is surplus agricultural labor and shortage of working capital, the task of the tenure system is to put people to work." [33, p. 274]

It has become an article of faith, at least among many professionals from the industrialized countries, that mechanization (mechanical technology and automation generally) always creates as many jobs as it destroys, sometimes more. According to this faith, there may indeed be some short-run problems of labor displacement and some structural unemployment. But given time, the new technology creates demand for labor in many areas of the economy through its various linkages, and eventually employment will rise to a higher level.

This assumption may be justified in a highly industrialized nation. But does the same assumption apply to a country that does not produce its own technology? In the United States, for example, the mechanical cotton picker displaced workers by tens of thousands.[5] Many of the workers displaced (though certainly not all) and especially the sons of these workers did find employment among the vast complex of industries interrelated with the production, sale, and servicing of cotton pickers—steel, rubber, oil, machinery manufacture, transport, farm implement sales and service, etc. But what about Nicaragua, which imports cotton pickers from the United States? Most of the vast complex of industries linked with the cotton picker does not exist in Nicaragua; it remains in the manufacturing country.[14]

The cotton picker case illustrates the general principle involved; it does not argue against all modern, imported technology. Much depends on what the machines will be used for. In an agriculture with an over-abundant and growing labor supply, it is unlikely that one can make a logical case for importation of labor-saving machinery if the problem is viewed from the standpoint of national policy rather than profit maximization of the firm.[19] If the agricultural sector is to make its most effective contribution to economic development, it must not only improve labor productivity for a select group but must also expand employment opportunities. [20, 40]

Mechanical power and equipment might sometimes be justified in terms of increased yields due to better tillage or timeliness of operations. But there is sufficient experience of countries where such needed machine services were provided to an agriculture otherwise based on labor-intensive production practices.

On the basis of his model of rural outmigration and urban unemployment, Todaro concludes:

Perhaps the most significant policy implication emerging from the model is the great difficulty of substantially reducing the size of the urban traditional sector without a concentrated effort at making rural life more attractive. [40, p. 147]

But how can rural life be made more attractive? Presumably public investments in rural education and health services would help; and funds used to accommodate rural migrants in the cities might be diverted to rural areas. Yet such services cannot be extended rapidly because of both capital and professional manpower shortages. Higher minimum wages for farm workers could be counterproductive so long as investment decisions in the farm sector are made by private entrepreneurs. A higher minimum wage might lead to a shift to labor-extensive enterprises or to an acceleration of machine substitution for labor. Even with low wages there is a strong incentive on large farms to mechanize and simplify labor supervision. It is almost

---

14 The problem is compounded if, as Singer has pointed out, the investments and the production processes are actually controlled by foreigners. "The main secondary multiplier effects, which the textbooks tell us to expect from investment, took place not where the investment was physically or geographically located but (to the extent that the results of these investments returned directly home) they took place where the investments came from. I would suggest that if the proper economic test of investment is the multiplier effect in the form of cumulative additions to income, employment, capital, technical knowledge, and growth of external economies, then a good deal of the investment in underdeveloped countries which we used to consider as 'foreign' should in fact be considered as domestic investment on the part of the industrialized countries." [37, p.475]

impossible to find farms of, say 1,000 hectares in rice or cotton that are planted, tended, and harvested mainly by hand labor. These farms either mechanize or operate with a sharecropper system. To get at the crux of the matter, "making rural life more attractive" in most cases means providing the farm family with *a secure opportunity on the land*. Land tenure arrangements and size of holdings must be included as variables in the analysis. But the basic assumptions underlying production and distribution theories take these as "given."[15]

2. Development of Human Abilities and Capacities. Another reason why the employment issue gets little attention is that in the less-developed countries, the most abundant potential resource usually is labor. I say *potential* because training and work experience are needed to transform raw labor power into the manpower resource (with skills, experience, and discipline) required for development. An abundance of people does not necessarily rule out labor shortages in selected occupations. The scarcest resource generally is capital. Given the abundance of people, there has been a tendency to ignore the need for investment in and development of the labor potential. Instead of viewing land as a vehicle for employing people and for developing the skills and experience required of the rural labor force, land has been viewed primarily as a resource to be efficiently combined with scarce capital so as to maximize agricultural output.

T.W. Schultz has written a good deal on the issue of investment in human capital [34], but he places primary emphasis on formal schooling. I do not deny this need, but formal schooling is not the only and not always the most significant dimension of education. Furthermore, many poor countries have not yet been able to supply even elementary schooling for large numbers of their people. Under these circumstances, economic activity should be designed to produce educational effects. Productive work can offer experience and discipline as valid as that gained in the classroom. It is different, to be sure, and neither kind of education is alone sufficient. Work experience can be directed and enriched by learning obtainable only from school situations; schoolroom education can be enhanced by work experience.

The manner in which increased production is achieved, and the number of people who participate and reap some benefits from the experience, may

---

[15] "Distribution theory today concerns itself, in essence, with tracing out the effects of various policies in distributing economic fruits among persons who own or otherwise command control over resources. . . . In current theory, distribution of ownership or other control of resources among people is 'given'. . . . In terms of the dynamics of economic development, however, the real problem of distribution is: 'How does ownership or other control over resources come to be distributed in the manner it is?'. . .The question is not, for example, whether a landlord and a tenant each receives the appropriate return for the resources he controls; but rather, is it appropriate, from the standpoint of the economic development of the country in question, for the landlord and the tenant to have these particular proportions of the nation's resources under his control." [24, pp. 729-730]

be as important as the production increase itself. One gets a different perspective regarding the role of land if (in addition to its accepted function in the production of farm products) it is viewed as a vehicle both for creating economic opportunities and upgrading the human skills and capacities required for their exploitation. [8, p. 12]

Man is a resource to be used (along with land and capital) as well as the user of resources. An individual plays a dual role—he is both the user and the used, the interested and the object of interest, the exploiter and the exploited.

In a society where economic and political power are widely shared, there is a continuous attempt to modify institutional structures and norms in order to keep this process of "using others" mutually beneficial. Procedures are designed so that individuals and groups, in pursuing their private interests, are not injuring (preferably, are furthering) the interests of other individuals and groups. When mutuality in the process breaks down and conflicts intensify, zones of discretionary behavior of the individuals and groups involved must be redefined in order to reestablish mutuality in the processes of associated living.

The common formulation in resource allocation-efficiency models is to view man as labor power—as the object of use. This view, far from being value-neutral, accepts the status quo power positions and ownership patterns of land and capital. In fact it places the weight of authority of "scientific analysis" in the camp of present owners. Under conditions of vast and increasing inequality, policy prescriptions based on such efficiency models are consistent with the poor man's view of the world: "Them that has—gets."

3. Inclusion of Income Distribution as a Variable in Analyses. Economic literature tends to deemphasize the income distribution consequences of the development process. Since land tenure arrangements are most directly associated with the creation of and access to income-earning opportunities and their distribution, these arrangements receive only passing mention in the economic literature on agricultural development policies.

If the task of development is conceptualized to include income distribution as an endogenous variable, some of the economists' most powerful ideas and tools lose some of their analytical leverage. For example, marginal analysis and the accompanying planning, programming, and budgeting tools implicitly assume certain nonchanging structural parameters. Yet once an elaborate and somewhat arbitrary measurement emerges, as from benefit-cost analysis, a strong faith is placed in it. The unstated assumptions remain unstated and are frequently ignored. The higher the benefit-cost ratio, the "better" the project.

However, the results of these calculations are directly conditioned by the pattern of income distribution. 16 Investments in the increased

---

16 "Cost-benefit analysis as generally understood is only a technique for taking decisions within a framework which has to be decided upon in advance and which involves a wide range of considerations, many of them of a political or social character." [32, p.685]

production of chickens and beans rather than airlines and television sets might give a good benefit-cost ratio if the pattern of income distribution were changed. Poor people, lacking the money votes, cannot register their needs or desires through the market mechanism. But when the income distribution is changed so is the structure of demand, thus changing the benefit-cost ratios of various projects and in turn altering investment priorities.[17]

Assumptions like those described in these examples allow certain strategic developmental questions to fall between the analytical slats: productive employment for the growing rural labor force; creation of opportunities for the development of human abilities and capacities; and ownership distribution of land and other resources. An agricultural economist, using a farm management approach, may ignore the displacement of workers or their need to find viable opportunities on the land. He is concerned with profit maximization from the resources available to the firm. Even an agricultural economist dealing with farm policy for the agricultural sector could ignore these questions on the assumption (well founded or not) that industrial and other nonagricultural activities are available for the absorption of excess rural labor. Nor does a macroeconomic approach assure that these strategic questions will be addressed in the analysis. While Keynes may have shown a deliberate disregard for the supply side of investments (and focused only on their demand-creating consequences) [23], post-Keynesian development economists seem to have overemphasized the supply consequences.

There is indeed an implicit assumption that somewhere policies are being implemented to maintain full employment and that when a laborer moves from one job to another it always results in increased productivity. But these are unwarranted assumptions in most cases of less-developed countries. Indeed, these assumptions point to some of the critical problems of development.[18]

---

[17] Hirschman speaks of the centrality of side-effects in judging investment projects. "The quest for a unique ranking device probably accounts for the hostility of economists toward side-effects and secondary benefits. Yet this quest is clearly futile. How could it be expected that it is possible to rank development projects along a single scale by amalgamating all their varied dimensions into a single index when far simpler, everyday choices require the use of individual or collective judgment in the weighing of alternative objectives and in the trade-off between them? There is much to be said, it is true, for facilitating decision making by reducing the many aspects of a project to a few crucial characteristics, one of which would of course be the rate of return. It is one thing to permit, in this way, the decision maker to use informed judgment in making critical choices and trade-offs; it is quite another, however, for the technician to aim at dispensing with such judgment altogether." [18, pp.162 and 179]

[18] "[The] process of labor transfer is typically viewed analytically as a one-stage phenomenon, that is, a worker migrates from a low productivity rural job directly to a higher productivity urban industrial job. The question is rarely asked whether or not the typical unskilled rural migrant can indeed find higher-paying regular urban employment. The empirical fact of widespread and chronic urban unemployment and underemployment attest to the implausibility of such a simple view of the migration process." [40, p.139]

Conclusions

What conclusions are to be drawn from the arguments set forth in this paper? First, we need additional criteria by which to assess development. This means inclusion of variables that are less measurable and quantifiable than the commonly accepted ones in use today. Second, both ends and means must be incorporated as variables in the analysis rather than accepting certain ends implicit in standard economic theories. Finally, distributional questions must be given higher priority on the research agenda.

Present theories may have much more relevance once we understand better the institutional context of specific country development problems and the "special case" out of which our own theories were constructed. If new theoretical extensions can accommodate the enlarged context, present theories may become more useful in guiding research in the very situations in which they are at present unsuccessful.[19]

New developments in theory are not simply willed into existence. The hypothesis suggested in this paper is that only as research concentrates on presently neglected policy issues within specific institutional contexts of individual countries can more adequate theories of agricultural development be constructed. It is obviously asking a great deal of a man to be guided by present theories and preconceptions and yet to be continuously suspicious and to question them at every stage in his research. Nevertheless, this would seem to be the nature of the present challenge.

[19] The theorist can be of help to the politician, the practitioner, ". . . if he refrains from trying to adapt uncritically models and measures designed in and for industrial countries, where priorities are different, but helps instead to develop policies, national and international, to mitigate the great social problems of the Third World. . . . above all, the aim must be to change international attitudes so that it becomes impossible for the political leaders and social scientists of Europe and North America to continue overlooking, and aggravating, often inadvertently, the obscene inequalities that disfigure the world." [36, p.6]

References

[1]   Benedict, Murray R. *Farm Policies of the United States, 1790-1950,* New York, The Twentieth Century Fund, 1953.

[2]   Boulding, Kenneth. "The Legitimacy of Economics," *Western Econ. J.* 5:299-307, 1966-67.

[3]   Buse, Reuben C. "Some Comments on Government Policy in Under-developed Countries," paper presented at AID Spring Review of the High Yielding Cereal Varieties, Washington, D.C., May 1969.

[4]   Currie, Lauchlin. "The Relevance of Development Economics to Development," paper presented at a Workshop on International Development at the University of Wisconsin, Nov. 1965.

[5]   Day, R.H. "The Economics of Technological Change and the Demise of the Sharecropper," *Am. Econ. Rev.* 57:425-449, June 1967.

[6]   Dewey, John. *Logic: The Theory of Inquiry,* New York, Holt, Rinehart and Winston, 1938.

[7]   Dorner, Peter. "Fourteen Million Rural Poor," (book review of *The People Left Behind,* report by the President's National Advisory Commission on Rural Poverty), *Yale Review* 58:282-292, Winter 1969.

[8]   ———. "Human Progress is Basic to Agricultural Growth," *Internat. Agr. Dev.* (a monthly newsletter, USDA, IADS) 35:12-15, Sept. 1967.

[9]   Dovring, Folke. "The Share of Agriculture in A Growing Population," *Monthly Bul. Agr. Econ. and Stat.* 8(8/9):1-11, FAO, Rome, Aug.-Sept. 1959, (Also in *Agriculture in Economic Development,* ed., Carl K. Eicher and Lawrence W. Witt, New York, McGraw-Hill, 1964, pp. 78-98.)

[10] Eagly, Robert V. ed., *Events, Ideology and Economic Theory,* Detroit, Wayne State University Press, 1968.

[11] Eckaus, R.S. "The Factor Proportions Problem in Underdeveloped Areas, *Am. Econ. Rev.* 45:539-565, Sept. 1955.

[12] Gardner, John W. *No Easy Victories,* New York, Harper and Row, 1968.

[13] Georgescu-Roegen, N. "Economic Theory and Agrarian Economics," *Oxford Econ. Papers,* (New Series) 12:1-40, Feb. 1960. (Also in *Agriculture in Economic Development,* ed., Carl K. Eicher and Lawrence W. Witt, New York, McGraw-Hill, 1964, pp. 144-169)

[14] Gerschenkron, Alexander. "History of Economic Doctrines and Economic History," *Am. Econ. Rev.* 59:1-17, May 1969.

[15] "Global Fallacies," *The Economist* 233(6586):75, Nov. 15, 1969.

[16] Griswold, A. Whitney. *Farming and Democracy,* New Haven, Yale University Press, 1948.

[17] Heady, Earl O. *A Recipe for Meeting the World Food Crisis,* CAED Report 28, Iowa State University, 1966.

[18] Hirschman, Albert O. *Development Projects Observed,* Washington, D.C., The Brookings Institution, 1967.

[19] Johnston, Bruce F. and J. Cownie. "The Seed-Fertilizer Revolution and Labor Force Absorption," *Am. Econ. Rev.* 59:569-582, Sept. 1969.

[20] Johnston, Bruce F. and John W. Mellor. "The Role of Agriculture in Economic Development," *Am. Econ. Rev.* 51:566-593, Sept. 1961.

[21] Keynes, John Maynard. *The General Theory of Employment, Interest and Money,* New York, Harcourt, Brace and Company, 1936.

[22] Kuhn, Thomas S. *The Structure of Scientific Revolutions,* Chicago, University of Chicago Press, 1964.

[23] Kurihara, Kenneth K. "The Dynamic Impact of History on Keynesian Theory," in *Events, Ideology and Economic Theory,* ed., Robert V. Eagly, Detroit, Wayne State University Press, 1968, pp. 127-146.

[24] Long, Erven J. "Some Theoretical Issues in Economic Development," *J. Farm Econ.* 34:723-733, Dec. 1952.

[25] Mitchell, Weseley. *Types of Economic Theory,* New York, Augustus M. Kelly Publishers, 1967.

[26] Nair, Kusum. *The Lonely Furrow: Farming in the United States, Japan, and India,* Ann Arbor, The University of Michigan Press, 1969.

[27] Owen, Wyn F. "The Double Developmental Squeeze on Agriculture," *Am. Econ. Rev.* 56:43-70, March 1966.

[28] ———. "Structural Planning in Densely Populated Countries; An Introduction with Applications to Indonesia," *Malayan Econ. Rev.* 14:97-114, April 1969.

[29] Paddock, William and Paul Paddock. *Hungry Nations,* Boston, Little Brown and Co., 1964. (Reproduced in part in *Selected Readings to Accompany Getting Agriculture Moving,* ed., Raymond E. Borton, New York, Agricultural Development Council, 1966, pp.716-721.)

[30] Parsons, Kenneth H. "The Logical Foundations of Economic Research," *J. Farm Econ.* 31:656-686, Nov. 1949.

[31] ———. "Poverty as an Issue in Development: A Comparison of United States and Underdeveloped Countries," *Land Econ.* 45:1-14, Feb. 1969.

[32] Prest, A.R. and R. Turvy. "Cost-Benefit Analysis: A Survey," *Econ. J.* 75:683-735, Dec. 1965.

[33] Raup, Philip. "Land Reform and Agricultural Development," in *Agricultural Development and Economic Growth,* ed., Herman M. Southworth and Bruce F. Johnston, Ithaca, Cornell University Press, 1967, pp.267-314.

[34] Schultz, T.W. "Investment in Human Capital," *Am. Econ. Rev.* 51:1-17, March 1961.

[35] Schumpeter, Joseph A. *Capitalism, Socialism and Democracy,* 3rd ed., New York, Harper Torchbooks, 1962.

[36] Seers, Dudley. "The Meaning of Development," *Internat. Dev. Rev.* 11(4):2-6, Dec. 1969.

[37] Singer, H.W. "The Distribution of Gains Between Investing and Borrowing Countries," *Am. Econ. Rev.* 40:473-485, May 1950.

[38] Southworth, Herman M. and Bruce F. Johnston. ed., *Agricultural Development and Economic Growth,* Ithaca, Cornell University Press, 1967.

[39] Taylor, Henry C. and Anne D. Taylor. *The Story of Agricultural Economics in the United States 1840-1932,* Ames, Iowa State University Press, 1952.

[40] Todaro, Michael P. "A Model of Labor Migration and Urban Unemployment in Less Developed Countries," *Am. Econ. Rev.* 59:138-148, March 1969.

[41] Wilcox, Walter W. and Willard W. Cochrane. "The Growth of Government in Agriculture," ch. 25 in *Economics of American Agriculture,* 2nd. ed., Englewood Cliffs, Prentice-Hall, Inc., 1961.

CHAPTER 2

Land Tenure Reform as a Policy Issue
in Modernization of Traditional Societies

DON KANEL

Professor of Agricultural Economics
and the Land Tenure Center
at the University of Wisconsin–Madison

Land Tenure Reform as a Policy Issue
in Modernization of Traditional Societies

DON KANEL

Economists frequently approach land tenure issues by emphasizing incentive effects and their consequences for productivity. They may ask: What is the effect of share tenancy on productivity? Or, more generally: Are land reforms advisable means for promoting economic development? This formulation views tenure as an instrumental variable (like fertilizer and credit) and as one that functions essentially the same way in different societies. It proposes as crucial the distinctions between ownership and tenancy (share or cash) and minimizes the importance of the social structure of which the tenure system is an integral part.

Actually, the tenure system functions very differently in the less developed than it does in the developed countries. In the development process, the relation of the tenure system to the social structure generates stresses and conflicts and land tenure reforms represent either spontaneous pressures forcing adjustments or opportunities for building new political coalitions. Land tenure, then, is not simply an instrumental variable easily manipulated by governments for economic reasons alone.

Land Tenure Systems in Industrialized Societies

The social significance of the tenure system in the developed countries is limited. For example in the United States, tenure arrangements function primarily to provide flexibility and to supplement the assets of farm operators. Tenancy is primarily an economic device for mobility of capital with relatively little social or political significance.

U.S. farmers have organized along a variety of lines. They have created marketing, supply, and bargaining cooperatives, frequently along commodity lines, as well as highly potent political organizations active in areas such as control over monopoly power in farm factor and product markets, farm price policy, regulation of imports, export promotion and subsidization, federal aid for local services such as education, conservation, credit, roads, etc. But farmers in the United States have not organized along land tenure lines in more than a century.[1]

In the less developed countries, on the other hand, the tenure system is usually a major component of the larger social structure. There are great social class divisions between groups having different tenure rights, and widening the accessibility of economic opportunities resulting from the process of development frequently requires change in the tenure system. Often the seizure of new opportunities by one tenure class is at the expense of the employment and income security of other classes.

A closer description of the features of the present U. S. land tenure system will clarify the contrast with the systems of the less developed countries. In U. S. agriculture, both land tenure and credit arrangements provide flexibility in organizing and reorganizing the farm firm. Assests are made available to the firm by combining the financial resources of the operator with those of creditors and landlords. Size of farm and factor proportions are determined primarily by relative factor prices which continue to change in response to changing technology. Farmers have adjusted to the increasing cost of labor by increasing land and capital per worker. These changes are apparent on farms in all tenure categories. Renting land and borrowing money both serve to supplement the resources required by the farm operator for organizing an efficient farm firm.

Leasing in U. S. agriculture places the resources of retiring older farmers or outside investors under the managerial control of the younger generation. Landlord-tenant relations may exist between a father and a son, between an unrelated older and younger farmer, or between a nonfarm investor and a farmer. As in any joint venture, it is necessary to protect the interests of the several participants in the firm to maintain individual initiative and incentives.

In the present state of economic development, factor proportions on U.S. farms change in approximately the same manner on rented and owned farms. Farms are continually reorganized to provide more production per man and per acre to meet changing conditions of factor costs resulting from technological change and the growing employment opportunities outside of agriculture. Those remaining in farming expand farm size by purchasing or renting more land. Landlords have found that to attract desirable tenants they either must have an adequate unit or be willing to lease to operators who farm other land besides that leased by the landlord.

Though changes in factor proportions and farm size are approximately the same for different tenure classes, U. S. farms are not highly uniform; size of farm and farm family incomes vary widely, and also differ by tenure classes. Yet similar changes occur among all tenure groups over time under the impact of economic development. The reorganization of U. S. agriculture

[1]Such organization along tenure lines did exist in the early years preceding and immediately following the American Revolution. However, in the United States, as in most developed countries, once the task of transforming feudalistic institutions was completed, organization was along lines other than land tenure. The U.S. South, both before and after the Civil War, resembled more closely the situation of the less developed countries; in the South, groups holding different tenure rights differed racially and socially.

toward bigger farms and higher incomes has affected the entire range of tenure classes. Small and large farms are still here, but what is a small farm in the 1970s was a relatively large farm in the 1920s. Changes in farm size and the factor proportions used in farming have been made by owners and part-owners as well as by tenants.

Characteristically, with some exceptions in the South, land tenure categories have not led to the creation of distinct, permanent, and socially separate classes. All tenure groups have been affected by the availability and access to alternative opportunities. Economic development continues to expand and improve incomes in alternative employments. Under such conditions the power of one party over the other in a landlord-tenant relation is limited. Incomes obtained by either party are influenced more by the relatively impersonal conditions in factor markets than by the personal ability of one party to dominate the other. Thus the U.S. tenure system is largely devoid of group interests and class oppressions along tenure lines.

Tenant-landlord situations are far from uniform. Landlord motives for owning farm land vary a great deal. They include ownership by virtue of retirement from active farming, leasing lands as an incidental outcome of buying land to obtain a rural residence, as well as ownership acquired for the specific purpose of obtaining rental income. Among the latter, rent is not usually the major source of income, and such landowners are an occupationally diverse group who find little common interest related specifically to their ownership of farm land.

The business arrangement between landlord and tenant may vary from the equivalent of a partnership, with many joint activities; to a separate business venture of the tenant alone, subject to rental payments; to conditions equivalent to farm labor with practically all managerial decisions made by the landlord. Interaction between the parties ranges from cordial and cooperative to strained and antagonistic. A bad relationship can be financially serious for either or both parties, but in these cases it is the individual landlord or tenant who will be seen as the enemy, rather than landlords (or tenants) as a class. There are a number of alternatives open to a landlord or tenant who wants to terminate an unsatisfactory relationship: the landlord can refuse to renew the lease or the tenant can refuse to sign a new lease; when a lease is not renewed for either reason, the landlord can seek a new tenant or sell his farm and the tenant can seek a new landlord or take up another occupation. In this sense landlords and tenants are more like corporate stockholders who, when dissatisfied, can sell their stock rather than organize against the management. On the other hand landlords, tenants and stockholders are unlike corporation management and organized labor in that the last two groups deal with each other as well as with the larger public as organized interest groups.

Land Tenure Systems in Traditional Societies

The role of land tenure in the institutional structure of traditional society contrasts sharply with its role in the developed nations, both when that structure is stable and relatively unchanging and when it is undergoing modernization. The difference between traditional and modern society will be distinguished here by the virtual absence of markets for rural land and labor in the former and the presence or emergence of such markets in the latter.[12]

The concept of traditional society is a highly artificial construct covering a great diversity of social structures. It tends to be misleading both in implication of uniformity among "traditional" societies and in implication of almost complete absence of change in such societies. Neither is assumed here. Our purpose is to highlight the contrasts and processes of transition from a traditional to a modern society, viewing changes in tenure and labor arrangements as a parallel to Polanyi's discussion of the emergence of markets for land and labor.2

2The tenure systems of traditional societies underlying this discussion are the feudal agriculture of medieval England (and more generally much of Europe), the Indian caste system [1; 9; 10], the Japanese pre-nineteenth century system [14], and the African "communal" tenure system.[2]

The general thesis presented here holds that almost everywhere in the underdeveloped world, modernization of agriculture involves a shift from relations governed by status to relations governed by contract, and that it is this shift which makes land reform a ubiquitous policy issue in the course of development.

At the same time, the starting point for these changes—the social structure from which changes proceed—varies widely; there are many possible models of status-oriented societies. Paths of transition also vary, so that the beginning situations and paths described here are only illustrative. No claims are made that beginning situations and paths of change must be the same everywhere; the illustrations are drawn from different areas and different historical times on the basis of their suitability for exemplifying issues. Perhaps one way of putting it is that pressures and challenges and their underlying causes are somewhat the same, but that the specific institutional content of the initial situations and the paths of transition differ greatly.

While this volume deals with Latin America, this region's evolution does not fit neatly into the patterns of traditional and transitional societies as described here. Since the Spanish and Portuguese conquests, Latin America has been a mixture of communal landholdings, an export-oriented agriculture, with essentially modern fee-simple property rights vested in the landowner, and an hacienda system with labor and tenure arrangements often resembling those of the medieval European manor. Though legally the relations between landowners and peasants were mostly contractual, in practice there was little labor turnover—peasants were bound to the land and often sold with the hacienda.[3] The attempts to bind labor to soil were sometimes reinforced by debt peonage and vagrancy laws.

The hacienda system is vulnerable to peasant unrest both when it is unchanging, traditional, and highly oppressive (note the Bolivian Revolution of 1952) and when it is modernizing via active entrepreneurship on the part of large landowners (as in Colombia, Central America and Brazil during the last decade).

Also, this article cannot attempt to treat the various twentieth century attempts to develop cooperative farming as an institutional form for modernizing agriculture. Besides such efforts in the Communist countries, important programs of cooperative farming

A society with limited nonagricultural production can provide for division of functions almost entirely through the land tenure system. The needs of government, army, and religion can be met by collecting food and other produce from the cultivators and disbursing it through designated agencies of the governing elite to the members of the political-administrative-religious superstructure (bureaucratic political structure). Alternatively, officials and other members of the superstructure can hold tenure rights and collect food from cultivators for their own support and for those who carry on governing functions (feudal political structure). The exchange of goods between food producers and artisans can also be accomplished by giving artisans tenure rights to share in the harvest, and giving cultivators the right to demand the service of the artisans (Indian caste system). The food producers themselves may be unequal in status. Arrangements for members of one family working for another, for admitting new families to the community, or for expanding the area under cultivation may all be provided through a set of complex rules governing the rights to land. Rights to land may be partly vested in the community as a whole and partly in individual families.

The absence of a labor market is equivalent to the absence of footloose labor, workers whose access to income depends on the decision of another person, an employer. In traditional societies a person's station in life and his occupation are not determined by bargains freely entered into but are primarily the result of status inherited from one's parents. Tenure arrangements involve access to a piece of land and an obligation to pass on some of the produce or to work for a social superior. Neither rights in land nor rights in labor are negotiable. While there are persons who resemble modern tenants, they do not get their rights to land by contract with a landowner. Tenants are persons who inherit that position, along with obligations to the landowner, but without their access to land dependent on a decision of the landowner to contract with them.

It is characteristic of such a system that no individual has a clear right to change the relations between parties. By way of contrast, an owner of a fee-simple title in the Anglo-American legal system can operate the land himself, he can sell it, or he can bring in a tenant under terms established by contract between himself and the tenant. The crucial point is that such an owner can eliminate the existing set of relationships between himself and others connected with his land and establish new ones. Such a right to "wipe the slate clean" does not exist in traditional societies. The whole structure with various customary commitments and obligations is such that no person within that system has a clear legal right to abolish one set of relationships

have been undertaken in Chile, Peru, and Cuba, in a number of African countries, and in Israel. The Latin American and North African attempts were influenced not only by ideological considerations but also by the disadvantages and costs which would have resulted if the existing infrastructure on large farms had had to be adapted to family farm parcels created from the large farms. Similarly, the use of description of the agricultures of the United States and other developed nations should not be taken to imply that such modern systems are necessarily the most desirable for or the best adapted to the needs of the less developed countries.

and to bring in people as workers or tenants on a new set of terms. In that sense there is neither a market for land nor for labor.

The basic feature of this kind of organization is stability of agricultural technology over long periods of time. The active concern of landlords (or more generally of the upper rural classes) is not changes in farming practices and gains that might be achieved thereby, but the extraction of a surplus from the peasantry (or more generally from the lower rural classes). To the landlords, management questions are primarily: How much can be squeezed out of the workers? How much are they holding back? How honest is the administrator? How can greater administrative effort be made to yield more income, and how can the disorganization and resistance resulting from such income gains be avoided? On the other hand, the technical organization, the tenure system, and the existing personnel are taken for granted. Alternatives with respect to these are hardly considered and rarely exercised.

Such tenure systems tend to be characterized by the personal dominance of the landlord over those in inferior tenure status. It becomes very important to those below whether the landlord is good and kind, or unfair, unpredictable, and violent. Economic alternatives which would temper abuses of landlords are absent; there is little security against unfairness and the whims of those above. On the other hand, there is much greater security and stability of occupations due to the absence of change in production techniques and the fixity of class lines. In other words, there is much less instability equivalent to that generated in modern times by changing technology and economic forces which alter market conditions and the decisions made by employers.

Landlord-tenant relations tend to be personal. Tenant access to the larger society is almost solely through the landlord; he may provide access to political power and protection from other powerful persons. In relation to the peasants, landlords combine in an undifferentiated manner social and political leadership with their economic roles (roles which in modern society would be differentiated by function and distributed among landlords, government officials, officials of interest groups and community leaders). Thus landlords may be responsible for the administration of justice. In the traditional setting, however, landlords are also likely to be imbued with an aristocratic and paternalistic tradition of meeting certain customary obligations to their clients.

This incomplete portrayal of landlord-tenant relations describes a society in which the capitalist or the entrepreneur has not yet emerged, and in which economic roles have not yet become differentiated from social and political roles (political roles may also not have become differentiated). The self-image of rural upper classes is apt to include the assumption of their right to leadership, superior status, and services from peasants combined with obligations to those below. The manipulatory social situations include intrigues and combinations with peers and with those of higher status, tightening or loosening control over peasants, and granting of favors; they do not, however, include an impersonal view of peasants as outsiders with whom one has no relations unless one chooses to contract with them over work or rental of land. This is not because such impersonal relations with a labor force are rejected as dishonorable, but more basically because the possibility of such a relation is something that emerges only gradually in history out of interrelated change in technology, organization of production, and attitudes.

Land Tenure Systems in Transitional Societies

The contrast between a traditional society and a modernizing society might be seen as a contrast between a relatively stable technology and social order on the one hand and a changing technology and more fluid social order on the other. More specifically, attitudes toward land and labor are closely bound to change in the society. The upper classes in traditional society view the product of the land as available because of the obligations of the lower classes and the work of the latter on the land; valuable rights stem from their superior role in the social organization rather than from ownership of land per se. In the process of modernization, land itself becomes valuable, and a fee-simple conception of ownership emerges along with the idea that the owner can cultivate the land with hired workers; the landowner learns that he can *create* the social order on his land by his choice of terms of labor and tenure arrangements.

The underlying shift in labor and tenure arrangements is influenced by the rapidity of technological change. Traditional systems are adaptations to relatively slow rates of technological change. This does not mean that they are simple or completely static. They are usually very complex systems that accommodate a diversity of occurrences of change, luck and misfortune: temporary transfers of land between members of a group, incorporation of outsiders into the group, bringing of empty land into cultivation, etc. However, land use by individuals is tied to group practices in a number of ways so that individual practice is locked in step with group controls. For example, in the three field system of medieval land use the stubble was open to pasture by the livestock of the whole community, effectively forcing uniformity in choice of crop and planting and harvest dates. Pasture and forest improvement were limited by group rights to graze livestock on and to collect firewood from lands belonging to the group.

The English enclosures, corresponding to our concept of a transitional system, attempted to group individual properties and to free them from group rights so that improvements by individual owners could proceed without need to await modifications of practices and attitudes acceptable to the group as a whole. This change, characteristic of the modernization of traditional society, signifies the emergence of greater individual rights over production decisions and the abrogation of group controls. The functional rationale is the need for individual adoption of technology, enabling individual owners to use credit on the security of landownership, and freeing innovating individuals from group claims to their gains.

The need for greater individual control in production decisions emerges regardless of whether modernization is dominated by the upper or the lower classes of traditional society. In either case the old social forms are loosened and transformed. If the upper class becomes active in attempting to gain from using new technology, then it tends to develop an interest in eliminating obligations to the peasants and in gaining full control over land. In terms of attitudes of the upper class there is a shift from the aristocratic tradition of a leader of a clientele group to a capitalist outlook recognizing the benefits from technological and economic opportunities—benefits realizable only if the power of the state is used to protect them in the use of their property and the enforcement of contracts. Whenever the rural upper classes become actively engaged in management they will seek to shed social obligations, gain a free hand in controlling land use, and obtain the services of a "law-and-order" state in protecting their property. In cases where modernization involves the emergence of a landowning peasantry, the peasants seek to eliminate the rights over individual holdings of both the upper class overlords and the peasant community.

The motives for these changes have varied in different areas and time periods, and have included: 1) a shift in the interest of the rural upper class to the political and economic opportunities in the national arena; 2) a shift in interest of the upper class from peasant labor obligations to share or cash rents; 3) opposition of the peasantry to displacement of workers or worsening of employment conditions due to increase in active management by the upper classes. While this opposition may in some cases stimulate repression of the peasantry, in other cases peasants may receive support from national governments attempting to preserve stability in rural areas or from political parties seeking to widen their popular base by gaining peasant allegiance. Attempts to remove the rights of overlordship thus stem from peasant desire for security in a changing situation, from loss of traditional functions of the upper class with resulting changes in peasant attitudes, or from shift in the political power of the landed upper class vis-à-vis the peasantry. Landowning peasantries have emerged through violent revolutions, orderly state-administered land reform, and even peasants' purchase of landlord properties.

A modern peasant community is usually quite heterogeneous with respect to farm size, economic efficiency, and tenure status. The typical range covers the landless, small part-time farms, full-time family farms, and larger farms that hire a few hired workers. In those cases in which successful service agencies have emerged (marketing, credit, and extension agencies which are public, cooperative, or private), commercialization eventually extends over the whole of peasant agriculture, and internal diversity does not harden into class lines.

The emergence of greater individual ownership rights in land is not an unqualified advantage for the peasants. The peasants clearly suffer when full modern landownership and the managerial function come into the hands of large landowners, and when the power of the state is used to support these powerful private interests. Even with widespread peasant proprietorship, modernizing peasants face problems of costly and inadequate credit, loss of ownership to lenders, low and uncertain market prices, and high cost of supplies. Increased security depends on farmer organization, the creation of farmer cooperatives, and many public programs and agencies to provide necessary services.

Despite all its imperfections, peasant proprietorship provides considerably more security to the agricultural population than ownership vested in large landowners. An agriculture of landowning peasants provides a shelter for the masses of people for whom outside employment is not available. It absorbs population increases up to the limits of capacity to support life. On the other hand, it does not necessarily act as a barrier to out-migration when employment opportunities appear elsewhere. It permits the use of new technological opportunities in farming, but those who have no alternatives or who cannot or are not ready to utilize new technology have access to subsistence. By contrast, in an agriculture dominated by large landowners, continued peasant employment depends on employer decisions, and for a variety of reasons, more active management by these landowners often leads to a relatively labor-saving path of modernization. These considerations are very important in the earlier stages of development when the growth in nonagricultural employment opportunities is low and the bulk of the population depends on agriculture.

The response of peasants to the stresses and insecurity associated with development has been different from that of the industrial workers because of the distinct conditions in the two sectors. Individual ownership of the means of production in modern industry is an impractical goal because of the decisive economies of scale. Workers have increased their economic power by unionization and by supporting the enactment of legislation requiring collective bargaining, particularly by setting up procedures to handle grievances and to govern dismissal of workers. Protection against unemployment is increased by expansionary fiscal and monetary policies and by special programs such as public unemployment insurance.

For several reasons it is easier to build both security and flexibility into industrial employment. If industrial jobs are being created at a sufficient rate, secure employment can be provided for those already in the industrial work force, and alternatives are available for new additions to the labor force. Industrial workers usually do not live in company-owned housing, and in an urban area they are usually in proximity to a number of potential employers. Thus urban conditions are more conducive to changes in place of employment and to a more impersonal relationship between employers and workers.

Rural conditions are different in all these respects. In most types of farming there are no decisive economies of scale so that family and larger farms can coexist. Development is less likely to increase demand for labor in agriculture, and in a sector dominated by large farms the tendency may be to decrease employment. Also, development involves basic changes in the long standing tenure and labor arrangements. Thus development in agriculture is likely to be much more disruptive than in industry. Further, housing patterns differ from those in urban areas. In many types of large scale agriculture, workers live on farms of their employers. Loss of job then means loss of home and home community as well; additionally, potential alternative employers are at a greater distance than in urban areas. Farm workers who live in homes of their own usually have employment on large farms only by the day and work at seasonal tasks when work requirements exceed the capacity of the resident labor force. Employment available to such temporary workers is usually the most insecure. They are often the most poverty-stricken of all rural classes.

For all of the above reasons, the peasants have not been able to utilize the protective devices used by industrial workers. The more typical peasant remedy has been the drive to achieve land ownership and to supplement this with public and cooperative service organizations.

The competitive strength of large and small farms depends on a number of factors. However, in the absence of decisive advantages to division of labor, the other factors do not generate overwhelming advantage to a particular size, and they can be neutralized or overcome. Existing infrastructure and government programs generally favor the large farms, which tend to have better and earlier access to improved technology, credit, and markets. But with the availability of an infrastructure and of cooperative and public service organizations that do not discriminate against them, the advantage often shifts to family farms.

A good example of this is found in the evolution of Danish agriculture, especially in the role of large farms and of peasants in the manufacture of butter. [13] Early in the nineteenth century peasants were given personal freedom and ownership of the plots they worked, but the landed aristocracy retained large portions of their former estates. In the immediate post-reform era the large farms made the best quality butter, largely because they could afford the facilities for on-the-farm cooling of milk. This technological advantage compensated for the difficulties of supervising hired labor. By the end of the century the situation was reversed because of technological and institutional changes.

The technological change was the invention of the centrifugal cream separator. The institutional factor was the emergence of a strong cooperative movement, including cooperative creameries, which had the necessary facilities for cooling the cream and making high quality butter. These two changes permitted the small farmers to separate and deliver the cream to the creameries instead of having to ship the bulkier milk or to make butter at home. The cooperatives were quality- and market-conscious (a major market outlet was exports to England, and quality was extremely important), and they were effective in influencing production practices on the farms which improved quality of the cream. As a result of these changes, small farms gained a competitive advantage over large farms; both had more or less equal access to improved technology, yet large farms were at a relative disadvantage due to higher labor costs and the difficulties in supervising hired labor.

Finally, a changing political and social structure has impact on tenure relations. At issue is the role of landlords as the sole agent of peasant access to the rest of society, and the emergence of competing power brokers such as government officials, peasant unions leaders and others. [see 5; 7; 6; 8; 15]

Wertheim discusses the class struggle in rural Java and describes the dominant role of landlords as the peasants' sole source of security and of access to the rest of society. [15] One study of a village shows that government had only a negative meaning to the villagers ("a government . . . does nothing but forbid"), and while rural workers did not trust their landowner, he was the only security they possessed—class solidarity of the workers with their peers is a luxury that they normally could not afford.[15, p. 7]

Wertheim constrasts Java with the Netherlands. He pictures the latter as a "pillarized" society in an industrial country. The "pillars" of Dutch society are Protestantism, Catholicism, and a-religious Humanism. Patronage relations are present within these "pillars" with preference in appointments and in customer relationships. The "pillars" are active in education, medical services, social and recreational activities and give group support in the economic and political field. But the protection of sources of livelihood and social security are largely provided through basic governmental or legal institutions which function in an objective and impersonal manner, and patronage arrangements are marginal rather than central in these areas.

It is the centrality of patronage arrangements that is characteristic of many of the less developed countries. Dominance of patronage relations in turn reflects the limited development of institutions of the state and their effectiveness in reaching all the citizens. On the other hand, the modern state, oriented to welfare and development as well as to protection of property rights, frees its citizens of dependence on client-patron relations.

The course of modernizing agriculture often proceeds in a series of stages, from a situation (a) where the state is weak (or nonexistent) in relation to the rural upper class, to a stage (b) where the rural elite needs and uses the state, to a further stage (c) where the rural elite's leadership and power over the peasants is challenged by other contenders, to a modern stage (d) where farm people and other interest groups build up organizations (pressure or lobbying groups) responsive to their needs and effective in influencing government policy. The second stage corresponds to landlord dominance of local politics, the third to political pressure on the landlord class and demands for land reform, and the last to a tenure system stripped of political and social significance, similar to that in the U.S. described earlier.

The transitions that occur can be illustrated with examples from Iraq and Chile. The Iraqi case is a transition from the sheikh as tribal leader in conflict with weak state authorities (nineteenth and early twentieth century) to the sheikh as large landowner in a stronger state (from about 1930 to the 1958 revolution). Fernea studied one community where irrigation agriculture was controlled by tribal groups.[4] The sheikh was a military leader in case of conflicts between tribal groups or in revolts against state authorities. He also had major roles in organizing group work to clean the canals, calling assemblies, and providing hospitality to travelling tribal members and visitors.

His legitimacy was highly dependent on his military prowess.

The situation gradually changed with pacification by British and then Iraqi authorities and with the enlargement of irrigation works by government projects and their administration by government engineers. On one hand the sheikh lost the role of the military leader and the legitimacy that went with it. On the other hand he emerged as a private landlord with a holding much larger than those of other tribal members, in part because his role in tribal society entitled him to larger holdings (some of the produce from his holdings were used for tribal functions) and in part because his role gave him opportunities to benefit himself. The new situation thus resulted from simultaneous changes: loss of traditional function and the legitimacy accompanying it; expansion of land holdings at the cost of other tribal members and made possible by pacification; state protection of property; and diminished need for loyalty from tribal members.

A Chilean example illustrates the decrease in the political power of the hacendado in the first quarter of the twentieth century.[11] The particular community included a large hacienda with resident workers as well as settlements of small peasant proprietors, communal farmers, and tenants of hacienda land. A small detachment of national police for the community was stationed at the hacienda, and its headquarters were transferred to a small town in the area only about thirty years ago. The hacendado was not just the owner and manager of his own hacienda, but the political and social leader of the whole community; the impression is that the presence of the state hardly reached the peasant, and its limited presence (such as the few policemen) was at the call of the hacendado.

Shifts in these relations after about 1920 resulted from construction of a road to the community, the appearance of trucks, and the establishment of merchants and officials of the national government in a small trade-administrative center that grew up in the community. The group of merchants and officials offered new linkages to the government and to the larger society and by-passed the hacendado. These developments limited his political and social leadership in the community and restricted his power to the management of his own hacienda.

In traditional society the elite and the peasants complemented and needed each other. The elite needed the peasants as its source of power (its "troops"), as well as for the work and the income obtained from them. The peasants needed the elite to protect them from and provide links with the outside world, as well as to provide organization and leadership in community affairs. The isolation of the local community, the dangers lurking from outside, and the stability of social relations gave legitimacy to the status of the elite.

On the other hand, the interests of the two rural classes diverge when the elite turns to modern economic opportunities in agriculture. It is no longer interested in peasants as followers but as workers, and it only needs limited numbers of them. Both in the elite's interest in keeping wages low and in keeping unneeded peasants off its property, it becomes antagonistic to the peasants. At the same time the elite ceases to be the defender of local interests against a distant government and other outside agencies. Instead of local leadership as a basic source of legitimacy, it needs a strong central governmental authority (enforcement of public order and property rights) to protect its possessions from the pressure of the peasants.

Members of the elite might in time acquire new legitimacy as large farm owners if they succeed in generating sufficient employment, or if they are lucky enough to have peasant land hunger dissipated by urban employment opportunities or settlement in frontier areas. But current rates of population growth and the tendency of large farms to generate only limited employment means that pressures for land reform are likely to be much greater than in eighteenth and nineteenth century Europe.

References

[1] Baden-Powell, B.H. *The Indian Village Community.* London: Longmans, Green, 1896.

[2] Bohannan, Paul and Laura Bohannan. *Tiv Economy.* Chicago: Northwestern University Press, 1968.

[3] Clark, Ronald J. "Agrarian Reform: Bolivia." Chapter 7 of this book.

[4] Fernea, Robert A. *Shaykh and Effendi.* Cambridge, Mass.: Harvard University Press, 1970.

[5] Galjart, Benno. "Class and 'Following' in Rural Brazil." *América Latina* 7, no. 3 (1964): 3-24.

[6] ———. "A Further Note on 'Followings': Reply to Huizer." *América Latina* 8, no. 3 (1965): 145-152.

[7] Huizer, Gerrit. "Some Notes on Community Development and Rural Social Research." *América Latina* 8, no. 3 (1965): 128-144.

[8] Lehmann, A. D. "Social Structure and Agrarian Reform in Chile: Preliminary Findings." Mimeographed. Brighton, England: Institute of Development Studies, 1970.

[9] Maine, Sir Henry Sumner. *Village Communities in the East and West.* 3rd (author's) ed. New York: Henry Holt, 1876.

[10] Neale, Walter C. *Economic Change in Rural India.* Yale Studies in Economics, no. 12. New Haven: Yale University Press, 1962.

[11] Pascal, Andres. *Relaciones de poder en una localidad rural.* Santiago: Instituto de Capacitación e Investigación en Reforma Agraria (ICIRA), 1968.

[12] Polanyi, Karl. *The Great Transformation.* New York: Reinhart and Company, 1944.

[13] Skrubbeltrang, F. *Agricultural Development and Rural Reform in Denmark.* Agricultural Studies, no. 22. Rome: Food and Agricultural Organization, 1953.

[14] Smith, T. C. *The Agrarian Origins of Modern Japan.* Stanford, Calif.: Stanford Press, 1959.

[15] Wertheim, W. F. "From Aliran towards Class Struggle in the Countryside of Java." *Pacific Viewpoint* 10, no. 2 (1969): 1-17.

PART II

LAND REFORM AND DEVELOPMENT

CHAPTER 3

The Economic Case for Land Reform:
Employment, Income Distribution, and Productivity

PETER DORNER

Professor of Agricultural Economics,
Director of the Land Tenure Center
at the University of Wisconsin-Madison

DON KANEL

Professor of Agricultural Economics
and the Land Tenure Center
at the University of Wisconsin-Madison

CHAPTER 3

The Economic Case for Land Reform: Employment, Income Distribution, and Productivity*

PETER DORNER and DON KANEL

Though ideological arguments on the best ways of organizing agriculture continue, no land tenure system can be judged best in the abstract. Any judgments concerning a particular system must take note of the institutional and technological conditions in the society and the stage at which that society lies in the transformation from an agrarian to an industrial economy. Judgments must also consider what specific groups and individuals in that society are attempting to accomplish.

Historical Perspectives

Several kinds of transitions from agrarian economies to industrial economies have occurred. The consequent reorganization of the agricultural sector in each of the following examples took place within a particular set of social and economic circumstances.

The system of European feudalism of several centuries ago is today, by most standards, an anachronism. Although comprising a total system of political, social, and economic institutions, it was at base an agrarian system built around the control of land. Eventually that system conflicted with the evolving goals of creating strong nation states; proved ill-equiped to respond to the requirements of expanding markets and too inflexible to accommodate the increased use of capital; and failed to meet the needs of man's evolving conception of himself.

Yet despite its inadequacies, its injustices, and its rigidities by present standards, the feudal system was an adaptation to the times. Growing out of a crumbling and disintegrating world empire, it organized people according to strict and rigid class structures with mutual obligations between classes, thereby assuring some degree of internal harmony and a measure of security from potential enemies external to the feudal manor. But these feudal structures were inconsistent with the requirements of changing from an agrarian system to an industrial society. The various attempts at reforming these agrarian systems, and their eventual transformation, define major landmarks in the economic history of the European states.

Russian collectivization may not have provided the individual incentives or the decision making freedom that family farms did; however, the Russian

* A slightly modified version of this is published by the United Nations Food and Agriculture Organization in *Land Reform, Land Settlement and Cooperatives*, No. 1 (1971): 1-16. Printed with permission.

planners' major concern was rapid industrialization. Russian agriculture was producing a substantial export surplus at the time collectivization policy was implemented, and a key requirement was to free labor from work in agriculture to provide manpower for the new factories. In addition, the state had to "squeeze" some of the surplus production from the agricultural sector in order to provide relatively cheap food for the growing population in the industrial sector. And of course collectivization of agriculture was perhaps necessary to assure party control over the economic system and to prevent decentralized political developments. The collective system functioned to achieve these ends.[24; 25; 26] In recent years modifications have been introduced, presumably because the system was not achieving present objectives and goals.

When the Soviet system was instituted more than forty years ago, the country had a relatively slow population growth and a low man-land ratio—a sharp contrast with the current situation in much of South and Southeast Asia, Latin America, and Africa. In the latter areas, the rapid population growth of recent decades (and capital intensive, low labor-absorptive industrialization) makes it imperative that the agricultural sector hold people rather than being forced to release them.

Throughout the nineteenth century the United States was also characterized by a low man-land ratio; despite massive immigration, population growth was lower than in many of today's less developed countries. Furthermore, industrialization in the nineteenth century was generally more labor absorptive than it is today. U.S. development, like Russian development, required production of an agricultural surplus and the release of labor from agriculture to meet the demands of the growing industrial sector. But the means employed in achieving these ends were wholly different from those used by the Soviet Union a century later. United States policy placed primary emphasis on new technology to increase the productivity of land and especially the productivity of labor, and relied on competition among small producers for allocation of production factors among alternative uses.[26]

In the past three decades U. S. agriculture has been substantially reorganized. The number of farms is now less than half what it was thirty years ago. Farms have been combined and their average size continues to grow. The 80-acre or even the 160-acre farm is an inefficient unit for most types of farming in the United States today. Present technology and factor costs and availabilities make them inefficient in terms of labor productivity and, since labor is relatively scarce compared with land and capital, labor productivity is a reasonably good measure for judging efficiency under U. S. conditions.[1]

[1] Labor productivity as a measure of efficiency in the agricultural sector ignores the social costs of people becoming stranded in rural communities and of large numbers of unskilled workers migrating to cities but failing to find employment within an occupational structure largely determined by the technological developments in industry. These are serious problems in the United States, and they are likely to become all but insoluble in the less developed countries if means cannot be found to hold more people in agricultural employment. [32; 9]

When the design of a U. S. system of land tenure and economic organization of agriculture was being debated, the major alternative to family farms appeared to be a system of large estates and plantations with some features of European feudalism. The latter had been challenged on both political and economic grounds and was in various stages of disintegration. Furthermore, the large land mass to the West had to be secured from threats by other nations. The family farm system that eventually emerged was perhaps the only reasonable way in which a relatively weak government, lacking major communication and transportation networks, could assure that this large land mass would be rapidly settled and incorporated into the nation.

There are very few places in the world today where such circumstances exist. For the most part, the problems then faced by the United States are not now central issues in agricultural development in most of the less developed countries. For both the Soviet Union and the United States, then, the land tenure system reflects specific historical, geographic, and political conditions; both systems continue to be modified as development occurs.

In most of Latin America, the land tenure system is dominated by the large estate or hacienda. There are of course some family farms, communal holdings, plantations, and large numbers of very small holdings—minifundios—in most countries, but the prevalent form of land tenure, in terms of the area of land controlled, is the large estate.

The tenure system resulting from Spanish conquest reflected the purposes of the conquistadores and the Spanish Crown: to gain control over and to settle this part of the new world, much of which had a larger indigenous population than then existed in North America.

However useful this land tenure system originally was for the Spanish colonizers, or is for national elites that now hold power, it has become obsolete and stands in direct conflict with the achievement of development goals. It needs to be changed to meet changing conditions, just as the land tenure systems of the industrialized nations have been modified and reformed in the process of development. Specifically, the basic land tenure institutions in Latin America must be reformed in order to create more employment, to achieve a more equal distribution of income, and to provide necessary increases in productivity.

The above sketches are not intended to imply a neat, logical relationship between tenure systems and concurrent social problems and policy needs. Tenure systems emerge from conflict and debate among contending groups—witness the Soviet debate on the rapidity and method of industrialization and the many U. S. experiments with land settlement policies in the nineteenth century. Tenure systems, as hammered out by experience and conflict, are nevertheless adaptations to prevailing circumstances. They cannot be easily transplanted into an entirely different set of conditions.

Economic Rationale for Land Redistribution

Even in the industrialized countries, agriculture still makes substantial contributions to overall economic development. However, its contribution to the supply of non-agricultural manpower, to capital formation, and to demand generation for industrial goods certainly becomes less critical in a highly industrialized country where the labor force in agriculture may be less than 10 per cent of the total. In the developing countries, by contrast, especially in countries with 50 per cent or more of their labor force engaged in farming, agriculture's contribution is critical in all these areas.[19] Although labor must move from agriculture to industry in the process of development, the problem under conditions of rapid population growth is not how to release laborers, but how to keep from releasing too many too quickly.[32] Under present circumstances rapid population growth seems to accompany and even to precede development rather than to follow the 19th century pattern where population growth seemed a response to development.

The less developed countries need a labor-intensive, capital-saving approach with heavy reliance on yield-increasing technical innovations in earlier phases of agricultural development, followed by a capital-intensive, labor-saving approach only in the later phases. These phases are determined by changing conditions in the areas of (1) demand for food and (2) employment opportunities.

Changes in the demand for food are determined largely by population growth and by the income elasticity of demand for food (which declines as average incomes rise). These changes are readily seen in the following formulation: $D = p + \eta g$, where D, p and g are annual rates of growth of demand for food, population, and per capita income, and η is the income elasticity of demand for food. As an illustration, assume that in a less developed country $p = 2$ and $\eta = .8$, while in an industrialized country $p = 1$ and $\eta = .2$, and that $g = 2$ in both cases. Then the demand for food will grow at a rate of 3.6 per cent in the less developed country and at 1.4 per cent in the industrialized country. The difference would be even wider if the population growth rate in the less developed country was more than 2 per cent, while a higher growth rate of income in the industrialized country would make little difference because of the low income elasticity. Thus the less developed countries need considerably larger increases in food output than do more developed countries.[2] The need to earn foreign exchange increases even more the importance of increasing agricultural production.

On the employment side the crucial considerations are high rates of population growth and the difficulty of absorbing a large share of this growth in the small urban sector. Even with large rural to urban migration, the rural population typically continues to grow, though at a slower rate than the total

[2] This discussion also assumes that the rate of growth in per capita income is widely shared. If increases in incomes are highly skewed in their distribution, the full impact of the income elasticity of demand for food would not be realized. For similar reasons, there may not be a one-to-one relationship in population growth and increased demand for food.

population. Urban population grows rapidly, and much of it is absorbed in precarious, low productivity urban jobs. Absolute numbers of rural people decline only in later stages of development, and only then is it necessary to reorganize agricultural production in a way that would decrease labor requirements.[12]

.The combination of the above two sets of circumstances yields the Johnston and Mellor policy prescription: a labor-intensive approach with reliance on yield-increasing technical innovations in the earlier phases of agricultural development.[19] This policy approach produces the required increases in agricultural production and avoids displacing labor prematurely from agriculture. It is a prescription for agricultural research, for large increases in the use of yield-increasing inputs such as fertilizer, improved seeds, insecticides and pesticides, for increases in irrigation facilities and for building service institutions in extension, marketing, and credit. It is also a prescription to minimize mechanization, especially when it serves to displace labor.

Under the large farm system in Latin America, however, it has been difficult to gain acceptance of such policies. Labor-saving machine technology is available from the industrialized countries. So long as investment decisions are made on the basis of private profit, large farm entrepreneurs may find it in their best economic interest to import labor-saving machinery. In fact it may be easier to transplant this type of technology than the biological type, which often requires additional research before it can be adapted to the specific conditions in new areas. The wide range of available production techniques now affecting employment contrasts with the more restricted options open to agricultural entrepreneurs in the nineteenth century. In this earlier period, labor-saving technology was largely a response to labor supply conditions, and the major innovations emerged from within the industrializing countries of the time—especially the United States and Western Europe.

The employment problem is worsened by the capital intensive-labor extensive patterns of development in manufacturing industries. In Latin America, manufacturing output is estimated to have increased by 140 per cent from 1950 to 1965. During this same period, manufacturing employment grew by only 45 per cent.[1]

Widespread population growth rates of 3 per cent and higher are a relatively recent phenomenon, but the low capacity of the manufacturing sector to absorb labor in early phases of economic development has been a feature of development in earlier times. Though manufacturing has become increasingly capital intensive over the past century, the early phases in the development of manufacturing have always had both a positive and a negative effect on employment. The shift from handicraft and cottage type industries to assembly-line manufacturing has resulted in less employment for a given amount of output.[23]

If agriculture were strictly comparable to industry, this employment dilemma would seem all but insoluble. In certain industries at least, capital intensive developments are frequently inevitable because the pattern of machine technology is set by that used in and available from industrialized countries. This technology may place limits on the substitution of factors (e.g., labor for capital) in production processes. If agricultural production were similarly restricted, there would be few alternatives to capital intensive developments in this sector since agriculture in developed countries is also capital intensive. But agriculture is different. There are alternative means of economic organization in agriculture which permit greater flexibility in production processes. Factor proportions (land, labor and capital) can more nearly be utilized in a manner consistent with their relative cost and availability. Market imperfections continue to obstruct more rational use of factors, but it is precisely at these imperfections (in land, labor and capital markets) that land reform is directed.

An important element in this argument concerns the factor proportions to be used in agricultural production. As one writer says, "the assumption of only a few alternative processes and a quite limited range for substitution of factors does not seem to fit well the technological characteristics of a number of important industries, as, for example, agriculture."[13] If factor substitution is possible over a fairly wide range, as here hypothesized, then the problem of major misallocations of resources is likely to be found in various market imperfections. The large, often redundant agricultural labor force in most Latin American countries lacks the economic and political power to gain control (either ownership or rental) over sufficient land and capital resources to increase its productivity. Nevertheless, present distribution patterns show a gross misallocation in terms of resource availabilities—too much land and capital and too little labor on the large farms, and too little land and capital and too much labor on the small farms. In Latin America, 30–40 per cent of the active agricultural population typically lives on and works less than 10 per cent of the land.[2]

Why do farmers with large extensions of land not employ more labor? There are many possible reasons. Farm owners may have outside interests that hold greater economic importance for them than farming. Abundant labor is not always cheap labor; minimum wages and a variety of social welfare laws may make the price of labor higher than it would by in their absence. A large unskilled hired labor force becomes difficult to manage on labor intensive enterprises. It also increases the risk in dealing with expensive machinery, improved livestock, and modern production practices which require constant use of judgment on the part of laborers. Given these circumstances, owners of large farms will frequently reduce their labor force and move in the direction of capital intensive, mechanized operations with a relatively small force of skilled workers (supplemented when needed by seasonal labor).[31]

On the apparent assumption that a developed agriculture must have the factor proportions now existing in the agriculture of the developed countries, government policy often encourages importation of farm machinery through favorable foreign exchange rates. Furthermore, most of the credit goes to the large farm sector (more credit-worthy by bankers' standards), with inflation often making effective interest rates minimal or even negative. Resource misallocations and poor performance are not surprising given the underlying assumptions and the monopolized control over land and capital, but the profitable course for the individual entrepreneur results in costs to society which cannot forever be postponed.

Reasoning from analogy, United States and European experience with farm enlargement and mechanization provides support for this type of development, but only if one ignores the widely differing situation with respect to factor proportions and real factor costs (in contrast to existing factor prices which are often controlled and distorted by some of the above policies). Given rapid population growth (and the inevitable continuing absolute increase in farm populations in most of the developing countries) and inadequate labor absorptive capacity of industry, agriculture must be organized to provide much more productive employment than it does at present.[33]

In a system built on private property in land, the size of farm operating units is a basic determinant in the development of a labor intensive agriculture. Data from India, the United States (Illinois), and Chile show the following relationships: the smallest farm group has 1.6, 74, and 1.1 acres per worker while the largest farm group has 15.6, 219, and 16.6 acres per worker for the three countries respectively.[20] These data certainly indicate some adaption to the factor proportions existing in each country. They also, however, illustrate the greater employment capacity of small farm units even though output per man may be (and usually is) lower on the small units. These figures also suggest a wider range of production techniques in the agriculture of the less developed countries: for example, the ratio of acres per man on large over small farms is about 3 in the United States but ranges from 10 to 15 in the cases of India and Chile.

A study of the Chateaulin area of Brittany reports the following results: "When one moved from holdings of less than 5 hectares to those of more than 25, the number of workers per 100 hectares fell from 105 to 18.7, the number of per-annum working hours per hectare from 1,500 to 480. Working capital also fell, but less markedly, from 210,000 to 119,000 francs, and gross yield from Index 163 to 88 (average for the area: 100)."[5]

Commenting on Mexico, Dovring notes that small-scale, labor intensive production is less costly than large-scale production in terms of the goods that are scarce in the Mexican economy. The large private farms are using more of the hardware that might otherwise have been invested toward even more rapid industrialization of the country. "There is no doubt," concludes Dovring, "that the owners or holders of large private farms make a good income by using more machines and somewhat less labor, but they render a less useful service to the struggling and developing economy of a low-income, capital-scarce economy."[11]

In the case of West Pakistan, Johnston and Cownie make a strong case for employment of more labor rather than more tractors in agriculture. They argue that "the existence of yield-increasing innovations which are neutral to scale and consistent with the existing systems of small scale agriculture increases the advantages of the labor-intensive, capital-saving alternative."[18]

Additional cases could be cited, but the evidence is quite clear that under a system of private property in land, a small farm agriculture can absorb more labor than can a large farm agriculture. Some have cautioned that a small farm agriculture of peasant proprietors may lead to an excess of capital equipment on small holdings (i.e., much duplication and underutilization of buildings and equipment).[14] However, the Japanese case shows that technology can be adapted to fit small farms if research is specifically directed to achieve these results.[10] Or, on the other hand, a reorganization of a large farm system on cooperative or communitarian principles can be designed to assure both labor absorption and efficiency in the use of capital.

Agricultural production processes, as mentioned, have characteristics which make many comparisons with developments in industry invalid. The superiority of a large farm system, argued on the basis of economies of scale, is an old idea. Marshall and Mill expressed serious doubts about its validity, but as Owen has pointed out, "It is probably fair to say that most economists have since attempted to resolve his [Marshall's] dilemma by avoiding it."[26]3 Moreover, the investment processes in agriculture and industry differ:

The process of economic growth in agriculture follows a distinct pattern. In its early stages, slow gains in capital stocks predominate. Investment decisions are typically made in small segments, spread over many seasons or gestation periods. Impressive amounts of capital are formed, but by many small, plodding steps. This is quite different from the large-scale, dramatic investment programs emphasized in much current economic development planning. The image of development conveyed by a hydroelectric dam or by a steel mill is misleading if applied to agriculture. Capital formation in farming is rarely concentrated either in space or time. It accumulates by an incremental process that is best described as accretionary.[27, pp. 267-314]

The development of a nation's livestock herds is a good example. But likewise is the use of available labor (due to the sequential nature of operations noted above in which slack periods inevitably occur) to construct buildings, drainage ditches, fences, maintenance of irrigation systems, etc. Raup concludes:

The prospect that subsequent economic development may create nonfarm employment opportunities has led many economists to condemn

3 With regard to the nature of employment in agriculture, Owen quotes John Stuart Mill: "Agriculture . . . is not susceptible of so great a division of occupations as many branches of manufactures, because its different operations cannot possibly be simultaneous. One man cannot be always ploughing, another sowing, and another reaping. A workman who only practiced one agricultural operation would be idle eleven months of the year. The same person may perform them all in succession, and have, in most climates, a considerable amount of unoccupied time." Mill's insight has been elaborated by Brewster. [3]

48

land distribution programs because of the "uneconomic" size of farm units that may result. In the long run this argument may have validity. In the shorter run, the waste of capital-forming potential represented by under-utilized labor is the more serious concern. In this sense, the political pressures leading to drastic land distribution programs may also be good economics.[27]

It is very difficult to make a case for large-scale, labor-extensive units in farming at early stages of economic development, especially in countries with a high man-land ratio. "Under a labor technology, costs cannot be cut by increasing the size of farm. Most of the cost economies from using modest capital items are largely exhausted as soon as the bullock team, horse or camel which provides the power are fully employed."[16]

The above arguments present the rationale for recommending farm enlargement under one set of circumstances (e.g., in the United States) and farm subdivision with smaller units (or in any event a more labor intensive agriculture) under another set of circumstances (e.g., in Latin America). The choice depends largely on the existing factor proportions and their relative real cost to society. What is good (i.e., profitable) for the individual entrepreneur may entail disastrous social costs.

The small farm cannot divert the cost of unemployed (or under-employed) labor onto society as can the large farm or industry working primarily with hired labor. It thus becomes a better vehicle for what Owen has referred to as farm financed social welfare.[26] A small farm agriculture (or one organized in such a way as to provide a greater correspondence between private and public costs and benefits) also has advantages in providing a more equal distribution of income and thereby an enlarged demand for the growing industrial sector.

Economic Performance of Small Farms

It may be conceded that a small farm or reformed agricultural system has the above noted advantages—more employment, more equitable distribution of income, a wider and more relevant demand structure for the growing manufacturing sector, a better base for farm financed social welfare, and more rational (in terms of existing factor availabilities) investment policies in both the agricultural and nonagricultural sectors of the economy. Yet all these advantages may seem less significant if increasing agricultural production, both for export and for feeding rapidly growing populations, is viewed as the main issue, and if the problems of unemployment and redistribution are thought to be resolved indirectly (rather than through policies directed specifically at their resolution) in the course of increasing agricultural output. None can deny the great importance of increased agricultural production, for which Ruttan has provided this rationale:

Demographic and economic forces are resulting in annual increases in the demand for agricultural output of 3-5 per cent. Sustained rates of growth in the domestic demand or in the supply of farm products in this range are completely outside the experience of presently developed countries. The annual rate of growth of agricultural output in the United States has not exceeded 3 per cent for a sustained period since 1860.[28]

But given the experience with agricultural modernization in Latin America, it is probably not feasible to institute a continuous process of development without specific attention to the growing problems of unemployment and redistribution.

Why should many agricultural production technicians (and some economists too) fail to give adequate recognition to the problems of unemployment and redistribution and concentrate instead on the more technical aspects of increasing production? (This is particularly true of U.S. technicians.) There is a general assumption that the large farm is more efficient. Under this assumption, it is natural to concentrate on ways and means of increasing the productivity of the larger farms through more favorable cost/price ratios, improved practices, better markets, more credit, etc. Speaking of U.S. research, Ruttan points out that "Research has been primarily oriented to providing information relevant to private rather than public decision-making. The same orientation is characteristic of American farm management and production economics specialists and U.S. trained farm management and production economics specialists working in less developed countries." [28]

The assumption that the large farm is more efficient has arisen because of the particular measure of productivity or efficiency employed. It is true that labor productivity is consistently higher on larger farms, but this is hardly a measure relevant to policy in a labor surplus economy. Higher labor productivity on large farms is primarily related to mechanization and labor-saving techniques. Land-saving technologies such as improved seed varieties, fertilizers, insecticides, and improved weeding can usually be applied equally well and efficiently on small farms. Under conditions of abundant rural labor and continuous rapid population growth, productivity per unit of land is a more relevant measure for policy purposes.[4] Obviously, it is the purpose of economic development to raise labor's producitivity—but not only for the few. And in order to raise labor productivity broadly for all those now in farming and those yet to be absorbed by the agricultural sector, land and capital must be redistributed—land reform must be implemented. Long has stated the case well when, writing on Indian agriculture, he notes:

Literally hundreds of American studies have confirmed that larger farms normally have correspondingly higher operator incomes, i.e., higher returns to the managerial and labor contributions of the farm operator and his family. In common usage this has erroneously been too often taken to be synonymous with greater "efficiency," leading to the conclusion that large farms are more "efficient" than small farms. They are! But only with reference to management and labor, i.e., with reference to returns to the human agent. They are not necessarily the most "efficient" in the use of other (non-human) resources. In the United States and similarly developed countries, this error creates little difficulty because the human agent is, from

[4] Actually, neither of these single-factor productivity measures is adequate. What is needed is a measure of efficiency or productivity based on output per unit of total inputs with inputs valued at their social opportunity costs. Unfortunately data are not available for the latter calculations.

a social viewpoint, the most scarce factor of production. Much more importantly, in the United States maximum returns to the human agent in agriculture, which is obviously the economic goal of the individual farmer, is also roughly congruent with the broad objectives of public agricultural policy. And since management and labor are usually supplied by the same social unit, the individual farm family operator's net income is the most relevant measure of the relative efficiency of farms of different sizes. Maximum operator's income serves as an adequate criterion of both private and public policy action. The situation in India and similar countries is very different.[21]

Figures 1 and 2 present the results from a number of recent studies on the relationship between farm size and output per unit of land.[30] In most cases measurement of output is in terms of gross value per unit of land. Value of output per unit of land above variable cost would be a better measure since it minimizes the distortions due to possible differences in amount of capital used by farms of different sizes. However, in those cases where some such concept was used, the results are consistent with the gross concept.[5] In fact, using the gross concept probably understates the small farm's margin over the large farm.

The evidence shown in Figures 1 and 2 is generally consistent with the hypothesis that output per unit of land is inversely related to farm size. Some may say that this does not *prove* an inverse relationship between farm size and productivity per unit of land. However, the data do show that the general presumption of a highly positive relationship—which underlies most arguments against land reform—is highly suspect.

In a Chilean study Morales analyzed output per hectare for farm size groups ranging from 10 to 500 hectares of irrigated land. In this study, soil quality, distance to market, and even type of farming were held constant. Even under these rigidly controlled circumstances there were no statistically significant differences in output per hectare for farms in the various size groups, despite the small farms' greater difficulties in obtaining credit and water for irrigation.[22]

The relationships of Figures 1 and 2 are cast in a static context. However, "the relationships revealed are the end products of such dynamics as have existed in the society." [21] In his analysis of India, Long has suggested that similar analysis from societies whose agriculture has had more dynamics might be more relevant. The data from Mexico, Taiwan and Japan are especially revealing in this regard. As Long points out, "if data for such countries [as Japan] reveal a negative relationship between size-of-farm and gross value productivity per acre above variable capital costs as the end result of a highly dynamic agricultural development process, then indeed the

[5] In the first Brazilian case, Figure I, the measure used was net sales per productive hectare. In Figure II, in the case of Japan, the measure is total receipts minus fertilizer costs per unit of land, and in the case of Taiwan the measure is net farm income per unit of land. Note also Dovring's point cited earlier that large farms use more of the hardware that might otherwise have been invested toward even more rapid industrialization. In the Indian case, Long notes: "Investigation of this point reveals, however, that empirically gross value of productivity per acre is equally adequate under Indian conditions. Variable capital inputs, in the form of seeds, fertilizers, insecticides, etc. are so small as not to affect comparison, even if there were some consistent bias in relation to farm size—which there appears not to be." [21]

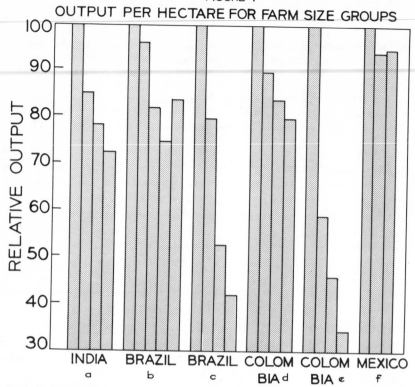

FIGURE I

OUTPUT PER HECTARE FOR FARM SIZE GROUPS

For each Country, bar at left represents output per hectare for smallest farm size group. Bars to the right represent successively larger farms with their output per hectare expressed as a per cent of that of the smallest size group.

a (India) From data for the mid- and late 1950s gathered by the Studies in Economics of Farm Management, Ministry of Food and Agriculture, Government of India, New Delhi. Output as gross value in rupees per acre. Long classified actual farm sizes into four size groups—smallest, second smallest, second largest, largest—for each of eight areas in seven states, and presented output per size group as the average of the eight areas. Data from more than 1,000 farms from seven states.[21]

b (Brazil) Output as net sales per productive hectare, in thousands of cruzeiros (1963). Actual farm sizes included in each size class are: 1) 0–10ha.; 2) 10.1–20 ha.; 3)20.1–40 ha.; 4) 40.1–100 ha.; 5) more than 100 has. Sample of 311 farms.[17]

c (Brazil, 1950) Output as per cent of value of sub-family (smallest) farm production per cultivated hectare. The authors classed actual farm sizes into four groups: sub-family, family, multi-family medium, and multi-family large. Based on National Census data.[2]

d (Colombia, 1960) Uses same measures of output and same farm size criteria as Brazil, above. Based on National Census data.[2]

e (Colombia, 1966) Output as gross value per hectare, in U.S. dollars. Actual farm sizes included in each size class are: 1) less than one ha.; 2) 1–2.99 ha.; 3) 3–9.99 ha.; 4) more than 10 has. Sample of 203 farms in a highland community of Colombia.[15]

f (Mexico, 1960) Output as gross value per hectare of arable land, in pesos. Actual farm sizes included in each size class are: 1) less than 5 hectares in the private sector (average about 1.45 has.); 2) ejido lands averaging about seven hectares per ejido member (only about 2 per cent of 1.6 million ejido members engage in collective farming); 3) more than 5 has. in the private sector (average about 27 has.). Based on National Census data.[11]

52

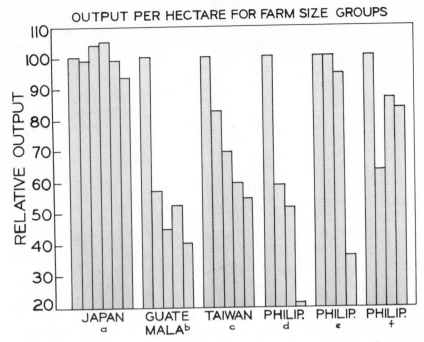

FIGURE 2

OUTPUT PER HECTARE FOR FARM SIZE GROUPS

For each Country, bar at left represents output per hectare for smallest farm size group. Bars to the right represent successively larger farms with their output per hectare expressed as a per cent of that of the smallest size group.

a (Japan, 1960) The author uses data from the Japanese Farm Household Survey of 1960. Output as total receipts per cho minus fertilizer costs per cho, for seven crops. Farm sizes are classified into six groups: 1) less than 0.3 cho; 2) 0.3–0.5 cho; 3) 0.5–1.0 cho; 4) 1.0–1.5 chos; 5) 1.5–2.0 chos; 6) more than 2.0 chos. One cho is slightly larger than one hectare.[4, p.36]

b (Guatemala, 1950) Output as value product per utilized hectare for nine selected crops, in U.S. dollars. Farms are classified into five groups: micro farms, sub-family, family, multi-family medium, and multi-family large.[8]

c (Taiwan, 1965) Output as net farm income per chia, in thousand N.T. dollars. Actual farm sizes are: 1) under 0.51 chia; 2) 0.52–1.03 chias; 3) 1.04–1.54 chias; 4) 1.55–2.06 chias; 5) over 2.07 chias. One chia is 0.9699 hectare. [6, p. 41]

d (Phillippines, 1963-64) Output in kilograms per hectare per year. Farms were placed in four groups: 1) below 1.0 ha.; 2) 1.1–2.0 has.; 3) 2.1–3.0 has.; 4) above 3.0 has. Graph depicts relative productivity for share tenants in Barrio Balatong B. [29]

e (Phillippines, 1963-64) Using same measures of output and same farm size criteria as Phillippines, above. Graph depicts relative productivity for share tenants in Barrio Santo. [29]

f (Phillippines, 1963-64) Using same measures of output and same farm size criteria as Phillippines, above. Graph depicts relative productivity for lease tenants in Barrio Santo. [29]

53

presuppositions of most land reform discussions—and also of much technical assistance work—need intense re-examination." [21]

The data for Japan certainly are not inconsistent with this view. In fact the multiple cropping ratio is consistently smaller as farm size increases. For the case of Taiwan, Figure 2 shows a very consistent inverse relation between farm size and net farm income per unit of land. From 1940 to 1965, cultivated land per farm was reduced by almost one-half while output per hectare *more than* doubled. [6, p. 41] The Mexican data also support this view. The ejido sector in 1960 had only one-fourth of the land but accounted for over one-third of all marketed farm produce. In terms of sales as a per cent of total output, the ejido sector sold practically the same proportion (65.2) as did the large farm sector (67.7). [11]

It might be argued that the higher productivity per unit of land on existing small farms is no real evidence that new units to be created by splitting up large farms would achieve increased productivity. But the evidence available on post-reform experiences—in Mexico, Bolivia, Chile, Japan, Taiwan, Egypt—shows that although in some cases there was an initial drop, average productivity per unit of land increased rather substantially after these reforms. All cases involved a reduction in the average size of farm. [30]

There has been much discussion of the drop in agricultural output following the Bolivian revolution and reform, yet this decline was not so much in output as in the amount marketed. [7] In fact, even the amount marketed was not reduced by as much as official statistics indicate because marketing channels were altered. Some of the produce marketed through the new channels did not get counted since market reports were obtained only at the traditional outlets.

These points are *not* presented to argue for small holdings per se or necessarily for a family farm system. Certainly the man-land ratio in Latin America, for instance, is immensely more favorable than in Japan or Taiwan, and presenting information on these countries is in no way meant to suggest such small farm systems for Latin America. The figures are meant to show that even in a system of extremely small holdings, the inverse relationship between farm size and output per unit of land exists.

Differences exist between today's less developed nations and those parts of Europe, the United States, and Canada where the family farm system was established some time ago. What is required for development is an agriculture organized in such a way as to (1) provide incentives for productive work and investment, and (2) use a combination of production factors consistent with the cost and availability of these factors at a given time.

In the United States, land tenure research has concentrated largely on improving leasing arrangements and on "modifications designed to help the tenant become an owner operator." [28] This research emphasis is also fitting for many of the landlord-tenant small farm systems in Asia (where land reform is a simpler process than in Latin America since such systems are already characterized by small operating units and the key to reform is to sever the landlords' control over the tenants). But such a research emphasis does not get at the issues in the Latin American situation. There, if the agricultural sector is to make a greater contribution to overall development, basic reorganization and redistribution of land and capital are required in order to: productively employ more people in agruculture, contribute more to capital formation in both the agricultural and the industrial sectors, and provide the income distribution necessary for broadening the market for locally manufactured goods as well as for the increased production from agriculture.

References
[1] Barraclough, Solon. "Employment Problems Affecting Latin American Agricultural Development." *FAO Monthly Bulletin of Agricultural Economics and Statistics* 18, Nos. 7/8 (1969):1-9.

[2] ――― and Arthur L. Domike. "Agrarian Structure in Seven Latin American Countries." *Land Economics* 42 (1966): 391-424.

[3] Brewster, John M. "The Machine Process in Agriculture and Industry." *Journal of Farm Economics* 32 (1950): 69-81.

[4] *Changes in Agriculture in 26 Developing Nations.* ERS Foreign Agricultural Report, no. 27. Washington, D. C.: Department of Agriculture, 1965.

[5] Chombart de Lauwe, J.B. and F. Morvan. "Les possibilitíes de la petite Entreprise dans l'agriculture française." Paris: 1954. Cited by Michel Cépède. "The Family Farm: A Primary Unit of Rural Development in Developing Countries." In *Rural Development Reader,* edited by R. Weitz, forthcoming.

[6] Christensen, Raymond. *Taiwan's Agricultural Development: Its Relevance for Developing Countries Today.* ERS Foreign Agricultural Economic Report, no. 39. Washington, D. C.: Department of Agriculture, 1968.

[7] Clark, Ronald. "Land Reform and Peasant Market Participation on the Northern Highlands of Bolivia." *Land Economics* 45 (1968): 153-172.

[8] Comité Interamericano de Desarrollo Agrícola. *Tenecia de la tierra y desarrollo socio-económico del sector agrícola: Guatemala.* Washington, D.C.: Pan American Union, 1965.

[9] Dorner, Peter. "Fourteen Million Rural Poor." Book review of *The People Left Behind,* Report of the President's Advisory Commission on Rural Poverty, 1967. *The Yale Review* 58 (1969): 282-292.

[10] ――― and Herman Felstehausen. "Agrarian Reform and Employment: The Colombian Case." *International Labour Review* 102 (1970): 221-240.

[11] Dovring, Folke. *Land Reform and Productivity: The Mexican Case, Analysis of Census Data.* Urbana, Ill.: University of Illinois, 1966. Revised and re-issued as Land Tenure Center Paper, no. 63. Madison, Wis.: University of Wisconsin, 1969.

[12] ―――. "The Share of Agriculture in a Growing Population." *Monthly Bulletin of Agricultural Economics and Statistics* 8 (1959): 1-11. Reprinted in *Agriculture in Economic Development,* edited by Carl K. Eicher and Lawrence W. Witt. New York: McGraw-Hill, 1964.

[13] Eckaus, R. S. "The Factor Proportions Problem in Underdeveloped Areas." *American Economic Review* 5 (1955): 539-565.

[14] Georgescu-Roegen, N. "Economiç Theory and Agrarian Economics." *Oxford Economic Papers* 12 (1960): 1-40. Reprinted in *Agriculture in Economic Development,* edited by Carl K. Eicher and Lawrence W. Witt. New York: McGraw-Hill, 1964.

[15] Haney, Emil. "The Economic Reorganization of Minifundia in a Highland Community of Colombia." Ph. D. dissertation, University of Wisconsin, 1969.

[16] Heady, Earl O. "A Recipe for Meeting the World Food Crises." *CAED Report,* no. 28. Ames: Iowa State University, 1966.

[17] Johnson, Roger G. and Rueben C. Buse. *A Study of Farm Size and Economic Performance in Old Santa Rosa, Rio Grande do Sul.* Land Tenure Center Research Paper, no. 27. Madison, Wis.: University of Wisconsin, 1967.

[18] Johnston, Bruce F. and J. Cownie. "The Seed-Fertilizer Revolution and Labor Force Absorption." *American Economic Review* 59 (1969): 569-582.

[19] Johnston, Bruce F. and John W. Mellor. "The Role of Agriculture in Economic Development." *American Economic Review* 51 (1961): 566-593.

[20] Kanel, Don. "Size of Farm and Economic Development." *Indian Journal of Agricultural Economics* 22 (1967): 26-44.

[21] Long, Erven J. "The Economic Basis of Land Reform in Underdeveloped Economies." *Land Economics* 37 (1961): 113-123.

[22] Morales Jara, Hector. "Productividad presente y potencial en 96 predios de la Provincia de O'Higgins y su relación con el tamaño de las propiedades." Memoria, Universidad de Chile, 1964.

[23] Myrdal, Gunnar. "The United Nations, Agriculture, and the World Economic Revolution." *Journal of Farm Economics* 47 (1965): 889-899.

[24] Nichols, William H. "The Place of Agriculture in Economic Development." In *Agriculture in Economic Development,* edited by Carl Eicher and Lawrence Witt. New York: McGraw-Hill, 1964.

[25] Nove, Alec. "The Decision to Collectivize." Paper presented at the Conference on the Agrarian Question in Light of Communist and Non-Communist Experience, August 23-26, 1967, University of Washington.

[26] Owen, Wyn F. "The Double Developmental Squeeze on Agriculture." *American Economic Review* 56 (1966): 43-70.

[27] Raup, Philip M. "Land Reform and Agricultural Development." In *Agricultural Development and Economic Growth,* edited by Herman M. Southworth and Bruce F. Johnston. Ithaca: Cornell University Press, 1967.

[28] Ruttan, Vernon W. "Production Economics for Agricultural Development." *Indian Journal of Agricultural Economics* 23 (1968): 1-14.

[29] ———. "Tenure and Productivity of Philippine Rice Producing Farms." *The Phillippines Economic Journal* 5 (1966): 42-63.

[30] Most of the evidence shown in Figures 1 and 2 was first assembled by Professor Lester Schmid and is published as Appendix III, "Relation of Size of Farm to Productivity." *Land Tenure Center Annual Report 1968.* Madison, Wis.: University of Wisconsin, 1969. That appendix contains summaries of additional studies.

[31] Schmid, Lester. "The Role of Migratory Labor in the Economic Development of Guatemala." Ph. D. dissertation, University of Wisconsin, 1967.

[32] Thiesenhusen, William C. "Population Growth and Agricultural Employment in Latin America with Some U. S. Comparisons." *American Journal of Agricultural Economics* 51 (1969): 535-752.

[33] Todaro, Michael P. "A Model of Labor Migration and Urban Unemployment in Less Developed Countries." *American Economic Review* 59 (1969): 138-148.

CHAPTER 4

Employment and Latin American Development

WILLIAM C. THIESENHUSEN

Associate Professor of Agricultural Economics,
Agricultural Journalism, and the Land Tenure
Center at the University of Wisconsin–Madison

CHAPTER 4

Employment and Latin American Development

WILLIAM C. THIESENHUSEN

In 1960 the United Nations estimated that about 40 per cent of the economically active labor force in Latin America was underemployed. At that time it showed that, when underemployment was converted to unemployment, some 27 per cent of the active population (equivalent to about 18 million persons) were jobless. [51] As the First Development Decade closed, the comparable figure was 25 million. [49] The startling fact is that the labor force will keep growing rapidly for a generation no matter what happens to the birth rate. [28; see also 30]

Between 1960 and 1969 the manpower supply in Latin America grew at an annual rate of 2.8 per cent compared to the 2.6 per cent recorded in the fifties. There is little likelihood that the rate in the seventies will drop since prospective entrants to the labor force have already been born. At its annual meeting in 1970 the Economic Commission for Latin America (ECLA) predicted that the yearly growth rate of the labor force in the seventies would be 3 per cent. [46, p. 36] By comparison, the working age population of industrialized countries is expected to increase by only about one per cent annually in this decade. Joblessness in Latin America will continue to grow unless far reaching policies are enacted. The only solution is more jobs.[1]

Despite the failure to design conscious employment policies, there is growing awareness that the issue is serious and that traditional remedies fall short of solutions. Speaking as president of the World Bank, Robert McNamara claims:

> We do not want simply to say that rising unemployment in LDC's is a "bad thing" and something must be done about it. We want to know its scale, its causes, its impact and the range of policies and options which are open to governments, international agencies and the private sector to deal with it.

> The issue is fully as urgent as the proper exchange rates or optimal mixes of the factors of production. ... Just as the censuses of the 1950's helped to alert us to the scale of the population explosion, the urban and employment crises of the Sixties are alerting us to the scale of social displacement and

---

1 Along with the writers of the Rockefeller Report, who relegated the employment problem to footnote importance [32], policy makers often prefer to repress the panoply of problems that joblessness raises. The Peterson Commission skimmed over the issue by saying, "the value of encouraging private intiative has been amply demonstrated. It has made possible more employment opportunities." [53]

general uprootedness of populations which are exploding not only in numbers but in movement as well. But we are still only picking up the distress signals. We still do not know how to act. [21]

The 1970 version of a text on economic development now carries a section entitled "The Labor Absorption Problem"—a topic not covered in the first edition. It notes:

One of the most perplexing—and serious—problems now confronting many LDC's is their growing level of urban unemployment in the modern sector... even if GNP rises, and even if per capita income also rises, some might still not consider the economy to have developed if the absolute number of unemployed has at the same time also increased. [22, pp. 430-431]

And a recent Organization of American States (OAS) analysis warns that unless meaningful employment programs are enacted, Latin America cannot hope to employ the steadily increasing proportion of the population in the economically active age group. [25, pp. 20-30] This says nothing about lowering present unemployment. As it wound up its conference in Lima on April 23, 1969, ECLA noted that to keep up with the increase in those seeking productive work, the number of available jobs must double every twenty-five years. [49, pp. 50-74]

Why is the problem not confronted directly? One reason that policy makers have not done more about unemployment is that the problem is so badly formulated: there are no definitive data on the number or the location of jobless people in the region. As John Kenneth Galbraith once observed, societies are loathe to do anything about problems that statisticians have not measured. But in his 1969 book, *Maximum Feasible Misunderstanding,* Daniel Moynihan reminds us that the United States guessed its way through the entire legislative program of the Depression without even knowing the unemployment rate; at the time, this information was gathered with the census each ten years. Now macro-economists would feel lost without the monthly decimal-accurate calculations of the Bureau of Labor Statistics. While more research into the matter is of crucial importance, Latin America cannot afford to stand by much longer waiting for a precise definition of its unemployment problem.

In Latin America no information (except perhaps personal income statistics) is harder to come by than reliable employment data. [48, p. 137] Unemployment figures that do exist may in fact understate the problem. Some of the unemployed have perhaps been without work for so long that they have ceased to look for regular jobs and are no longer considered part of the economically active population. Frequently such individuals are taken in by their extended families or compadres to do odd jobs. Others may eke out a living in some menial occupation, such as shining shoes, or they may work a day or two a week and remain unemployed the rest of the time. Usually, they are not listed as unemployed if they do anything at all; even though they are "underemployed," they are not technically jobless. A further problem is that some unemployed workers are not counted because they are hard to find and are never approached in a survey. [49]

Another reason that policy makers have not done more about employment policy is that many assume that more jobs will come as a by-product of economic growth. The essence of economic development is too often equated with maximizing GNP per capita. Paul N. Rosenstein-Rodan argues that Latin America must

aim at absorbing unemployment at a high level of productivity through large-scale, capital intensive but highly productive industrialization. This implies high savings and investment, and a high rate of economic growth—5.5 to 6.5 per cent for the economy as a whole, and around 9 to 10 per cent per annum in the industrial sector. It will take at least five to ten years to reach full employment that way—but it is the way of defeating poverty. [33, p. 58]

figures debatable, but emphical, clear

Along these lines, even though the Pearson Report states, "the failure to create meaningful employment is the most tragic failure of development," it seems to imply that the prime economic target for less developed countries is that they attain a rate of growth of GNP of 6 per cent annually in the seventies as contrasted to the 4.8 per cent rate actually reached from 1950 to 1967. [27, p. 58] It has been estimated that in Brazil a growth rate of 12 per cent is necessary to absorb new entrants to the labor force over the next few years. [10, p. 4] Speaking of Latin America as a whole, the United Nations claims that, in order to absorb those now underemployed as well as new additions to the active labor force, total output would have to grow by not less than 8 per cent yearly in 1970-80. Increases of even 6 per cent per annum, which would preserve the 1960 level of unemployment into 1980, are unprecedented. [51; 29]

While we know that a slower growth rate will undoubtedly aggravate the situation, it does not seem to follow that stepping it up will solve the employment problem. Seers reports that in Trinidad the growth in per capita income averaged more than 5 per cent a year during the whole period 1953 to 1968 while overt unemployment showed a steady increase to more than 10 per cent of the labor force. [37] Reynolds observes that total employment in Puerto Rico fell between 1950 and 1960 in spite of an average annual rate of growth in GDP of 5.2 per cent. [31] Seemingly paradoxical situations are not uncommon. In Brazil and in Venezuela between 1950 and 1960 annual manufacturing output grew very rapidly (9.2 per cent and 13.0 per cent), but manufacturing employment expanded only moderately (2.6 per cent and 2.1 per cent), while in Peru, output grew only moderately (6.6 per cent), but employment expanded fairly rapidly (4.4 per cent). [10, pp. 4-5] This situation seems quite general in less developed countries. Eicher et al. assembled similar data from various African studies and reported that between 1954 and 1964 manufacturing output in Kenya rose by 7.6 per cent per year in current prices while manufacturing employment fell by 1.1 per cent. A similar phenomenon was experienced in Zambia. [11, pp. 11-12] In

Uganda between 1954 and 1964 the total recorded employment fell 13.2 per cent, a decline of 1.4 per cent yearly, while gross domestic product increased by 60 per cent. [5]

Why does industry not absorb more labor? Available macro-data seem to suggest that the *nature* of the industrial process may be as important as its growth rate. Myrdal explains the slow absorption of labor early in the contemporary development process by noting that where manufacturing implies rationalization of earlier and more labor intensive firms, the new factories "will out-compete craft and traditional production and the net effect on labor demand will be negative." [23]

Much of the economic growth that has occurred in Latin America since World War II can be traced to the conscious policy of manufacturing domestically the simple consumer goods that used to be imported. Largely because of the skewed pattern of income distribution, the demand for these goods was soon satisfied; investment funds began to move from industries which manufactured more labor intensive goods like textiles, processed foods, and furniture to more complex products (refrigerators and even automobiles).

These consumer durables require more imported equipment and materials. To make it easier to ship in these intermediate products, local currencies were overvalued in relation to the dollar, so imported capital (often labor-saving machines) became cheaper relative to labor. At the same time, credit rates were subsidized to encourage industry.

Dziadek reports that recent records in less developed countries show manufacturing output expanding most rapidly in the more capital intensive industries. [10, p. 5] Indeed, in many less developed countries an increase in capital intensity in manufacturing seems to accompany the sector's lack of ability to absorb more labor. [2; 47]

Schuh catalogues a number of policies designed to foster import substituting industrialization which have contributed to its capital intensity:

The overvaluation of the currency, the multiple exchange rate, and the subsidized interest rates in the capital market have in part contributed to the implantation of a capital-intensive industrial sector. The granting of special tariff exemptions and lower exchange rates have kept the relative cost of foreign capital equipment below that of other types of imports.

He concludes:

The capital-intensive nature of the industrial sector must in part be due to the cheapening of the price of capital as a result of the direct and indirect subsidies to capital goods and a low real rate of interest. [35]

He also believes that the overpricing of labor as a result of minimum wage laws and other government regulations has contributed to the capital intensive tendency. This is corroborated by Turner, who reports that in many Latin American countries, average real wages in the urban sector are rising some 4 to 5 per cent annually compared to an increase in real product per capita of only some 1 to 1.5 per cent. [42]

Moreover, aid from developed countries often comes with "strings," making it mandatory for the recipient to buy equipment from the nations contributing the aid. This encourages the use of the latest capital-intensive (or labor-saving) machinery, even when less costly and perhaps secondhand equipment might be just as useful and would probably provide more jobs. Indeed, it often proves impossible for private entrepreneurs to use more labor intensive methods because the appropriate equipment does not exist—or at least it cannot be imported economically; technology in the industrialized countries is produced in accordance with factor proportions existing there and these tend to reflect conditions of labor scarcity. Therefore, as manufacturing has moved from artisan shops into factories and from less to more complex goods, machines have been replacing labor. By private calculation this results from economically rational decisions. But from the public's perspective it is often a losing proposition, mainly because it increases joblessness. A high tariff wall which protects finished products of even very inefficient producers is the capstone to the process.

Thus industry has done little to relieve the pressures of rising unemployment. Modern Latin American manufacturing has employed labor at a lethargic pace. Between 1925 and 1960 modern manufacturing absorbed only a little over 5 million of the 23 million people added to the urban labor force in that period.

Put differently, an estimated 35.4 per cent of a relatively small nonagricultural labor force was engaged in manufacturing in 1925; but by 1960, as urbanization advanced, this percentage dropped to 27.1. [47] Examining the history of most currently developed countries, one finds that the ratio of manufacturing jobs to urban employment remained essentially constant over long periods of time—and at much higher levels. [47, p. 36]

In exemplifying the problem, Dorner and Felstehausen report that the total labor force in Colombia increases by an estimated 168,000 to 200,000 persons per year while modern manufacturing currently provides only 10,000 new jobs annually. They conclude that, "These numbers will grow even larger as young people already born reach working age. New Jobs in manufacturing are falling further and further behind growth in the labor supply, despite the fact that in recent years manufacturing employment appears to have been growing more rapidly in Colombia than in Latin America as a whole." [9; see also 54]

In sum, between 1960 and 1965 in Latin America, a 5.6 per cent average annual increase in manufacturing output was associated with a 2.1 per cent average annual growth in employment. While hopefully investment and effective demand can remain high enough to increase both rates, the output-to-labor ratio will probably become more unfavorable to employment in the future. Manufacturing in Latin America is likely to become less rather than more labor-intensive.

It may be possible to retard this trend in a few industries from time to time, but it is difficult to see how enough jobs can be created thereby.[2] Yet,

---

[2] For example, income redistribution policies could shift the demand structure for manufactures (in the short run) away from its current emphasis to more labor intensive consumer nondurables. This development would also ease balance of payments difficulties.

as Barraclough explains: "A new factory in Medellín or São Paulo will generally adopt the labor saving technology of industries in present-day Detroit or Pittsburgh, not that of 19th century Birmingham or Manchester." [3]

The increase in capital intensity in city-based industry is not confined to manufacturing: "Even construction, while much less capital-intensive than manufacturing, has apparantly become more capital-intensive with cranes and bulldozers and other labor-saving machinery being substituted for labor." [10, p. 6]

Where are the unemployed and underemployed located? Open unemployment in Latin America is predominantly urban in nature, and it has grown steadily in the last decade. The prime locus of the misery brought by idleness is the city slum or shantytown. Latin American city populations are growing at a rate of at least 5 per cent a year; and although the region now has its population about equally divided between urban and rural areas, it is rapidly becoming predominantly urban. Projections indicate that by 1980 metropolitan Buenos Aires, Mexico City, Rio de Janeiro, and São Paulo will each have 10 million inhabitants while greater Santiago, Lima, Caracas, and Bogotá will each have 4 million. In other words, the population of each of these cities will just about double in one decade. About 5 million people already live in shantytowns and slums in these and other Latin American cities. This "marginal population" is growing at a rate of an incredible 15 per cent per year—about 10 percentage points higher than city populations as a whole.

Since the nonfarm goods-producing sectors have not absorbed a substantially larger percentage of a growing labor force, more workers drift to the tertiary sector (such as government service) and to what the United Nations has called "unspecified activities"—mainly disguised unemployment. In absolute numbers, 1965 employment in these subsectors was nearly double that for 1950—a growth seemingly not in line with the need for services engendered by the region's rate of economic growth. [56; 45, pp. 62-63, Table I-XIII] The most poignant illustration of the problem is that in this period "unspecified activities" absorbed labor at an annual rate of 8.2 per cent and "employed" far more new entrants to the labor market than did manufacturing.

ECLA recently investigated the hypothesis that all sectors have high-, medium-, and low-productivity subsectors. [48, pp. 132-164; 50] It estimates, for example, that in manufactures, construction, and technological services, the work force allocated to each productivity subsector would be about 20, 60, and 20 per cent respectively. ECLA also indicated that the distance between the upper and lower extremes of per capita income and productivity is increasing in all sectors. Currently, 11 per cent of the working population generates 40 per cent of the regional product—a labor productivity similar to that of Western Europe. At the other end of the scale the level of productivity of 40 per cent of the working population is at the same level as that of the poorest countries in Asia. [48, p. 136] As urbanization proceeds at a rate faster than industrialization, new entrants to the job market—if they are absorbed at all—are employed in the medium- and low-productivity subsectors. It stands to reason, that if the economies of Latin America do not grow much faster and if they continue to become more capital-intensive while population growth in the cities continues at the projected pace, the capacity of this subsector to provide jobs will become even less adequate, thereby raising open unemployment to even higher levels. [50]

Migration and Employment

One reason for the rapid increase of urban populations is the high birth rate. While demographic studies of all Latin American countries are not available, one recent study has shown that almost 70 per cent of the total population growth of Chile's major cities (Santiago, Valparaíso, Concepción) can be accounted for by natural increase; the remainder was due to migration from rural areas. [1; 55; 43]

Although migration-related unemployment is certainly not negligible in Chilean metropolitan complexes, the step-wise nature of migration patterns (from rural areas to towns and then to cities [16])[3] indicates that the unemployment strain resulting from rapid rural-to-urban migration may be even greater in small towns that in large cities. In any event, major cities in Latin America are experiencing heavy in-migration. For example, three-fourths of the population of Bogotá aged fifteen to fifty-nine years was born outside of the city. Even so, population in rural Colombia continues to grow by more than 100,000 people each year. Between 1941 and 1964 adults living on farms increased by a figure twice that for the period 1938 to 1951. [9; 36] The United Nations reports that half or more of the population increase in large Latin American cities comes from in-migration and "a similar proportion of the annual natural increase of the rural population is moving out of the countryside." [44, p. 60]

However, "it does not follow that the peripheral settlements are occupied mainly by uprooted peasants." [44, p. 60; 14; 19; 20; 26] Actually several processes keep these shantytowns' populations growing rapidly: (1) Increasing numbers are apparently moving from downtown areas. Campesinos with the least financial resources may well move first to the central city unless they have family ties in the shantytown. [14] While downtown, they may accumulate enough capital to buy a plot or at least they may organize for an invasion of fringe property. The natural increase in poor areas in general and peripheral areas in particular is higher than in the rest of the city. (2) Peripheral settlements seem to have a more youthful population than the

---

3 Some evidence leads us to belive that this phenomenon may be quite common in Latin America. In a sample study of one shantytown in Bogotá, Flinn points out that 34 per cent of the in-migrants had changed their residence at least once before moving to Bogotá. [14]

rest of the city; younger couples with growing children are most highly motivated to escape from the crowded urban centers. At the time of the 1960 census, fertility rates in low income areas of Santiago amounted to 44 per 1,000—about 10 per 1,000 above the national rate. [44, p. 58, footnote 8] (3) Many people come from smaller towns. Flinn shows that in one barrio clandestino (illegal settlement) in Bogotá, 32 per cent of the in-migrants had last resided in towns with 2,000 to 20,000 persons. [14] (4) Some, of course, come directly from the farm.

But whether migrants go first to the central city, to its periphery, or to smaller towns, they are often jobless when they resettle. Given the bleak prospects that most Latin American urban areas offer to many of these newcomers, why do they go? The answer often lies in a combination of "push" and "pull" factors. [17] Economists have tended to concentrate on pull factors: a significantly higher wage in town is likely to attract in-migrants. Furthermore, the educational opportunities and social services offered are usually substantially better in urban than in rural areas. Other social scientists regard push factors as more important: displacement of labor by mechanization, the high degree of soil exhaustion in some overcrowded rural areas, and shifts from crops to livestock.

Within a framework recently developed by Harris and Todaro out of East African experience, it becomes rational for a rural resident to migrate to the city, even if there is only a 33-50 per cent probability of finding a job, provided that average wage earnings in the modern sector are two or three times the average agricultural income. [41;15] This leads Harris and Todaro to the conclusion that efforts to reduce urban unemployment by expanding urban jobs will be self-defeating: a flood of new migrants will be attracted because the large wage differential will likely persist, if not become greater, as urban employment expands. Presumably these observations also fit the case of most Latin American countries where the rural-urban wage gap is as great, if not greater, than in East Africa. Todaro claims, in interpreting this analysis:

Perhaps the most significant policy implication emerging from this model is the great difficulty of substantially reducing the size of the urban traditional sector without a concentrated effort at making rural life more attractive. For example, instead of allocating scarce capital funds to urban low cost housing projects which would effectively raise urban real incomes and might therefore lead to a worsening of the housing problem, governments in less developed countries might do better if they devoted these funds to the improvement of rural amenities. [41]

Yet far from despairing of more rural-to-urban movement, some argue that this trend should be encouraged and claim that Latin American agriculture retains too many people. [6; 8] Shuh has decried what he calls "damming up labor in the agricultural sector" [35] and in a similar tone and idiom FAO claims that:

farmers and farm population in the developing countries are 'dammed-up' in an agricultural reservoir. . . . There are really far more people on farms than are needed, even with present low levels of technology. They stay there

66

because—in the absence of adequate employment in the towns—they are at least reasonably sure of some food, of housing—no matter how primitive—and of the protective care of the family.[52]

No doubt labor productivity in Latin American agriculture is low, but if industry in Latin America cannot be structured so that it is substantially more labor absorptive, the consequence of faster rural-to-urban migration means trading underemployment on the farm for unemployment in town.

Latin America badly needs development policies which, with a minimum of capital expenditure, allow more people to be more productively employed while stimulating industry to catch up with population growth. This is a large order. One can only hope to discover and take advantage of slack somewhere in the economy—idle resources that can be combined cheaply with labor to produce a needed product. Meier believes it will be difficult to reduce the rural-urban wage differential, making it "all the more important to emphasize the 'supply side' of the problem. When the urban sector cannot absorb the inflow of labor from the rural sector, special consideration must be given to policies that will remove the causes of the rural 'supply push' and help contain the labor force in rural areas." [22, p. 437] He suggests that the modern sector must avoid manufacturing whatever can be produced in the rural sector, and he advocates a full scale program of rural development including public works; incentive prices for agricultural products; wider dispersal of public services in the countryside; more labor-intensive technology in farming, industry, and the tertiary sector; and removal of monetary distortions. [22, pp. 437-439]

The "pull" factors are important in the latin American context, but Meier's contention that "push" factors also figure in determining migration deserves more attention.

Structure of Latin American Agriculture

Besides its failure to produce adequate food supplies (meaning, among other things, that progressively higher wages must be paid in the industrial sector to provide sustenance to workers while scarce foreign exchange must be used in some countries to import food rather than industrial equipment), agriculture in Latin America is not providing adequate opportunities for the underemployed. In brief, agriculture in Latin America is not as labor absorptive as it might be. One reason is the way farming is organized—the minifundio-latifundio system.

Both minifundios and latifundios have their peculiar employment problems in Latin America. Focusing on minifundios in Guatemala, Schmid found that they often cannot support a family even at subsistence levels and that this often forces micro-plot owners to search for work on large farms.

Recruitment of these workers (cuadrilleros) is done by farm representatives called habilitadores who hire a total of roughly 150,000 seasonal workers per year. The habilitadores are paid commissions equalling 10 per cent of the wages earned by the workers they contract. Such contracts are generally for a period of thirty days. The habilitadores commonly give the cuadrilleros advances of two to five dollars to defray trip costs, to provide needed cash for family, or to buy food on arrival at the large farm; these advances are later deducted from wages. [34, pp. 7, 12-16]

Schmid considers this temporary rural-to-rural migration important in somewhat alleviating the employment problem. He notes that separate export and subsistence sectors characterize Guatemalan agriculture. The export sector consists of large farms producing cotton, coffee, and sugar cane; the subsistence sector produces corn and other food crops on very small farms—much of it for consumption by the farm family—and provides the large farms with needed migratory labor. The number of people, including dependents of the workers, involved in this kind of work in 1965-1966 in Guatemala was estimated at about 1 million, most of them migrating from the altiplano (highlands). [34, pp. 1-2] Yet, if the minifundios cannot absorb adequate labor because they have too little land, latifundios cannot do so because of the way they are organized.

Large estates encompass much of the best land—except in Mexico, Bolivia, and Cuba—and are worked by hired laborers who have little or no bargaining power. When farming is structured in this manner, it does not provide either the security of employment or the income necessary to keep workers in farming until industry can employ them; low incomes for most people in farming mean that certain segments of the industrial sector are stifled for lack of purchasers. Furthermore, this structure does not permit a flourishing community organization which would support an educational system capable of developing literacy skills and attitudes needed for urban employment or for upgrading the abilities of the rural labor force.

When management is separated from labor, and when labor is ample and poorly organized—as it is in the estate system in Latin America—there is little to stop landowners from firing workers, who have few employment alternatives. On the other hand, an owner-operator may sell out when the situation becomes acute, but he cannot fire himself or his family labor when caught in a cyclical cost-price squeeze. Consequently, in a system dominated by family farms, a large proportion of surplus labor takes the form of involuntary underemployment in the countryside rather than involuntary unemployment in town.

In the United States for example, family farm agriculture harbors a surprisingly large amount of surplus labor. These redundant labor resources have not only funded their own sustenance but have also been called upon to cover a substantial percentage of the schooling costs of their children and to supply a large proportion of other necessary social overhead capital. Owen has called this usually unnoticed phenomenon "farm-financed social welfare." [24]

Recent congressional hearings and special study commissions have revealed that, by relying too much on farm-financed social welfare, the affluent U.S. society has consistently overlooked its rural poor. We may abhor this neglect but must also admit that the "agrarian dualism" which developed throughout this century had some important advantages: one subsector of farming provided immense production while the other's contribution to the economy was primarily in retarding premature cityward migration. Through primarily locally-financed schools, agricultural communities have helped to prepare farm people to be more productive in agriculture if they remained or in urban employment if they migrated.

The U.S. type of agricultural dualism is not static; land harboring redundant labor constantly "moves" into more active uses in response to changes in the market. Labor saving capital has now become so cheap relative to labor that farms are being rapidly combined into larger units, with a resulting release of workers. Labor has not always benefitted from these land and capital "flows." That some individual farmers—even entire communities—have been "left behind," in the words of a recent government report, is but one indication that farm-financing of welfare does not work altogether smoothly.

In some parts of the United States, including much of the South, farm-financed social welfare never was a part of the institutional framework. To the degree that the southern sharecropping system separated ownership-management from labor (which had little countervailing power) and discouraged the education of the farm work force, it can, albeit roughly, be compared to the Latin American estate. Indeed, the southern cropper may be considered a U.S. analogue of the Latin American hacienda worker.

These farming systems seem to have serious urban repercussions. In the United States the problems of today's ghetto are not due to racial prejudice alone (in boom periods black unemployment in cities does drop somewhat). They are at least partly due to the release of an unskilled labor force which could not be fully hired by industry at the stage of development it was passing through.

We may thus pose several plausible hypotheses from U.S. experience with relevance for contemporary Latin America: had a land tenure system that was labor absorptive over the long run been established in the rural South after the Civil War, recent out-migration would not have been as rapid. When it occurred, it would have represented a more genuine response to viable economic opportunities. And if that land ownership system had fostered farm-financed social welfare, laborers would have reached the urban labor market more adequately prepared for urban life. [39]

Like the remnant southern plantation, the Latin American estate is not known for its ability to absorb labor. Research by the Inter-American Committee on Agricultural Development shows that production per acre is inversely related to farm size in several Latin American nations; while latifundios average 400 times larger than many tiny farms called minifundios, they employ only 15 times more workers. [4] The reason for this phenomenon is not hard to find. Pressures for the adoption of labor-saving farm technology in Latin America are similar—if not yet so pervasive—as those in industry. Accordingly, the trend on large farms in Latin America is toward use of less and less labor per unit of output.

Some countries appear to be following policies which encourage this effect. Import subsidies enable those who mechanize to obtain machinery at reduced cost with cheap credit and long term repayment arrangements. In addition, minimum agricultural wage laws in many countries are making labor more expensive in relation to capital. A point that these policies fail to note is that mechanization—which is primarily labor displacing—usually does not elevate production as much as equivalent expenditures on yield-increasing inputs such as fertilizers, hybrid seeds, and insecticides, unless double cropping is possible and speed in harvesting one crop and planting the next is of the essence.

Some have suggested that a progressive land tax would result in a more intensive agriculture and a more active land market. Laying aside the difficulties of effectively administering such a law, large landowners may find it profitable—at least as long as inflation continues—to dislodge workers and substitute capital for labor to meet this fixed cost instead of intensifying their production or selling their land.

What is the possibility of a "reform policy?" The argument here is that a concerted effort should be made to slow the rate of farm-to-city migration in Latin America until industry can absorb labor at a faster pace. This slow down would undoubtedly be one effect of a land reform program which emphasized the need for increased employment. One plan for Latin American countries with a traditional land tenure structure—a plan with historic parallels in our North and West and in post-revolutionary Mexico—might be "contrived dualism." [39; see also 40] This plan involves two subsectors and involves giving far more policy emphasis to the second than to the first.

(1) *A subsector which emphasizes growth in marketable surplus.* On the progressively managed large farms as much employment and income security as possible should be required without creating disincentives for management. At the same time, incentives should be created for the achievement of greater productivity through the application of more yield-increasing inputs. This is not out of the question in the Latin American context where credit supply, experiment stations, extension services, and market and educational facilities are already "in place" and are serving the large-acreage farmer.

(2) *A subsector which emphasizes growth in employment.*

(a) The existing subsector of very small farms can probably continue to absorb some population increase until development-created employment begins to catch up with population growth. If technology can be adapted to their needs (as it has been in Japan and Taiwan) and if markets and credit can be made available to them, some small farms might employ even more people and make a greater contribution to marketable surplus.

(b) Programs to provide secure, legal titles for present occupants may be inexpensive and very important in some areas. Most Latin American countries have farmers who are "squatters" on public lands, and thousands of other farmers do not have title to the land they farm. Neither status is conducive to employment stability, nor does either offer the security required for long term investments in agriculture.

(c) Since underutilized and poorly managed land on traditional large-scale farms contributes little to production or to employment and since the absentee ownership and paternalistic labor patterns do not permit farm-financed social welfare, such land should be transformed into new peasant farms, which may take the form of "family farms" or "co-operatively-worked" operations. As with existing small farms, policies should try to move reform-created farms as rapidly as possible toward commercial agriculture with limited mechanization but increased use of inputs such as fertilizer which increase yield per acre without cutting down on labor use.

Dorner and Felstehausen suggest that there is "direct competition between small and large farmers for land, capital, and services" and that the "small farmer is at a serious disadvantage in competing for cost-reducing technologies and services without specific policies aimed at reallocating resources in his favor." They believe, in the Colombian context, that a policy of contrived dualism requires development of some separate technologies for the small farm sector, modification of the rual service structure (like schooling facilities and marketing) to assure access to small farmers, and development of dual credit systems.[9]

Certainly reforms at the producer level require reshaping of secondary level institutions also. But given the exceedingly scarce supply of resources available, it will not be possible to do everything at once. Even if (for the time being) reform does no more than provide sustenance for large numbers of rural people, it will contribute to economic development by retarding migration until industrial development can catch up with population growth. Nevertheless, just giving people land will do more than just feed them. As people discover that they can buy consumer goods by raising their incomes, they will make an effort to do so. As they increase their city sales, urban food problems will be ameliorated. As the labor market tightens, more land and capital should be freed for the "predominantly marketable surplus" sub-sector.

Aside from slowing cityward migration by providing more farm jobs, this strategy should also increase the demand for simple consumer goods since the economy would rest on a broader base. Because income sources will be appropriated from the rich, the demand for luxury consumer durables might be somewhat stifled. Manufacture of such products as textiles, furniture, clothing, and processed food is typically more labor-intensive than manufacture of either consumer durables or intermediate products. Therefore, in addition to creating more farm employment, land reform should yield more city jobs too. Agriculture input industries should also be stimulated by land reform and balance of payments should be affected favorably since simpler goods require fewer imported inputs than more complex goods. Moreover, the government may be able to increase its revenues from agriculture. If these public funds are invested wisely, economic development should be stimulated.

Land reform seems a logical first step to development. It must be followed with proper fiscal and monetary measures. And if the program is not adapted to the country's needs it may stifle rather than promote development. For example, if executed too slowly, it may result in investor insecurity; if too expensive, it may fuel inflation; if conceived of as indiscriminately splitting up productive farms in which there are substantial economies of scale, it may cut exports and exacerbate balance of payments problems.

Does substantial increased agricultural employment necessarily accompany all "agrarian reform?" It has not been widely recognized that a primary goal of any agrarian reform program must be to provide more jobs. Hence reform is often defended on other grounds, and employment goals are forgotten or at least shortchanged.

In some cases the provision of more employment through agrarian reform has been considered so politically infeasible that "in general, it is taken for granted that most of the new jobs that must be created will be outside agriculture." [44, p. 61] Recent studies by the Inter-American Committee on Agricultural Development proposed "as a 'reasonable objective' for agrarian reform—programmes benefiting half the families of landless workers now in agriculture, minifundio holders and cultivators with insecure tenure within the next decade, or 5 per cent of such families annually plus an allowance for increase in their numbers." [18; 4] In citing these, the United Nations claims, "it does not seem likely. . . that more than one or two countries in which the rural population is already a minority will attain the proposed rate of agrarian reform in the near future." [44, p. 61, footnote 18]

Feder reserves special ire for recent reform efforts and claims they were so slow-moving that their employment impact has been all but negligible.

During the 1960s, Latin America's so-called land reform has been an unqualified failure. . . . Actually families receiving land from the governments' land reform institutes are outnumbered by *new* families joining the poor rural proletariat by a ratio of something like 20 to 1. [12]

The Colombian case seems to illustrate Feder's contention. Felstehausen reports that the Colombian land reform agency (INCORA) titled 88,200 parcels of land from its founding in 1962 through July 1, 1969. But this did not affect the employment problem significantly because 91 per cent of these titles represented de facto recognition of settlers' claims to public lands they already occupied. Meanwhile, he reports, "Expropriation procedures have been almost wholly unsuccessful. The legal procedures are complex, slow, and cumbersome.... Using both expropriation and amicalbe purchase procedures, INCORA has acquired 123,889 hectares of land through June 1969. Of this amount, only 18,000 were obtained by outright expropriation." He explains that much of this land was acquired by INCORA for reclamation and public works projects and not necessarily for settlement; through mid-1969 INCORA had titled only 1,194 farms representing 13,600 hectares of this land. Since about 21,000 farm families are added to rural Colombia each year, Felstehausen claims that INCORA's program to date has scarcely dented Colombia's employment problem. [13]

Chile's recent record is somewhat brighter than Colombia's although it did not begin to become so until 1965. There are, however, certain disturbing signals about employment effects of the Chilean reform. In some cases it seems the reform settlers themselves may be becoming a closed group with no more willingness than a latifundista to pay decent wages to labor. Of course, if Chile's asentamiento system results in more employment than would be the case in the absence of reform, the net social result may still be positive.

Some agrarian reforms can have a profound employment impact. It has been reported that the man-land ratio on the Bolivian side of Lake Titicaca is more than eight times that on the other side of the lake in Peru. [7] Since the agrarian reform in 1953, population seems to have increased between 50 and 100 per cent in this region of the Bolivian countryside. In 1965 the Peruvian departamento of Puno was declared an "agrarian reform zone" with one stipulation being that owners can retain more land (up to 8,000 hectares) if they pay campesinos a minimum wage. This provision resulted in campesino firings and evictions and their flight to small towns in the area, as well as to Lima and Arequipa. Population density per square mile is 8.3 in Puno and 67.9 in the Titicaca area of Bolivia. Marketable surplus per hectare is similar in both areas. The level of living of the Bolivian campesinos is higher in this region than the level of living of the nearby Peruvian campesinos.

Likewise, a recent analysis of Mexican agriculture revealed, "at this stage of Mexico's development the micro-farms in the ejido and private sector of agriculture fulfill the important function of providing a subsistence base to millions of people who would otherwise be far worse off than they are now." Even so, "one of the gravest problems of Mexican agriculture at the present time is the extensive un- and underemployment of the rural labour force." [38]

The high population growth Mexico has experienced of late means that the landless labor force in Mexico has grown equally fast. Indeed, as Stavenhagen indicates:

The agriculture labor force has almost doubled from 3.6 million in 1930 to over six million in 1960. And though the number of farms has more than doubled during the same thirty year period ... the size of the landless agricultural population (wageworkers, day labourers, sharecroppers, etc.) has likewise increased and it now represents one half of the agricultural labour force ... [numerically] more than the whole peasant population taken together at the time of the revolution. [38]

The experience of Mexico bears lessons for countries now embarking on a land reform: if the current population growth rate continues for several decades, no stopgap expedient of agricultural employment will be able to provide enough jobs to accommodate the burgeoning work force.

References

[1] Arriaga, E. E. "Components of City Growth in Selected Latin America Countries." *Milbank Memorial Fund Quarterly* 46 (1968): 241-253.

[2] Baer, W. and Herve, M. H. "Employment and Industrialization in Developing Countries." *Quarterly Journal of Economics* 80 (1966): 88-107.

[3] Barraclough, Solon L. "Rural Development and Employment Prospects in Latin America." Prepared for the Second Conference on Urbanization and Work in Modernizing Areas. Mimeographed. St. Thomas, Virgin Islands, 1967.

[4] ––– and Arthur Domike. "Agrarian Structure in Seven Latin American Countries." *Land Economics* 42 (1966): 391-424.

[5] Baryaruha, Azarias. "Factors Affecting Industrial Employment." *Development Digest* 7 (1969): 17-21.

[6] Berlin, Lawrence H. "A New Agricultural Strategy in Latin America." *International Development Review* 9 (1967): 12-14.

[7] Burke, Melvin. "An Analysis of the Bolivian Land Reform, by Means of a Comparison between Peruvian Haciendas and Bolivian Ex-Haciendas." Ph. D. dissertation, University of Pittsburgh, 1967.

[8] Currie, Lauchlin. *Accelerating Development: The Necessity and the Means.* New York: McGraw-Hill, 1966.

[9] Dorner, Peter and Herman Felstehausen. "Agrarian Reform and Employment: The Colombian Case." *International Labour Review 102 (1970): 221-240.*

[10] Dziadek, Fred. *Unemployment in the Less Developed Countries.* Discussion Paper no. 16. Washington, D.C.: Agency for International Development, 1967.

[11] Eicher, Carl; Thomas Zalla; James Kocker; and Fred Winch. "Employment Generation in African Agriculture." Draft discussion paper prepared for the African Bureau. Mimeographed. Washington, D.C.: Agency for International Development, 1970.

[12] Feder, Ernest. "The Campesino Is Still Waiting." *CERES* 2 (1969): 25-29.

[13] Felstehausen, Herman. "Agrarian Reform: Colombia." Chapter 8 of this book.

[14] Flinn, William L. "The Process of Migration to a Shantytown in Bogotá Columbia." *Inter-American Economic Affairs* 22, no. 2 (1968): 77-88

[15] Harris, John R. and Michael P. Todaro. "Migration, Unemployment and Development: A Two-Sector Analysis." *American Economic Review* 60 (1970): 126-142.

[16] Herrick, B. H. *Urban Migration and Economic Development in Chile.* Cambridge, Mass.: The M.I.T. Press, 1965.

[17] Horowitz, Irving Louis. "Electoral Politics, Urbanization, and Social Development in Latin America." In *Latin American Radicalism.* Edited by Irving Louis Horowitz, Josué de Castro, and John Gerassi. New York: Vintage Books, 1969.

[18] Inter-American Committee on Agricultural Development. *Policies of Agrarian Reform.* LARC/65. CONF. 3. Presented to the Latin American Conference on Food and Agriculture, 1965.

[19] Mangin, William. "Latin American Squatter Settlements: A Problem and a Solution." *Latin American Research Review* 2 (1967): 65-98.

[20] Manaster, Kenneth A. "The Problem of Urban Squatters in Developing Countries: Peru." *Wisconsin Law Review* 1 (1968): 23-61.

[21] McNamara, Robert S. "Address to the Columbia University Conference on International Economic Development." New York, February 1970.

[22] Meier, Gerald. *Leading Issues in Economic Development.* 2d ed. Oxford: Oxford University Press, 1970.

[23] Myrdal, Gunnar. "The United Nations, Agriculture and the World Economic Revolution." *Journal of Farm Economics* 47 (1965): 889-899.

[24] Owen, Wyn F. "The Double Developmental Squeeze on Agriculture." *American Economic Review* 56 (1966): 43-70.

[25] Pan American Union. *The Alliance for Progress and Latin-American Development Prospects: A Five Year Review, 1961-1965.* Baltimore: Johns Hopkins Press, 1967.

[26] Patch, Richard W. "Life in a Callejon." *American Universities Field Staff Report* (1961).

[27] Pearson, Lester B. *Partners in Development: Report of the Commission on International Development.* New York: Praeger, 1969.

[28] Prebisch, Raúl. Confidential report to Governor Nelson Rockefellor. Reported in *The New York Times,* May 12, 1969.

[29] ———."Transformación y desarrollo, la gran tarea de America Latina." Mimeographed. Santiago: Inter-American Development Bank, 1970.

[30] República del Perú, Ministerio de Trabajo. *Recursos humanos del Peru, 1965-1975.* Lima: Editorial Servicio de Empleo y Recursos Humanos, 1967.

[31] Reynolds, Lloyd G. "Wages and Employment in a Labor Surplus Economy." *American Economic Review* 55 (1965): 19-39.

[32] Rockefeller, Nelson A. *Quality of Life in the Americas.* Washington, D.C.: Agency for International Development, 1969.

[33] Rosenstein-Rodan, Paul N. "The Alliance for Progress and Peaceful Revolution." in *Latin American Radicalism,* edited by Irving Louis Horowitz, Josue de Castro, and John Gerassi. New York: Vintage Books, 1969.

[34] Schmid, Lester. *The Role of Migratory Labor in the Economic Development of Guatemala.* Land Tenure Center Research Paper, no. 22. Madison, Wis.: Land Tenure Center, 1967.

[35] Schuh, G. Edward. "Effects of Some General Economic Development Policies on Agricultural Development." *American Journal of Agricultural Economics* 50 (1968): 1283-1293.

[36] Schulz, T. Paul. *Population Growth and Internal Migration in Colombia.* Memorandum RM-5765-RC/AID. Santa Monica, Calif.: The Rand Corporation, 1969.

[37] Seers, Dudley. "The Meaning of Development." *International Development Review* 11 (1969): 2-6.

[38] Stavenhagen, Rodolfo. "A Land Reform Should Answer the Questions It Raises." *CERES* 2 (1969): 43-47.

[39] Thiesenhusen, William C. "Population Growth and Agricultural Employment in Latin America with Some U.S. Comparisons." *American Journal of Agricultural Economics* 51 (1969): 735-752.

[40] ——— and Marion R. Brown. "Problems of Agriculture." In *Survey of the Alliance for Progress.* U.S. Congress, Senate, Committee on Foreign Relations, 90th Congress, 2nd session, 1968.

[41] Todaro, Michael P. "A Model of Labor Migrations and Urban Unemployment in Less Developed Countries."*American Economic Review* 59 (1969): 252-261.

[42] Turner, H. A. *Wage Trends, Wage Policies, and Collective Bargaining: The Problems for Underdeveloped Countries.* Cambridge: Cambridge University Press, 1966.

[43] United Nations. *Population and Vital Statistics Report,* data available as of July 1, 1968, statistical papers, Series A, Vol. 20, no. 3.

[44] United Nations, Department of Economic and Social Affairs. "Recent Changes in Urban and Rural Settlement Patterns in Latin America." In *International Social Development Review* 1 (ST/SOA/Ser. X/1), 1968.

[45] United Nations, Economic Commission for Latin America (hereafter cited as ECLA). *Economic Survey of Latin America, 1965.* (E/CN. 12/752/Rev. 1), 1967.

[46] United Nations, ECLA. *Economic Survey of Latin America, 1969* (E/CN. 12/AC.62/2), 1970.

[47] United Nations, ECLA. *The Process of Industrial Development in Latin America* (E/CN. 12/716/Rev. 1), 1966.

75

[48] United Nations, ECLA. *Social Change and Social Development Policy in Latin America* (E/CN. 12/826), 19 February 1969. Prepared for the Thirteenth Session, Lima, Peru, April 1969.

[49] United Nations, ECLA. "Some Aspects of the Latin American Economy towards the End of the Nineteen-Sixties." In *Economic Survey of Latin America, 1968,* Part One (E/CN. 12/825), March 1969.

[50] United Nations, ECLA. "Structural Changes in Employment within the Context of Latin America's Economic Development." *Economic Bulletin for Latin America* 10 (1965): 163-187.

[51] United Nations, Economic and Social Council. "The Employment Problem." *Development Digest* 7 (1969): 3-11.

[52] United Nations, Food and Agricultural Organization. *Provisional Indicative World Plan for Agricultural Development.* Vol. 1 (C69/4), August 1969.

[53] U. S. Presidential Task Force on International Development. *U.S. Foreign Assistance in the 1970's: A New Approach.* Mimeographed, Washington, D.C., 1970.

[54] U.S. Senate, Committee on Foreign Relations. "Colombia: A Case History of U.S. Aid together with a Report of the Comptroller General." In *Survey of the Alliance for Progress,* Document No. 91-17, 91st Cong., 1st. sess., 1969.

[55] Weeks, John R. "Urban and Rural Natural Increase in Chile." *Milbank Memorial Fund Quarterly* 48 (1970).

[56] Wolfe, Marshall. "Social Trends in Latin America." ECLA Draft. Santiago: ECLA, 1967.

PART III
SELECTED CASE STUDIES

CHAPTER 5

Agrarian Reform Legislation: Chile

JOSEPH R. THOME

Professor of Law and the Land Tenure
Center at the University of Wisconsin-Madison

CHAPTER 5

Agrarian Reform Legislation: Chile*

JOSEPH R. THOME

The role of law in the process of change is often neglected, even though it is evident that legal structures to a large degree set the framework within which policies leading to economic and social change must operate. As Friedman puts it: "No major social change occurs or is put into effect in a society which is not reflected in some kind of change in its laws." [10, p. 29]

Chile's attempts at reforming its land tenure system illustrate the ways in which a social and cultural context may both shape and be shaped by legal institutions. Chilean Agrarian Reform Law 16.640 of 1967—particularly its expropriation provisions—also supplies an important Latin American example of the process ·by which policy consideration and values concerning land reform are translated into legal objectives and means—institutions, rules, powers—to reach the objectives, as well as of the actual functioning of these legal means.

Development of Land Tenure Structures in Chile

As in most Latin American nations, the Chilean tenure structure has its origin in the Spanish colonial system, and its basic forms were reinforced after the establishment of the Republic. Contrary to some notions, the Spanish Crown made serious attempts at curtailing the abuses of the encomienda system, under which Indian labor was "entrusted" to Spanish colonizers. These attempts included regulation of land grants (mercedes) by subjecting them to conditions of possession and use similar to the U.S. homestead acts, guarantee of access to water, pasture and wood by declaring these public goods for the common use, and protection of Indian lands by establishing Indian reserves and ejido or common village lands. [8, pp. 113-115; 24, pp. 47-50]

The king held ultimate and absolute control over all matters regarding the "Kingdoms of the Indies"; the colonies, in fact, were the domain of the crown, not of the Spanish state. Directly under the monarch was the Council of Indies, which through royal delegation exercised vast powers over all phases of the colonial administration: legislative, judicial, financial, military,

* From *American Journal of Comparative Law* 19, no. 3 (Summer 1971); with some modifications. Reprinted with permission.

commercial, and even ecclesiastical. But only here, at the top, was the imperial bureaucracy highly centralized. While the principal crown agents in the colonies ostensibly held supreme power over civil and military matters in their areas of jurisdiction, their powers were in reality rigidly limited. [25] The functions of the colonial officials were not those of modern executives, with planning or other delegated powers, but were limited to interpreting and enforcing the vast number of minutely detailed and often contradictory laws and directives of the Council of Indies. Lines of authority or jurisdiction were blurred and often overlapped; each official was supposed to oversee the other, and almost any colonial official or Spanish settler could appeal over the heads of his superiors directly to the Crown. Moreover, any colonial official could, while recognizing the authority of the king, refuse to comply with a particular royal directive on the grounds that it was against the interests of the crown to do so. [13]

According to Phelan, the prevalence of conflicting standards and ambiguous goals prevented subordinates from enforcing all of the laws and gave them a voice in decision making without jeopardizing the centralized control of their superiors. [25] To Heise, this situation "determines the formation—in all of Spanish America—of a proud, aristocratic class." [13] This class was very independent from state power, conscious of its rights, and, in practice, devoted to making sure that its interests would prevail.

In Chile, as elsewhere in Latin America, the colonial bureaucracy proved unable or unwilling to effectively control the encomenderos and land grantees. A large migration of settlers from southern Chile into the central zone occurred between 1577 and 1600; consequently, the number of land grants as well as the usurpation of Indian land increased substantially. By 1603 hardly any land was left undisturbed, and conflicts over boundaries and titles were settled through a complete land survey that covered all the area between the Choapa and Maule Rivers. Some of the usurped land was returned to the Indians, and many small and middle-sized farms still remained. [8, pp. 181-183]

By 1650, however, the increasing demand for leather and tallow began to make cattle ranching very profitable. The resulting pressure for larger holdings led to the acquisition of the smaller mercedes by the more ambitious or stronger of the landowners, and the large, extensively exploited latifundios started to form.

In 1680, the Peruvian market was opened for Chilean wheat. Together with the still important market for cattle products, as well as the growing importance of other crops, such as grapes and other fruits, this led to a greater concentration of ownership, particularly of the more fertile and irrigable lands. [8, p. 264] The mayorazgos (lands granted in primogeniture) and the large landowners' tendency to leave the land to one son, even where primogeniture was not required, solidified the large fundos. Moreover, by 1700 almost all available cultivable land had been distributed throughout central Chile and south to Talca and Concepción. Land prices rose, and land began to be treasured not only for what it could produce, but for speculative purposes as well. [8, p. 264]

Though official crown opposition to ownership concentration continued throughout the eighteenth century, many attempts to tighten state control only served to further alienate the creoles from the Spanish crown, and to strengthen the position of the landed oligarchy. The public sale of Church lands after the expulsion of the Jesuits in 1767 resulted in either the extension of already existing latifundios or the creation of new ones. Likewise, the abolishment of taxes on Chilean wheat exported to Peru, while beneficial to commerce, also consolidated the wealth and power of the Chilean landowners. [8, p. 266]

When independence finally came in the early nineteenth century, it was not the result of a social revolution or even a process of "decolonization," but was merely an alteration of political ties, substituting local creole rule for European rule. [16] Nevertheless, ideology played an important role in the movements for independence and in the subsequent development of the new nations. The creole leaders were influenced by the French (and to a lesser degree, the American) revolution and the prevalent ideologies of the times. These new ideas contrasted the emergent bourgeois-capitalist society with the remnants of feudal, static structures; among the main new principles were those of economic liberalism and individual rights. These principles were reflected in legal norms which guaranteed equality under the law, freedom of contract, and private property rights. However, their result was "an exaggerated emphasis on private property and liberty of contract, similar in effect to the exaggerated individualism of nineteenth century England and America." [21, p. 18]

Particularly important was the concept of individual or private property rights, a concept formally incorporated into that most influential of nineteenth century legal documents, the Napoleonic Code, which was in turn the model for most Latin American Civil Codes. [11, pp. 44-45] Thus, Article 582 of the Chilean Civil Code reads as follows: "Ownership is the real right in a corporeal thing to enjoy it and dispose of it arbitrarily, provided no other law or right is violated." [translated in 23, p. 14] While the final phrase of the cited article would allow the application of almost any restriction, civil law jurists or legal scholars have nonetheless traditionally considered that ownership provides absolute, exclusive and perpetual rights. [23, p. 14] In effect, and in rural areas at least, these concepts have provided legal protection to individual property rights (haciendas, fundos) against almost any attempt aimed at their restriction.

The concept of "exclusiveness," for instance, was used in Mexico and other countries as a means for justifying the subdivision of the still extant communal landholdings into individual plots, many of which were subsequently incorporated into adjoining latifundios. [12]

It is of course very difficult to document whether the landowners of that period consciously adopted the concept of absolute ownership in order to preserve or extend their power, or whether they were merely following the ideas then in vogue. Nevertheless, in referring to this period in Chilean

The constitution of 1833 was made by the landowners for the landowners, and it lasted as they were the only really viable political force in Chile. After 1833, a period of authoritarianism developed a sense of respect for tradition, for property interests, and for judicial order. Mayorazgo was finally abolished as a result of laws passed in 1852 and 1857. A list of the families that enjoyed these rights coincides with those who controlled the political life of Chile. These laws led to some inroads on the absolute power of the landholders, but they still managed to maintain the haciendas as one-family units, and, as the price of land rose, they maintained their economic power. [1] [1]

Whatever the reasons which led to the adoption of these legal rules concerning ownership, and whatever the objectives of these rules, the fact remains that during the balance of the nineteenth century and well into the twentieth, the Chilean landed class did extend its holdings and power.

The effects of independence were particularly burdensome to native Indian communities. Even such legal reforms as the proclamation of equality before the law, for instance, were used against them, as Lambert points out: "When the Indians' special status that sealed their inferiority was abolished, so was a meticulous legislation which, although discriminatory, aimed at protecting these inferiors against excessive exploitation by the colonists." [16, p. 56]

Throughout the nineteenth century, wholesale usurpation or absorption of Indian lands and other small holdings by the hacendados was accomplished, often through means either patently illegal or of dubious legality, including such practices as debt peonage. [30] This process "gave to the landowning oligarchies a measure of absolute local power that would have exceeded even the dreams of the conquistadors." [22, p. 167]

Generally speaking, the almost unrestricted power of the landed oligarchy lasted until well into the twentieth century. Around 1920, however, certain other countries, particularly Mexico, started what Morse labels Latin America's "truly 'National' Period." New political regimes, social programs, and cultural statements began to emerge and to evince a new preoccupation with historical realities and needs. [22, p. 169] Chief among these programs were the processes of agrarian reform, receiving their legal rationalization from the concept of "the social function of property," which posited that ownership involved obligations as well as rights; among these obligations was to use the property for the common welfare, under penalty of losing some or all of the rights. [23, pp. 20-22]

[1] The relevant clause protecting private property rights in the 1833 Chilean Constitution, Article 10, Section 5, reads as follows [cited in 1]:

No. 5—The inviolability of property of all kinds, whether belonging to individuals or communities. No one shall be deprived of his property or any part thereof, however small, or of any right therein, except by virtue of a judicial decision, or when the interest of the state, declared by law, requires the use or condemnation thereof; but in this case proper indemnification to be determined either by agreement with the owner or by valuation made by a jury of competent men shall be previously made.

Previous Attempts at Agrarian Reform

With the election of President Arturo Alessandri in 1920, Chile entered a new era, marked by the gradual erosion of the political power of the landed oligarchies and the emergence of urban and industrialist elites, more modern in outlook than the traditional landlords, though often intimately related to or allied with the landed class. [20; 28; 1] This shift or sharing of political power also represented an awareness that new legal responses were required to satisfy or at least palliate the growing social and economic demands of the less favored classes. The pressures for change resulted in 1925 in the promulgation of a new constitution, which provided the legal framework for the moderate social legislation enacted in the following years. [26, pp. 51-58]

With regard to property rights, the new constitutional provisions established somewhat clearer limitations on private property rights and committed the state to look after the proper division of property and the formation of family homesteads. [20, p. 16; 23, pp. 26-27; 1] [2] The most relevant section of the 1925 Constitution reads:

No one shall be deprived of his property, or any part of it, or any right he might have to it, except by judgment of a court of law or by expropriation for reason of public utility declared by law. In such case, the owner shall be previously indemnified either by agreement with him or by judgment of a court of law.

The exercise of the right of property is subject to the limitations or regulations required for the maintenance and progress of the social order and, furthermore, the law may impose obligations or servitudes of public utility in favor of the general interests of the State, the welfare of the people, and public health. [translated in 23, p. 27]

The requirement of prior compensation for any condemnation process was retained in almost identical form from the 1833 Constitution; nevertheless, the last clause represented a very important legal innovation. By subjecting the exercise of property rights to the "social order," and empowering subsequent legislation, for reasons of the common welfare, to impose limitations and obligations on property rights, the new constitution opened the way for a series of new laws. The Water Code, General Law on Constructions and Urbanization, and others under which property rights were limited, would probably not have been possible prior to 1925. [7, pp. 13-14, 25]

The new constitution also signaled that the hacienda or latifundio should somehow be restricted and that the family farm should be promoted. [1] To this end, Law 4.496 of 1928 established the Caja de Colonización

---

2 The subcommittee in charge of discussing and drafting the new provisions was bitterly split between a small faction that would do away with the principle of individual property altogether, and a larger faction that would retain the relevant section of the 1833 Constitution untouched. [23, pp. 26-27; 1] The final result emerged from the urging of Alessandri, who personally directed the subcommittee, and who based his position on the writings of Leon Duguit. [26, pp. 272-274]

Agrícola (Agricultural Colonization Bank) to carry out land redistribution and settlement activities. [28, p. 33] The Caja was to colonize virgin land, or to purchase land in the open market for subsequent resale under long term mortgages. It also had limited expropriation or eminent domain powers, but they were never exercised. After initial financing, the Caja was to operate with the mortgage payments of the colonists. [1]

The Caja's efforts were not particularly successful. By 1962, when it ceased to exist, it had settled only 4,206 families in the entire country. It failed primarily because of inadequate government financing, the requirement of paying cash for properties acquired, and inflation, which made the outstanding mortgages practically worthless. Moreover, its process for selecting beneficiaries made it very difficult for farm laborers to qualify. [1; 28, pp. 34-36]

Under increasing pressure from both the Chilean peasantry and the Alliance for Progress to implement a land reform, a new Agrarian Reform Law, No. 15.020, was enacted by the Chilean Congress and signed by President Jorge Alessandri in November 1962. Under this law the Caja was eliminated and two new agencies—the Corporación de Reforma Agraria (CORA) and the Instituto de Desarrollo Agropecuario (INDAP)—were established, with new and better defined powers and functions.

CORA was made solely responsible for carrying out land reform in Chile; given its own credit department for new colonists; and empowered to acquire or expropriate land for its subsequent subdivision into small family farms (parcelas) and garden plots (huertos), to regroup minifundios, and to establish cooperatives. INDAP was to provide supervised credit and assistance to established colonists and other small farmers. In addition, it was charged with operating government experiment stations. Both agencies were to be semi-autonomous, but under the administrative umbrella of the Ministry of Agriculture. [28, pp. 37-45]

Lands used by CORA for the reform were to be obtained from purchases at public auction, direct purchases from the landowners, contributions of public lands from the government, or expropriation, which is the means of particular interest here. Law 15.020 had very elaborate provisions regarding the categories of expropriable land [19, pp. 8-9] but did not supply clear criteria as to when or under what circumstances expropriation should be exercised.

At any rate, existing constitutional provisions forced CORA to pay in cash the full value of any property expropriated before that property could enter CORA's possession. [28, pp. 39-40] [3] This requirement severely limited

---

[3] A new constitutional amendment was adopted in 1963 which permitted deferred compensation (10 per cent in cash and the balance in equal installments). The new amendment, however, stipulated that deferred compensation could only be applied when the law provided judicial review of the expropriation action as well as a procedure to annually readjust the unpaid balance in accordance with the rate of inflation. The required new legislation was never enacted; consequently, this amendment was never implemented, and was replaced in 1967 by a much broader amendment. [28, p. 40]

the potential application of Law 15.020, since it is simply impossible to compensate expropriated landowners under these conditions and still have a land reform that will benefit a significant number of landless peasants. [3] CORA, of course, could still enter purchase agreements with landowners in which installment payment procedures were voluntarily stipulated. Quite obviously, landowners would only do so when it was to their advantage.[4]

A plethora of exceptions to expropriation, as well as procedural complexities in Law 15.020, made the expropriation process cumbersome and time consuming. Furthermore, all CORA's determinations were subject to judicial review by a special agrarian court, whose decisions were in turn appealable to the overloaded regular court system.

The most generous estimate of land distribution under the Jorge Alessandri government (up to May 1964) was that CORA had effected 1,354 land divisions totaling 51,442 hectares. Most beneficiaries had yet to receive a land title to their new "parcela" or "huerto." [28, p. 42] In short, Law 15.020 fell into the pattern of Latin American land reform laws so aptly described by Thomas Carroll: "Land reform laws are invariably long, complicated and detailed. This makes their implementation very difficult." [2, p. 198] The law was badly drafted, provided too many safeguards to landlords, had too limited objectives (small family farms), did not solve the issue of prior compensation, and was poorly implemented. Nevertheless, Law 15.020 served a very useful function. The mere fact that a land reform agency had been organized proved immensely valuable to President Frei's program after 1964.

New Agrarian Reform Legislation: Law 16.640 of 1967

In November 1965 the Frei Government submitted for approval by the National Congress an agrarian reform bill to supplant Law 15.020 of 1962. Over a year in the drafting, the proposed bill represented the result of lengthy and careful study and the participation of distinguished agronomists, sociologists, economists, farmers, and lawyers. [9, p. 5]

Frei's campaign had criticized the Alessandri land reform as not going beyond a colonization program and had promised more comprehensive reform programs. There were several reasons for this prominence of agrarian reform: the economic stagnation in the agrarian sector; the failure of the Alessandri government to make any headway against this problem; and finally, the growing political awareness and independence of the peasantry. [20, pp. 48-49] The first clear statement of reform goals was contained in the message which Frei presented to Congress along with the new reform bill. According to this document, the basic objectives of the bill were:"(1). . .to

---

4 However, once Frei introduced to the Congress his land reform program, which included a proposed constitutional amendment to allow deferred compensation, CORA was able to reach "negotiated" agreements with landowners with terms much more favorable to the goals of agrarian reform. [17]

provide thousands of families, capable of working it, with their own land . . . [and] thus fulfill their ancient desire to be owners of the land they work, providing them with the chance to improve themselves and to contribute to the progress of the greater national community. (2) . . . [to make] substantial improvement of agricultural productivity. (3) . . . to bring about an effective and authentic improvement in the conditions of [the] rural population by integrating them into the national community and into the country's social, cultural, civic, and political activities." [9, pp. 12-14]

The conceptual underpinning of the first objective was that of "extending" and "perfecting" property rights by providing them with a "social sense" which would permit their full exercise. The second objective, of course, was based on economic and pragmatic considerations, but the basic rationale for the agrarian reform was clearly derived from the idea of "social function" of ownership, as well as from the more progressive teachings of the Catholic Church. [20, p. 63]

Limitations of ownership should be founded on an adequate technical base, such that an effective and profitable redistribution may be carried out, while respecting the property rights of those who are already exercising these rights with social awareness. Property should be maintained and respected. However, it should be socially regulated. No property rights should be allowed to exist which, in their implementation, damage the common well-being and rights of the community. When this happens it means that the basic principle of the primacy of the general well-being over the rights of the individual is not being adhered to, impelling the State to reorganize, regulate, and redistribute those rights, in order to prevent their abuse.

The agrarian reform will guarantee and respect the property rights of those persons who meet the social functions these rights demand. The social functions are: not to have accumulated vast properties, to have adhered to the existing social legislation, to have included the peasants in the benefits acquired from the land, and to have created conditions of stability, justice, and well-being. [9, p. 13]

No attempt will be made to analyze all the elements that played a role in the variation of the means-goals of the agrarian reform process during the Frei government (nor have those elements been documented well enough to permit anything beyond reasoned speculation).

Certain variables, however, can be identified as important factors in this process. One, of course, was the lack of a unified agrarian reform policy within the Christian Democratic Party (PDC). While Frei and his followers (the so-called oficialista, or official, sector within PDC) were proclaiming a goal of individual family farms, members of the tercerista and revelde wings of PDC were talking in terms of "communitarian" farms and similar concepts, and many of the PDC members charged with drafting the new law and with its subsequent administration belonged to the "communitarian" wing.

The voluntary establishment by the Chilean Church in 1963 of land distribution programs on many of its rural landholdings also seems to have been influential. INPROA, the institute organized by the Catholic Church to undertake its land distribution programs, had experimented with the asentamiento type tenure patterns that were later adopted by the government. Moreover, members of the INPROA staff were among the first technicians recruited by the Frei government to help run the agrarian reform. [28, p. 23]

Another factor in this process probably was the experience gained by CORA between 1965 and the promulgation of the law in 1967, experience which seemed to indicate than an asentamiento stage was required. Also, the PDC needed the support in the Senate of both the Communist and Socialist parties in order to pass the land reform law, so their viewpoints were influential. In January 1967, the Chilean congress amended Article 10, Section 10 of the 1925 Constitution, a crucial prelude to action on Frei's new bill, particularly as regards the question of deferred compensation. While the 1925 version of Article 10 did allow for some expropriation of private property for reasons of public utility, it also stipulated that the compensation for said property was to be determined by the courts, using the commercial value as a basis. Moreover, it required the payment of this compensation in full *before* the expropriating agency could enter into possession of the property.

The 1967 amendment effectively removed these limitations by extending the expropriation power of the government over all properties not meeting their "social function," by providing that the basis for compensation was to be the property tax valuation, and finally, by permitting that this compensation be paid over a period of up to thirty years. The amendment also stipulated that new expropriation procedures and norms could be establish by law, thus facilitating the quick-taking of expropriated properties.[5]

In short, the constitutional amendment opened the way for translating the agrarian reform policy of the Christian Democratic government into law. Several months later, Agrarian Reform Law No. 16.640 was enacted by Congress, and it was put into effect on July 29, 1967.

Law 16.640 is a very ambitious statute. Notwithstanding other very important and complementary new statutes and programs improving the

---

5 Relevant sections of Article 10 read:

When the interest of the national community should require, the law shall be empowered to reserve in the State the exclusive dominion of natural resources, productive goods, or others which might be declared of preeminent importance for the economic, social, or cultural life of the country. It will also favor the proper distribution of property and the establishment of family property.

No one shall be deprived of his property except by virtue of the general or special law which authorizes expropriation for the cause of public utility or social interest declared by the Legislator. He who is expropriated shall have a right to indemnization which amount and condition of payment shall be determined by taking into consideration both the social interests and those of the individual. The law shall determine the norms for fixing the indemnity, the court which shall have jurisdiction of appeals as to the amount fixed, which in every case shall pass judgment according to the law, the form of extinguishing the obligation, and the conditions and means by which the expropriator shall take physical possession of the expropriated property.

As to the expropriation of landed estates, the indemnity shall be equivalent to the current assessment for the territorial tax, plus the value of improvements not included in the assessment, and may be paid part in cash and the balance in payments not to exceed thirty years, all in the form and condition determined by the law. [translated in 23, pp. 29-30] status of rural labor, extending rural education, and providing credit and technical assistance to small holders, the heart of the new agrarian reform program depended and still depends on this law. It was supposed to provide for cheap, quick, and efficient redistribution of farm-estates among landless campesinos and for nationalization and reallocation of water rights. These and other measures provided by the law were to be the chief legal mechanisms for ending the stagnation in agricultural and cattle production, and integrating nearly 3 million campesinos into the social, economic, and cultural life of the country. [9] Consequently, Law 16.640 is very complex and lengthy; its official text—160 pages of small type—contains 357 excruciatingly detailed and legislistic articles which, in addition, cross-refer to each other and to articles in other laws. It is a difficult law to understand and to explain. Nevertheless, it is a good law: complete, thorough, and with the basic legal means to achieve a substantial agrarian reform.

In addition, Law 16.640 has spawned a vast number of complementary statutes, regulatory decrees, and other legal regulations, resolutions, and the like. A complete summary and analysis of all these legal provisions is impossible here. Our purpose here is limited to the examination of that basic legal mechanism on which the rest of the agrarian reform process depends: the acquisition or expropriation of rural properties for the purpose of redistribution.

The Process of Expropriation under Law 16.640

A major obstacle to agrarian reform processes in other countries—and in Chile under Law 15.020 of 1962—has been the complexity and excessive length of expropriation procedures. Law 16.640 was supposed to enable CORA to acquire the necessary land in the easiest possible way while at the same time providing affected landowners with adequate legal remedies. [9, p. 27] Application of these provisions, however, brought forth problems not foreseen by the drafters of the law. For purposes of clarity and organization, the process has been divided into different categories; but with few exceptions they are all interrelated and contain both substantive and procedural elements.[6] Procedures are summarized first, and the more important legal considerations and complications are detailed later.

1. *The Expropriation Procedure.* Law 16.640 was supposed to provide a quick-taking expropriation procedure which would permit the adequate planning of agrarian reform projects and shorten the period during which the property, because of the insecurity of the landowner, would remain unproductive. Under this procedure the landowners were to receive adequate

---

[6] The author is indebted to German Lührs [17] for many portions of the following evaluation of the expropriation process under Law 16.640. Also, conversations with various CORA officials were of much help, and several publications of the Chilean government [4; 6] were especially useful.

judicial protection of their rights, particularly regarding compensation of their expropriated lands. If any conflicts should arise they were not, in most cases, to postpone the taking of possession by CORA so that it could proceed with its land settlement programs.

As of late 1970, the procedural stages occurring in an expropriation were as follows: A branch office (one of the 12 Zonal Offices of CORA) conducts field studies (soil, production, etc.) and gathers other socio-economic data on an area or specific property which is potentially expropriable, and reports to the CORA central office in Santiago. The head office, after further studies by the Technical and Legal Directorates, prepares an expropriation decree and submits it to the Consejo of CORA for approval, which requires a majority vote of the Consejo.[7] The decree must contain all basic information about the expropriated property, including its location, its property tax roll number, the legal grounds for its expropriation or acquisition, and the form of compensation. Notice of the decree must be provided to the affected parties, both through personal delivery and through publication in the *Diario Oficial* (Official Gazette).

Once the decree is published, Law 16.640 prohibits, under civil and penal sanctions, all acts which tend to destroy or reduce the value of the land and its accretions.[8] Provided he acts within thirty days of publication, an affected landowner can oppose the decree either by petitioning the Consejo to reconsider its decision, or, under certain circumstances, by challenging it before a Provincial Agrarian Tribunal. Judicial review by the Agrarian Tribunal usually prevents CORA from taking possession of the property until a final judgment is issued.

CORA assesses the expropriated land and the improvements (this assessment must be approved by the Consejo), and deposits at the Superior Civil Court with jurisdiction that part of the compensation that must be paid in cash, in accordance with CORA's own determination.

At this time, CORA is legally entitled to take possession of the property and may request the use of public force if so required. Nevertheless, if at this time there are unharvested crops on the farm, CORA will postpone possession until the end of the agricultural year so that they can be harvested by the owner. CORA can, in most cases, still decide to take possession, provided it indemnifies the owner in cash for any damages, or allows him to enter the property to harvest the crops.

7 The Consejo, or Council of CORA, is made up of the following persons as stipulated by Law 16.640: the Minister of Agriculture, the Executive Officer (Vice-President) of CORA, the Executive Officer of INDAP, one campesino representing the beneficiaries of CORA's programs, one campesino representing the Comités de Asentamiento (Land Settlement Councils) and two delegates named by the President of the Republic.
8 Nevertheless, there are no provisions preventing the owner from stripping the farm of movable or personal property, such as cattle or machinery. About the only power CORA has to prevent the removal of this type of property is the provision that such goods must be compensated in cash. By bargaining with the owners over the value of these goods, CORA has managed, in most cases, to prevent the stripping of necessary implements from the expropriated farm. [18, p. 42]

These are the basic steps in expropriating a rural property for the purpose of agrarian reform. More often than not, however, CORA did not follow the entire legal procedure to its end, but rather negotiated an agreement with the landowner to save both CORA and the landowner much time and expense.

2. *Private Lands Subject to Expropriation.* If a fairly substantial agrarian reform is to be accomplished, quite obviously as much land as possible must be made available for distribution. The legal classification as to which privately owned properties are subject to expropriation, as well as the various criteria that condition their acquisition, provide a fairly accurate measure of the potential reach of any agrarian reform legislation.[9]

Causes for subjecting properties to expropriation in Chile are: (a) *Excess size.* All rural properties in excess of 80 basic irrigated hectares (BIH) in size, regardless of the efficiency of operation. Only the hectares exceeding 80 BIH are expropriable. However, *all* the properties of any given owner are added together for this purpose. (b) *Voluntary transfers.* Properties voluntarily offered to CORA which are necessary for carrying out a reform program.[10] (c) *"Corporate" ownership.* With certain exceptions, such as small cooperatives, and land reform settlements, all farms owned by corporations or other "legal persons." (d) *Pending cases.* Properties over which expropriation proceedings were pending at the time Law 16.640 came into effect. (e) *Unauthorized subdivisions.* Properties originally larger than 80 BIH which were subdivided after November 4, 1964 in order to avoid the agrarian reform. (f) *Low productivity.* Abandoned or poorly exploited farms of any size.[11]

[9] Law 16.640 also made available to CORA most lands in the public domain or owned by government agencies which were susceptible to agricultural use. With the exception of lands owned by welfare agencies, which have to be compensated under the same terms as private property, all other public lands are to be transferred gratis to CORA. Certain public lands are exempted from these provisions. By the time Law 16.640 was promulgated most public lands had already been transferred to CORA, so they will not be the subject of further discussion.

[10] Strictly speaking, such acquisitions are not expropriations but simple purchase agreements. However, they are categorized as "expropriations" by the law in order to subject them to evaluation, compensation, and other conditions. Thus CORA is prevented from purchasing properties at market value but at the same time is given some flexibility in acquiring otherwise non-expropriable properties. Moreover, the provision encourages landowners who fear expropriation to offer the land to CORA voluntarily, as it provides better compensation terms than most of the other expropriation provisions.

[11] Properties which as of November 1964 were smaller than 80 hectares will be subject to this provision for only three years after the publication of the law. Subsequent regulations, according to Article I (a), would provide the criteria for determining the minimum economic, technical and social conditions which must be met in order that a property not be classified as "poorly exploited." Nevertheless, Article 1 (a) also states that there is always a presumption of poor exploitation when a landowner cultivates less than 80 per cent of the normal irrigable area, or 70 per cent in the case of dry land, or when he violates one or more of certain specified labor law provisions at least twice during the two-year period preceding the expropriation resolution.

Minifundia, or properties too small for economic exploitation, are also subject to expropriation, but only for the purpose of land consolidation projects.[12] There are other grounds for expropriation, such as absentee ownership and location within a land reclamation or irrigation project, but these have seldom if ever been applied. Table I shows the number of times each of these potential causes for expropriation was used in 1967-69.

The major reasons for the frequent use of "excess size" expropriations are the simplicity of application and the fact that judicial review over them is very restricted. Most other grounds for expropriation are more difficult to establish and are subject to much more thorough judicial review, particularly "low productivity" expropriations. The growth of the "declarations of abandonment or inadequate exploitation" attached to excess size expropriations is probably due to the promulgation of Regulation 281 of July 1968, which contained the rules for determining abandonment and inadequate exploitation. Once CORA developed experience with these regulations, it became advantageous to attach the declaration to the excess size expropriations, as it has the effect of reducing the cash payment from 10 per cent to 1 per cent. Moreover, this declaration is also not reviewable by the courts.

At the same time, the increasing number of farms voluntarily offered to CORA probably indicates a realization by landowners that they run the risk of being expropriated, and consequently might as well offer their farms voluntarily and obtain the better terms that go along with this. For CORA this method signifies a more rapid acquisition of lands for its programs.

Some rural properties are either specifically or potentially excluded from expropriation. Subject to various conditions or limitations, Law 16.640 specifically exempts those rural properties smaller than 80 BIH; family farms (that area of land, operated personally, which allows a family group to live and prosper due to rational use of the land); experimental farms; and those used for timber operations. Also, the President of the Republic can exclude properties through special decrees: those with soil rehabilitation or improvement plans approved by the Ministry of Agriculture, as well as vineyards that bottle wines and satisfy other stringent conditions.

Law 16.640 also grants some expropriated landowners the right to retain a portion of the affected property. This "reserve right" applies *only* to expropriations affected in "excess size" and "corporate ownership" cases. In the latter instance the right applies only when the property is owned by a "personal association" (e.g., limited liability partnerships), and when certain other conditions are satisfied.

The basic reserve right is 80 BIH or the equivalent; however, if compliance with very stringent conditions regarding productivity and labor relations, etc., can be demonstrated by the landowner, the reserve will be extended to 320 BIH. The reserve right is computed by taking into account *all* the rural properties owned by the expropriated landowner. Thus, it can

12 The reassignment will be either in the form of a family farm or a share of a cooperative farm. Few, if any, minifundia have been expropriated to date.

TABLE I—Number of Properties Expropriated and Legal Grounds Used in CORA Expropriations, July 1967–December 1969

Expropriation Dates	Excess Size A¹	B²	Low Productivity	Unauthorized Subdivisions	Corporate Ownership	Voluntary Transfers	Transitory Articles	Sub-Total	No Data Available	Total No. of Expropriations
July 67-Dec 67	51	7	1	4	12	4	8	87	19	106
Jan 68-June 68	26	3	2	–	5	34	15	85	4	89
July 68-Dec 68	30	19	–	–	15	53	14	131	–	131
Jan 69–June 69	29	20	1	5	5	56	2	118	13	131
June 69-Dec 69	16	47	–	7	8	54	4	136	47	183
Totals	152	96	4	16	45	201	43	557	83	640

Source: Compiled by German Lührs and Joseph R. Thome, from unpublished data of CORA, Dirección de Planificación y Control.

¹By reason of excess size alone.

²Excess size **plus** declaration of abandonment or inadequate exploitation.

only be used once. There are no known cases in which the 320 hectare reserve has been granted.

On lands voluntarily offered, the amount retained depends on the bargain the landowner can strike with CORA. Although no specific data are available, it is obvious that in most cases the reserve retained by the landowner will equal at least 80 BIH.

3. *Compensation Schemes.* Latin American nations usually cannot afford to base the compensation of expropriated properties on their market value or to pay for them in cash and still have an agrarian reform that will benefit a large number of the landless campesinos. [27, p. 139; 15] Moreover, agrarian reform implies much more than the purchase and resale of real estate; it also involves a redistribution of wealth and power, and paying in cash or basing payment on market value is inconsistent with this objective. [29]

In Chile, regardless of the particular grounds for an expropriation, compensation to any expropriated landowner is limited to the amount of the current appraisal of the land for property tax purposes, plus the market value of new "improvements" not included in the appraisal, both determined as of the date of the expropriation decree for the particular property. Furthermore, "improvements" incorporated into the expropriated property subsequent to November 4, 1964—the date Frei took office—are to be compensated in cash. This provision tries to prevent a reduction in investments by landowners fearing expropriation.

There are, however, differences in the form of compensation according to the grounds for the expropriation. When the acquisition is based on excess size, "corporate" ownership, or voluntary offers to CORA, the landowner is paid 10 per cent in cash and the balance in twenty-five-year Class "A" bonds.[13] Nevertheless, if CORA can show that a property so acquired was either abandoned or inadequately exploited, then the form of compensation is the same as for properties expropriated because of abandonment or poor exploitation: 1 per cent or 5 per cent in cash respectively, with the balance in thirty-year Class "C" bonds. (As explained, an expropriation on grounds of abandonment or poor exploitation per se gives the landowner recourse to judicial review, not available under other grounds, and may delay the process for years; also, CORA prefers to acquire properties through amicable settlements with landowners, rather than following the entire expropriation process to its lengthy and costly conclusion.)

---

[13] The three classes of bonds. "A," "B," and "C," are amortized in twenty-five, five, and thirty annual quotas respectively. Each of the three classes is divided in two series. An expropriated owner receives 70 per cent in bonds of the first series, which are readjusted annually in accordance with the official consumer price index, and 30 per cent in bonds of the second series, which are not readjusted to reflect inflation. Each annual amortization quota, which follows the seven to three proportion, shall include a 3 per cent interest return on the nominal value of the bonds. As regards the first series, the nominal value is increased for this purpose by 50 per cent of the readjustment figure cited above. The bonds are not negotiable, but can under certain conditions be used to purchase stocks or to satisfy tax bills or public assessments.

The remaining types of land acquisition also have different forms of compensation, ranging from 100 per cent cash for minifundia farmed personally by the owners to 1 per cent in cash and the balance in thirty-year bonds for lands subject to the jurisdiction of the Law of Southern Property. Because of their rarity, they are not discussed here.

4. *Judicial Review: The Agrarian Tribunals.* Law 16.640 established one trial agrarian tribunal in each province (for a total of twenty-five) and ten appeal agrarian tribunals. These have exclusive jurisdiction over all conflicts arising from application of the law, particularly questions of expropriation. Each trial tribunal has one judge and two agronomists, while the appeal tribunals are staffed by two regular appeal judges and one agronomist.

This special court system was a conscious attempt to keep all land reform conflicts out of the regular civil court system, which is notoriously slow and conservative. To get the expropriated properties into CORA's possession as quickly as possible, Law 16.640 stipulates that there are *no* appeals from judgments of the Agrarian Appeal Tribunals. Furthermore, the technical expertise of the members of the agrarian tribunals, and their concentration on agrarian reform conflicts, together with special procedural rules, were supposed to ensure a more rapid process while guaranteeing the basic rights of affected individuals. [9, pp. 28-29]

In practice, however, these goals have not been fully achieved. The Supreme Court, for instance, was quick to accept jurisdiction over land reform conflicts where the landowners claimed that the transitory articles of Law 16.640 were unconstitutional even though these cases were being heard before Agrarian Tribunals. Although the Court in these and most other cases found that the applications of Law 16.640 did not violate the constitution, nevertheless the appeals did postpone taking possession of the affected properties by CORA.

The goal of obtaining more technical and relevant judgments through the use of agronomists as judges has not worked well either. The agronomists, faced with the procedural complexities of a trial, have tended to unhesitating-ly follow the lead of the judicial members of the tribunals.

Nor has the goal of a quick trial been attained. The principle that makes all trial proceedings in Chile extremely slow has not been eliminated from the supposedly summary proceedings of the agrarian courts: judges are passive; they only act when petitioned to do so by one of the parties. While it was anticipated that an entire process before the agrarian court would only take thirty-two days, in reality it is more likely to last several months or even years. [17, p. 2]

For reasons already discussed, CORA usually uses excess size and voluntary offers as expropriation grounds, both of which are rarely susceptible to judicial review by the Agrarian Tribunals. The bulk of the judicial review by the Tribunals, then, involves other matters which are not so important and which do not interrupt the taking of possession by CORA. These include claims that CORA assigned a compensation scheme different from that stipulated by law, that the required reserve right was not granted, and that the assessment by CORA of the "improvements" was erroneous.

Findings from the province of Valparaíso show that relatively few expropriations result in cases before the Agrarian Tribunals. Of the twenty-six expropriations in Valparaíso between July 1967 and March 1969, only six were contested in these courts. [17, p. 21]

5. *Taking of Possession.* Clearly the drafters of Law 16.640 tried to minimize the time period between the decision to expropriate and the actual taking of possession of an affected property. [9, p. 28] The law provided that CORA could take possession of a property after depositing with a Civil Court that part of the compensation that must be paid in cash, but as noted, this goal has not been achieved, at least in those cases where the landowners decided to "fight" the expropriation.

Although no exact data are available on the length of expropriation processes, a fair idea can be obtained by comparing the date of the expropriation decree for each property and the date of the organization of an asentamiento on it. Table III shows that very few of the properties expropriated under Law 16.640 had reached the asentamiento stage by October 1968. CORA, as of this time, was still concentrating on constituting asentamientos on those properties expropriated under Law 15.020 between January 1965 and June 1967. Yet, as Table II demonstrates, 208 of the 478 properties so expropriated were still waiting for an asentamiento stage in October 1968.

Some of these delays in taking possession can be traced to CORA itself. CORA has often waited until almost a year (the maximum period allowed by the law) after the date of the expropriation decree before depositing the amount required for taking possession. This was probably due to scarcity of funds, though the endemic inflation in Chile may also have played a role—the longer payment of a fixed cost can be delayed, the cheaper it becomes. CORA officials admit that it has often taken a long time to set the necessary valuation figures, particularly as regards "improvements." This may have been due to a shortage of sufficiently trained personnel, or to extended negotiations with affected owners.

Many of the difficulties with quick-taking, however, are the results of legal loopholes in Law 16.640. CORA could not take possession until it deposited with the Superior Civil Court the required cash compensation (1-10 per cent of the valuation), and until the judge ordered the inscription of title in CORA's name at the appropriate Registry of Property. Landowners, aided by the conservative nature of most civil court judges in Chile, were quick to object to CORA's deposit on the grounds that valuations were incorrect. Many judges accepted these complaints for consideration, which then became subject to regular civil court procedures, notorious for their complexity and length. In many cases, appeals to higher courts occurred. Not until a final judgement was made could CORA enter possession of the property. [14]

In the face of such problems, the Government introduced an amend-

TABLE II
**Pending Expropriation Processes Under Law 15.020 (January 1965-
June 1967) as of October 30, 1968
(asentamientos not yet organized)**

Length of Cases	Pending Number of Cases	Number of Settled Cases (Asentamientos Organized)	Total Expropriations Under 15.020
Under 6 months	19	—	—
Over 6 and less than 12	19	—	—
Over 12 and less than 18	8	—	—
Over 18 and less than 24	59	—	—
Over 24 months	103	—	—
TOTALS	208	270	478

Source: Compiled by J. R. Thome and Hector Mora from unpublished data
provided by CORA, Dirección de Planificación y Control

TABLE III
**Expropriations Under Law 16.640: Length of Time From
Expropriation Decree to Constitution of Asentamiento
(data as of October 30, 1968)**

Length of Process	Number of Expropriation Cases	Cases Where Asentamiento Organized	Cases Where Asentamiento Not Yet Constituted
Under 6 months	89	11	78
Over 6 and less than 12	111	8	103
Over 12 and less than 18	20	—	20
Over 18	—	—	—
SUB TOTAL	220	—	—
No Data	28	—	—
Total	248	19	201

Source: Compiled by J. R. Thome and Hector Mora from unpublished data
provided by CORA, Dirección de Planificación y Control.

ment to Law 16.640. It was passed, and Law 17.280 of January 17, 1970 substituted new Articles 39, 40, and 41 for the original ones in Law 16.640. Among many important changes, the new articles provide: that the deposits will be made at the appropriate Municipal Treasuries rather than at the Civil Courts; that, in the absence of any tax assessment on the land, CORA will set a proxy assessment for the purpose of determining the deposit (subject to subsequent tax assessment by Internal Revenue Service); that CORA can obtain the inscription of titles of expropriated properties by presenting the necessary documents at the Registry of Property rather than doing this through a judge; and that, after complying with the above conditions, CORA can enter possession of its own accord and can request and obtain the assistance of the local public authorities. In addition, the new Article 41 provides that possession is no longer to be delayed by the existence of unharvested crops and establishes a new compensation scheme to take care of this situation. Finally, the new law establishes that all expropriations pending at the time of its enactment are subject to its provisions, thus enabling CORA to start all over again, under better conditions, to acquire possession of properties in the process of expropriation.

It is too early to determine the effects of the new amendments, although they certainly seem to close many loopholes. In any case, more recent data show that CORA has improved its internal administrative procedures and is now moving faster in organizing asentamientos. By March 31, 1970, CORA had established 597 asentamientos, covering almost 2.5 million hectares, on which about 20,000 peasent families had been settled. [5]

Conclusions

Expropriation is the basic legal mechanism on which the rest of an agrarian reform process depends. Far too many "land reforms" have been doomed to failure by constitutional provisions or legislation which did not allow efficient and broad ranging expropriation processes. Three examples come immediately to mind: the Colombian land reform law of 1961, the Peruvian law of 1964, and the Chilean law of 1962. If the legal framework for an expropriation process, at least in Latin America, is to provide the means necessary for a substantial agrarian reform, it must at least: (1) make the bulk of privately owned rural property subject to expropriation; (2) establish a compensation scheme of deferred or long-term payments based on a valuation other than market price; and (3) have a quick-taking procedure which enables the reform agency to obtain possession of the land in the shortest time possible, while at the same time providing affected landowners with adequate legal remedies.

In Chile, the expropriation process, as established by Law 16.640 (and its regulatory decrees) and implemented by CORA, has more or less satisfied the first two of the minimum "legal conditions." However, the procedure for taking possession of expropriated properties has not proven to be nearly as expedtious or uncomplicated as planned. As we have seen, certain legal formalities established by Law 16.640 have, with the cooperation of the courts, been utilized by landowners to suspend the taking of possession for months and even years. Moreover, CORA itself has in the past contributed to such delays through it administrative practices. Consequently, it cannot be said that the agrarian reform carried out by the Frei administration in Chile was a massive one. On the other hand, it was certainly much more than a mere colonization program or one of token expropriation and redistribution.

References

[1]   Becket, James. "Land Reform in Chile." *Journal of Inter-American Studies* 5 (1963): 177-211.

[2]   Carroll, Thomas F. "The Land Reform Issue in Latin America." In *Latin American Issues: Essays and Comments,* edited by Albert O. Hirschman. New York: The Twentieth Century Fund, 1961.

[3]   Chonchol, Jacques. "Razones económicas, sociales y políticas de la reforma agraria." In *Reformas agrarias en América Latina,* edited by Oscar Delgado. México: Fondo de Cultura Economica, 1965.

[4]   Corporación de Reforma Agraria (CORA). *Cuatro años de reforma agraria.* Santiago, 1968.

[5]   ———. Dirección de Planificación y Control, Sección Control y Estadística. Unpublished data. March 1970.

[6]   Departamento de Investigación. *Organización, planificacción y coordinación de las instituciones del sector público agrícola de Chile, a nivel de terreno.* Anexo 22. Santiago: Instituto de Capacitación e Investigación en Reforma Agraria (ICIRA), 1966.

[7]   Evans de la Cuadra, Enrique. *Estatuto constitucional del derecho de propiedad en Chile.* Santiago: Editorial Jurídica, 1967.

[8]   Eyzaguirre, Jaime. *Historia de Chile.* Tomo I. Santiago: Editorial Zig Zag, 1965.

[9]   Frei, Eduardo and Hugo Trivelli. "Mensaje del ejecutivo al Congreso proponiendo la aprobación del proyecto de Ley de Reforma Agraria." In *Ley de Reforma Agraria,* by Antonio Vodavonic. Santiago: Editorial Nascimento, 1967. Translations by Philip Hazelton.

[10] Friedman, Lawrence M. "Legal Culture and Social Development." *Law and Society Review* 4 (1969): 29-44.

[11] Friedman, W. *Legal Theory.* London: Stevens and Sons, Ltd., 1944.

[12] Gonzalez Navarro, Moisés. "La tenencia de la tierra en México." *Cahiers de Monde Hispanique et Luso-Brésilien* 12 (1969): 115-134.

[13] Heise Gonzalez, Julio. *Historia constitucional de Chile.* Colección de Apuntes de Clase. Santiago: Editorial Jurídica 1954. Cited by Gonzalo Figueroa in "El origen de la propiedad agrícola en Chile." Mimeographed. Santiago, 1968.

[14] Informe de la Comisión de Agricultura y Colonización del Estado. Cited by German Lührs in "Proyecto de ley modificatorio de la Ley 16.640." Unpublished report. Santiago: ICIRA, 1969.

[15] Karst, Kenneth. "Latin American Land Reform: The Uses of Confiscation." *Michigan Law Review* 63 (1964): 327-372.

[16] Lambert, Jacques. *Latin America, Social Structures and Political Institutions.* Berkeley: University of California Press, 1969.

[17] Lührs, German. "Expropiaciones bajo las Leyes 15.020 y 16.640." Unpublished report. Madison, 1969.

[18] Lyon, Michael. "The Agrarian Reform Law of Chile: A Description of Its Basic Elements." Unpublished report. Santiago: ICIRA, 1968.

[19] Martin, Kent. "Expropriation under the Venezuelan and Chilean Land Reform Acts." Unpublished seminar paper. Madison, 1967.

[20] McCoy, Terry. "Agrarian Reform in Chile, 1962-1968: A Study of Politics and the Development Process." Ph.D. dissertation, University of Wisconsin, 1969.

[21] Merryman, John. The Civil Law Tradition. Stanford: Stanford University Press, 1969.

[22] Morse, Richard M. "The Latin American Heritage." In The Founding of New Societies, edited by Louis Hartz. New York: Harcourt, Brace and World, 1964.

[23] O'Connor, Theron. "Some Aspects of the Development and Erosion of the Right of Private Ownership in the Civil Law System." Unpublished seminar paper. Madison, 1968.

[24] Ots Capdequi, José María. España en América: Las Instituciones Coloniales. 2d ed. Bogotá: Universidad Nacional de Colombia, 1952.

[25] Phelan, John Leddy. "Authority and Flexibility in the Spanish Imperial Bureaucracy." Administrative Science Quarterly 5 (1960): 47-65.

[26] Silva Bascuñan, Alejandro. Tratado de derecho constitucional. Tomo II. Santiago: Editorial Jurídica, 1963.

[27] Silva Solar, Julio and Jacques Chonchol. El desarrollo de la nueva sociedad en América Latina. Santiago Editorial Universitaria, 1965.

[28] Thiesenhusen, William C. Chile's Experiments in Agrarian Reform. Madison: University of Wisconsin, 1966.

[29] Thome, Joseph R. "The Process of Land Reform in Latin America." Wisconsin Law Review 9 (1968): 9-22.

[30] Weeks, David. "The Agrarian System of the Spanish American Colonies." The Journal of Land & Public Utility Economics (1947): 153-168.

CHAPTER 6

Agrarian Reform: Chile

WILLIAM C. THIESENHUSEN

Associate Professor of Agricultural Economics,
Agricultural Journalism, and the Land Tenure
Center at the University of Wisconsin–Madison

CHAPTER 6

Agrarian Reform: Chile

WILLIAM C. THIESENHUSEN

When Eduardo Frei took office as President of Chile in 1964, he pledged a frontal attack on the developmental problems plaguing agriculture. As he defined it, rural development was to include not only an increase in agricultural production but also a more socially desirable distribution of income and provision for more secure jobs on the land to ease the growing employment problem. His government emphasized the improvement of living conditions for landless laborers and small acreage farmers to an extent unprecedented in Chile. Since there would not be enough land for all landless laborers to receive even a minimum-sized parcel, increased wages and improved public service were to be provided for those who couldn't be assigned land. Unionization of farmers was to be encouraged. And minifundistas would be helped, mainly through credit and cooperatives.

Evaluation of the Frei government's reforms is somewhat premature since the policies followed tend to have medium-term and long-run as well as more immediate payoffs. However, even a partial evaluation and extrapolation from short-term results can be useful.

Extent and Procedures of Reform

The predecessor government's reform efforts provided fewer than 1,250 families with land of their own. Under the Frei reforms, 18,618 families were settled on farms through December 31, 1969. Estimates are that about 20,000 had been settled by the end of February 1970. Over 65 per cent of these were located in the rich heartland of the country, the Central Valley (from Aconcagua to Nuble Provinces), an area traditionally dominated by the hacienda or fundo. Nearly 85 per cent of the more than 192,000 irrigated hectares on which there are reform settlements (about 41 per cent of the total area in the reform program) is also located there. As of early 1970, about 10 per cent of the "farmland"—and over 15 per cent of the irrigated land—in Chile was part of the agrarian reform.

Appropriations for the Corporación de Reforma Agraria (CORA) continued to rise and, in real terms, its budget in 1970 was about 30 per cent higher than in 1969. Furthermore, one could detect no appreciable change in the speed at which expropriations occurred in the late 1960s; if anything it quickened (Table I). Yet the Frei administration recognized that there was no chance to fulfill the campaign promise of settling 100,000 families during its term in office (a goal which would have required the expropriation of about half of the irrigated land in the country, according to CORA officials). In

TABLE I
Expropriations of CORA Through January 1970
Total Properties, Acreage, and Per Cent of Total

Exprop. Dates (in three-month periods)	Exprop. Properties	% of Total Exprop. Properties	Irrigated Hectares Exprop.	% of Total Irrigated Hectares Exprop.	Dry Hectares Exprop.	% of Total Dry Hectares Exprop.	Total Hectares Exprop.	% of Total Hectares Exprop.
[June/65-July/68]	693	60.8	169,990.1	67.5	1,315,194.4	46.0	1,485,184.5	47.8
Aug./68-Oct./68	36	3.2	4,859.6	1.9	20,044.2	0.7	24,903.8	0.9
Nov./68-Jan./69	90	7.9	21,947.6	8.8	544,461.8	19.1	566,409.4	18.3
Feb./69-April/69	75	6.6	14,200.3	5.7	94,525.7	3.4	108,726.0	3.5
May/69-July/69	66	5.7	11,888.4	4.7	223,069.8	7.8	234,958.2	7.6
Aug./69-Oct./69	87	7.7	14,505.7	5.7	251,123.5	8.8	265,629.2	8.5
Nov./69-Jan./70	93	8.1	14,332.2	5.7	405,152.8	14.2	419,485.0	13.4
Total	1140	100.0	251,723.9	100.0	2,853,572.2	100.0	3,105,296.1	100.0

Source: Computed from Corporación de la Reforma Agraria (CORA), unpublished data.

1970, approximately 250,000 families were still either landless or held too little land to enable them to earn the increased, though still modest minimum wages set by the government.

Under the Chilean plan of agrarian reform the fundo is converted into a cooperatively worked asentamiento. There is usually a time lag between expropriation and asentamiento organization, and sometimes several expropriated properties are combined into one asentamiento. An estimated 575 asentamientos were in operation in January 1970, while about one-third of the expropriated land had not been so reorganized. [6] On the usual asentamiento the physical layout of the fundo is not changed; large fields continue to be operated intact. Work is accomplished communally in "field crew" fashion, much as it was before the reform. But now the former owner and usually his on-farm representative, the administrator, have left. Many field foremen also elect not to take part in the reform.

The settler selection process usually gives preference to former permanent workers on the expropriated estate, but others may be admitted providing they have had experience as an agricultural worker, renter, or sharecropper; do not own a parcel of land larger than an "economic unit" (as defined in Chilean law); and are over eighteen years old and the head of a family.

Settlers elect a five member "settlement committee" (president, vice president, etc.), and CORA and the committee draw up a contract which formally establishes the asentamiento organization called the Sociedad de Reforma Agraria (SARA). Each SARA is governed by an administrative council—the settlement committee and, where CORA desires, two members of its staff. A prime function of the administrative council is to draw up plans for what will be grown—and where—and which are later formalized in a general assembly of all campesinos on the property.

Settlers agree to live on the farm, carry a share of the work as directed by the administrative council, not cede their rights to another, and market all cooperatively-grown produce through official SARA channels. Those crops grown individually on each member's houseplot and privately owned animals for which each member is granted some free grazing rights are exempted from this marketing provision.

The settlement committee divides work responsibilities among members. Some are appointed as field-work overseers but, contrary to the old system of supervision by a field foreman, all are expected to do physical labor.

During the year, campesinos are advanced a lump sum each month. If they have a special skill, a bonus is added to this basic amount. Male family members of working age usually work under the same arrangement (in some cases, however, they are paid wages as hired laborers—as are those laborers who are sometimes brought in from outside) and at the end of the year the farm's net income is divided by a pre-agreed-upon formula. Family allowance payments that used to be paid through the government social security program are also subtracted as an operating cost. These government payments are available to hired workers, but asentados are considered self-employed. In the usual case, CORA takes from 10 to 20 per cent of the net farm income

MAP I

ZONAL OFFICES OF CORA (TOP NUMBER REFERS TO THE ZONE;
THE MIDDLE ONE TO THE NUMBER OF ASENTAMIENTOS AND THE
BOTTOM TO THE NUMBER OF BENEFICIARIES IN THE ZONE)
ZONE X IS UNDEFINED AT PRESENT
COMPUTED FROM [6]

for administrative expenses and leaves 80 to 90 per cent to be divided among
the asentados according to days worked. Of course, monthly advances are
subtracted in calculating the net income to be divided.

Under the asentamiento system, productive inputs for the agreed-upon
farm plan are supplied by CORA. A team of extension specialists usually
visits each asentamiento weekly. Just over them in responsibility is the area
chief; his administrative superior is the zonal director (there are now fifteen
zones in the country—see Map 1). CORA also supervises some investment
projects—for instance, bringing in nursery stock for orchards and helping
peasants buy dairy cattle.

The asentamiento is an intermediate step in reform which will last for
three to five years (though in order to cut costs CORA is attempting to
shorten this period on properties with fewest production and administrative
problems), after which time the settlers will decide whether the asentamiento
is to be divided into individual farms or whether the former work pattern will
continue. Judging from early experience (only a few SARA's have completed

their asentamiento phase), an intermediate alternative may become quite general: commonland farming may continue on part of the old asentamiento while plots are given out on the remainder.

The main objectives of the asentamiento are to train the campesinos in farm management and marketing, to maintain full production during the first crucial years after expropriation, and to encourage the asentados to retain a cooperative type of operation once the land is distributed to them—or, at the very least, to foster a "spirit of cooperativism." Working the property as an undivided farm lowers initial cost of land reform; division of infrastructure—such as the irrigation system—and installing a road network to each individual farm can be a costly proposition.[1]

The asentamiento period also serves to test the capacity of the asentados. They are graded each year by a committee of three of their colleagues and one CORA official, each with equal vote. Once the proving period has elapsed, only those who meet certain requirements will be eligible to receive land titles to the property. In practice it is difficult (but not impossible) to drop asentados, whatever the charges against them.

At the end of the asentamiento period actas de asignación—certificates of eligibility for land—are given to each asentado. As soon as possible, titles and mortgages are delivered. The first actas were distributed in November 1968. As of September 20, 1969, titles had been granted to twenty-four cooperatives (now "former" asentamientos) which had 1,621 families as members.

Beneficiaries are expected to pay off their land debt within thirty years after this assignment. Payments are based on tax assessed value of the land the year of assignment, CORA's infrastructure investment, and a 2 per cent fee to CORA. It has been shown that debt installments are adjusted in such a way that the deflated value of total installments will be less than the original debt even if a fairly conservative 20 per cent inflation rate is assumed.[14, pp. 75-79][2] A three-year grace period on these payments will be offered (but a down payment of half an annual installment will presumably be required immediately) during which time the livestock and machinery (plus a 2 per cent CORA fee) are to be paid off; these latter payments may be extended over a five-year period. Payments that settlers make while they are asentados will reduce their future debt.[14, pp. 75-79] But under high rates of inflation, extending the period of repayment will also progressively lighten

---

1 Much ideological discussion during the Frei government focused on whether the reformed farm should be cooperatively worked or parcelled out to individual owner operators. One wing cf the Christian Democratic party favored "communitarianism" and there were many professionals with this philosophy in CORA. They claim that cooperative farming is the most desirable alternative for the post-asentamiento period. Peasants have exerted some pressures for having their own parcels, however. It is possible that de facto subdivision—and individual management—may become common even if the large property is still, de jure, intact.

2 Installments are readjusted to only 70 per cent of the rise in consumer price index and no interest is charged on the first three installments.

the debt burden. Regardless of the post-asentamiento type of tenure decided upon, a cooperative to purchase inputs and sell produce will continue.

Campesino Unions

Perhaps better than the agrarian reform program per se, the expanding power of campesinos is illustrated by the spread of unionization and organization in Chile's countryside. The unionization law of 1967 (16.627) may prove to be the most important facet of the Frei government's rural development program. Even if a later government tries to reverse gears on reform—or even to slow the program appreciably—pressure from rural unions may make it impossible to do so.

Before the Christian Democrats came to power, it was virtually impossible to unionize peasants. In 1964 there were only 24 unions with 1,658 members. By early 1969 there were over 3,500 union organizations involved in some degree of bargaining with landlords at the fundo level. They represented, according to government figures, more than 190,000 farm workers. In 1960-64 there were only 97 strikes of agricultural workers. In 1965 there were 141, and in 1966 there were 586, indicating that the government was allowing action that was, by the strict letter of the law, illegal. After Law 16.627 was passed in 1967, there were 693 strikes, and in 1968 there were 618.

Another 500 unions—again according to government count—were comprised of small landholders. Many of them were organized by INDAP (the Institute of Agrarian Development), which has also organized campesino cooperatives for the purpose of purchasing inputs and selling produce. INDAP is the government agency charged with providing credit for small holders who are not beneficiaries of land under CORA programs. INDAP credit is given through cooperatives which serve as guarantors for the credit disbursed to individual borrowers.

The Macro-Economy and Its Relation to Reform

A. The Agricultural Sector. However determined the effort, when judged by the total number employed in agriculture, the Frei government's agrarian reform program cannot be considered as very extensive. Even the reform that has taken place must be regarded as a long run investment. To look for short term effects of reform in the macro-economy by examining such indicators as production, employment, and income distribution is a premature exercise. Hence, much of the evidence in this report will deal with the economic effects at the micro-level—and even this will have to be highly qualified because of the short time period involved. While the Frei government utilized the law passed by the previous administration to settle 6,000 families, the more comprehensive agrarian reform law was not passed until July 1967.[3]

Besides the impossibility of measuring the effects of agrarian reform on total agricultural production, given its limited scope and short time horizon, a great many factors other than the reform have been operating and influencing agriculture during this period. It will be worthwhile to enumerate a few of them since some undoubtedly had positive effects on agricultural production and employment while others affected economic performance adversely:

1. In 1970 Chile was just recovering from one of its worst two-year droughts in history. The 1968 drought (affecting the 1969 harvest) was considered the worst in 100 years, and 1967 was not much better. Most analysts trace the decline of agricultural production in the central provinces—one of the most productive agricultural areas of the world which becomes a virtual desert without irrigation—to shortages of water.

2. Chilean wheat production in 1970 was likely influenced positively by the favorable forward price announced during the planting season, with promises that this price would be adjusted upward with inflation.

3. Chile's agricultural planning office (ODEPA) had completed an agricultural development plan covering the next decade. In addition to spelling out the need for continued agrarian reform, it called for increased acreage in truck crops, orchards, and vineyards; a doubling of improved pastures, more irrigation facilities, and a two-fold increase in the cattle and sheep population.

The government claimed a 4.6 per cent annual growth rate in Chile's agricultural sector during the Frei presidency. This compares with a 1.8 per cent rate of growth in the years immediately preceding 1965. These figures are open to much dispute. In 1969, rice was only 39 per cent and corn 61 per cent of 1968 production. Slightly less wheat was harvested in 1969 than in 1968. Furthermore, yields per hectare for some of the major crops do not show a clear upward trend (Table II). Besides, Chile had a negative trade balance for agricultural products amounting to $96 million in 1967 and $141 million in 1968; the deficit for 1969, reflecting the severe drought, was likely even higher. The country still imports many products—some economists put the figure at 60 per cent of agricultural imports—which could be grown domestically.

One problem often associated with agrarian reform concerns the disinvestment that may occur in the large-farm sector which, admittedly, contains some well managed properties. The extent to which this may have happened is as yet unknown. The legislation does permit owners of the best worked farms to retain larger reserves, and terms of payment for land expropriated from these farms are likewise more favorable. Ringlein compares the results of a 1968-69 study of a sample of forty-three privately operated

---

[3] From the beginning of its term through July 31, 1967, the government expropriated 479 farms and organized 156 asentamientos.[6] Payment for property during this period had to be negotiated with owners, some of whom feared less favorable terms were they to await passage of the new law. This applied with special force to those who held notoriously badly exploited or abandoned property.

fundos in Santiago Province with 1963-64 data obtained for these same farms by Chile's Ministry of Agriculture. His comparison shows that in all categories investments per hectare in the latter period were higher (in real terms).[17]

  B. *Developments in Other Economic Sectors.* If it is difficult to assess the impact agrarian reform to date has had on agriculture, it is likewise impossible to determine its effect on the rest of the economy. But the progress of reform will depend to some extent on how well the economy performs, and the expansion of the Chilean economy was less at the close of the decade than in either 1965 or 1966. In 1966 per capita growth of GNP in real terms was 6.5 per cent. The Chilean economy did not grow in terms of GNP per capita in 1967 or 1968, and there was very little improvement in 1969 and 1970.

  Industrial production increased 6.4 per cent in 1965 and 8.6 per cent in 1966, but it rose only 2.8 per cent in 1967 and 2.0 per cent in 1968. When the Frei administration assumed office, there was a great deal of idle capacity in industry: manufacturing output could be expanded without incurring as much inflation as Chile had experienced under the previous administration. But the economy failed to generate sufficient new capacity and by the middle of Frei's term, industrial production slowed and as a partial result (but only

TABLE II
Yields of Various Crops: Chile

| Product | Quintales Per Hectare | | | |
	64/65	65/66	66/67	67/68
Wheat	15.4	17.3	16.7	17.4
Oats	n.a.*	16.2	16.8	15.0
Barley	19.3	22.8	23.3	21.9
Rye	11.9	16.1	13.0	11.4
Rice	29.1	20.8	30.2	28.8
Corn	30.8	35.4	39.3	36.2
Beans	10.1	10.6	13.1	10.9
Lentils	3.9	4.4	5.8	5.1
Peas	7.7	13.0	10.5	6.8
Chick Peas	6.0	4.9	8.6	4.7
Potatoes	77.2	105.3	92.6	90.6
Sugar Beets	379.7	n.a.	n.a.	378.7
Sunflowers	14.1	13.3	14.8	14.9
Rapeseed	12.5	12.5	13.5	12.8
Onions	n.a.	n.a.	260.0	325.0
Garlic	n.a.	49.2	50.0	n.a.

*n.a. = not available.

Source: Computed from AID, unpublished memorandum, November 28, 1969, Santiago.

partly for this reason) inflation boomed again.[4]

Because of the high price of copper on the world market, Chile's foreign exchange earnings continued high. Total exports rose from U. S. $783 million in 1965 to U. S. $1,042 million in 1968. But total imports rose to U. S. $1,040 million in 1968. A balance of payments surplus resting on a very high copper price could easily become a deficit.

C. Population and Employment. While high, the rate of population growth in Chile is well under the 1963-67 Latin American annual average of 2.9 per cent, and it dropped from about 2.3 per cent in 1961 to slightly under 2 per cent in 1967. The total population of the country was estimated at about 9.4 million on July 1, 1969, and is expected to increase to between 12.5 and 15.6 million by 1991. The potential work force (the population aged fifteen to sixty-four years) will likely increase at a slightly faster rate and reach a total of between 8.5 and 9 million by 1991.[16]

One important problem currently confronting Chilean society is unemployment and underemployment. Official data show that the unemployment rate rose to 7.1 per cent in greater Santiago by June 1969, compared with 5.9 per cent a year earlier [4, p. 590], and these data may even understate the full dimensions of this problem. [see discussion in 3; 21; 18; and 10]

In addition to production targets then, economic programs must have employment objectives. As a result of off-farm migration, the active labor force in Chilean agriculture is either remaining constant or dropping slightly. Unless the urban economy becomes more dynamic, the underemployment and unemployment will continue to be transferred from farms to cities and towns.

D. Redistribution of Income and Resources. There are conflicting reports concerning the actual redistribution toward poor sectors during the Frei administration. There was a notable rise in the minimum wage after 1964 and in 1969 Frei reported that real incomes for white and blue collar workers had risen 54 per cent during his administration.[9]

Ringlein's sample of private fundos shows that over the 1963/64-1968/69 period, farm workers' real wages, including payments in kind, nearly doubled.[17] This was a direct response to the reforms and to Frei's insistence on increasing wage workers' earnings. While there is no way of knowing how many landowners paid their workers at a rate other than the minimum, Agency for International Development (AID) figures (Table III) show that between 1966 and 1969 real minimum wages dropped slowly.

---

4 Officially, inflation was 17 per cent in 1966 and about 40 per cent in 1969. Both of these figures probably understate the true rise in the cost of living since the many government-controlled items included in the price index may be disproportionate to their relative importance in consumer budgets.

TABLE III
Legal Minimum Agricultural Daily Wages[a]

	Nominal (Escudos)	Real[b] (Escudos)
1965	3.264	3.264
1966	4.104	3.340
1967	4.800	3.285
1968	5.851	3.100
1969	7.483	3.067

Source: AID, unpublished memorandum, November 28, 1969, Santiago.

[a]Since 1965 agricultural and industrial minimum wages for workers were fixed at the same level. The escudo in 1969 averaged about U. S. $0.13.

[b]Deflated by General Price Index 1965 = 100. For 1969 it was assumed that the G.P.I. would increase by the same per cent as for 1968.

The reform to date has not changed the basic structure of Chilean agriculture where, as revealed by the last census—in 1965—13,478 farms (5.3 per cent of the total) of 200 hectares or more constituted nearly 87 per cent of the country's farmland. As of January 30, 1970, after 1,140 properties had been expropriated, approximately 5.0 per cent of the properties still comprised 76.7 per cent of the land area. (This observation does not, of course, consider the likely possibility that there has been some private subdivision of land in the 1965-69 period.) The other end of the spectrum, of course, was unchanged by reform; in 1965, 123,693 farms of under five hectares, or 49 per cent of the total number of farms, occupied 0.7 per cent of the land. And 45,233 farms of less than one hectare or 17.8 per cent of the total number, held 0.1 per cent of the land (Table IV).

Another indicator of redistribution is the amount of agricultural credit going to agrarian reform beneficiaries or small-plot agriculturists over the past years. This can be evaluated by comparing disbursals by CORA and INDAP as opposed to those of the Banco del Estado and the Corporación de Fomento de la Producción (CORFO), both of which direct the bulk of their agricultural loans to large farms.

Agricultural credit trebled between 1964 and 1968 (see Tables V and VI); likewise, the number of farmers receiving loans increased three times. Banco del Estado credit disbursals were up 300 per cent while CORFO credit increased much more slowly. Meanwhile, INDAP credit more than trebled, and that extended by CORA rose by more than sixty times from an exceedingly low level.

It is also revealing, however, that 72.1 per cent of all 1968 institutional agricultural credit in 1968 was still granted by the Banco del Estado (as compared to 79.9 per cent in 1964). CORA's share rose from 0.8 per cent in 1964 to 15.7 per cent in 1968 while CORFO's share dropped from 14.3 per cent to 6.5 per cent. Average loan size by the Banco del Estado doubled while average loan size by INDAP remained fairly stable.

Private Sector Subdivision, 1965—Jan. 30, 1970

Farm Size Groups	Number of Properties 1965*	Number of Properties Jan. 30, '70	% of Total Properties Jan. 30, '70	% of Total Properties 1965	Number of Hectares 1965	Number of Hectares Jan. 30, '70	% of Total Hectares 1965	% of Total Hectares Jan. 30, '70	Average Number Hectares/ Property '65	Average Number Hectares/ Property Jan. 30, '70
Less than 1 hectare	45,233	45,233	17.8	17.8	22,378.5	22,378.5	0.1	0.1	.495	.495
1-4.9 hectares	78,460	78,460	31.0	31.0	184,480.2	184,480.2	0.6	0.6	2.351	2.351
5-49.9 hectares	92,412	92,386	36.5	36.4	1,556,049.7	1,555,234.7	5.1	5.1	16.838	16.834
50-99.9 hectares	14,785	14,699	5.8	5.8	1,022,655.9	1,016,150.9	3.3	3.3	69.168	69.131
100-199.9 hectares	9,164	8,993	3.6	3.5	1,261,513.3	1,235,187.6	4.1	4.0	137.660	137.349
200 and more hectares	13,478	12,621	5.3	5.0	26,597,053.1	23,525,402.7	86.8	76.7	1,973.368	1,863.988
Reformed Sector*	1,140			0.5		3,105,296.1		10.2		2,723.944
TOTALS	253,532	253,532	100.0	100.0	30,644,130.7	30,644,130.7	100.0	100.0		

Sources: The numbers and extent of properties in 1965 are from [7]. Figures for 1970 were arrived at by subtracting the numbers and extent of all properties taken over by CORA, 1965 to December 1969 [6], from the appropriate categories.   *1965 Agricultural Census

TABLE V—Number of Agricultural Loans
By Institution: 1964-1968

Institution	1964	1965	1966	1967	1968
CORA[a]	465	1,089	4,980	8,347	23,000
INDAP[a]	20,360	49,340	52,446	45,475	78,000
Banco del Estado	31,217	38,344	48,866	55,000	47,000
CORFO	3,918	2,842	3,619	2,841	4,330
Total	55,950	91,815	109,911	111,663	152,230

Average Size of Loan by Institution
1964-1968 in 1965 Escudos

	1964	1965	1966	1967	1968
CORA[a]	5,161	3,398	6,927	10,015	6,457
INDAP[a]	702	582	606	811	699
Banco del Estado	7,275	9,049	12,655	12,636	14,543
CORFO	10,311	17,628	24,316	28,159	14,273
Total					
Average	5,079	4,678	7,034	8,019	6,229

Source: Computed from [20]. [a]INDAP lends to small acreage farmers who have not received land rights under the agrarian reform program; CORA lends to beneficiaries of the land reform. While INDAP loans go to many more campesinos than CORA, the land base of beneficiaries is smaller.

TABLE VI—Agricultural Credit Extended by Institution, 1964-1968
in Millions of 1966 Escudos

Institution	1964	1965	1966	1967	1968
CORA	2,4	3.7	34.5	83.6	148.5
INDAP	14.3	28.7	31.8	36.9	54.5
Banco del Estado	227.1	347.0	618.9	695.0	683.5
CORFO	40.4	50.1	88.0	80.0	61.8
Total	284.2	429.5	773.2	895.5	948.3

Per Cent of Total Agricultural Credit Contributed
by Institution, 1964-1968

	1964	1965	1966	1967	1968
CORA	0.8	0.9	4.5	9.4	15.7
INDAP	5.0	6.7	4.1	4.1	5.7
Banco del Estado	79.9	80.8	80.0	77.6	72.1
CORFO	14.3	11.6	11.4	8.9	6.5
Total	100.0	100.0	100.0	100.0	100.0

Source: AID, unpublished memorandum, November 28, 1969, Santiago

This seems to indicate that the government is tending to favor agricultural development programs but that most of the agricultural credit is still going to the large farm sector. But vastly more low income farmers are now benefitting from official credit than in 1964. And the data presented may somewhat understate the institutional credit going to small farmers: asentamientos are increasingly encouraged to turn to the Banco del Estado for credit. Also, CORA is favoring contract farming to channel private-sector funds to asentamientos.

Regardless of reservations and qualifications, one can now at least begin to question the continued validity of McBride's classic 1936 statement: "In so far as a middle class has existed at all, it has existed only in the cities. In rural life it must be master or man. There has been no alternative." [13, p. 183]

But reform is a difficult process in the Chilean context:

Those groups that wish to oppose change are strong and well entrenched. ... Moreover, it is perhaps misleading always to speak of the Christian Democrats as a reformist party: while reform elements certainly predominate numerically and often control the party, President Frei's ministerial choices have given plenty of power and opportunity to those supporters who come from and feel more comfortable with the right wing of the Chilean political spectrum.

Nor, of course, do the Christian Democrats enjoy a monopoly of reformist sentiment. They won the elections of 1964 and 1965 only because of the support of the right. It is very difficult to wield a reform coalition in a country like Chile; those groups who want reform often tend to want partial reform in their own interests; these interests may clash with those of another group.[2, p. 84; see also 1 and 15]

Any program which involves redistribution of opportunities and resources must be examined on the basis of its contributions to development. One explicit purpose of President Frei's rural development program was to give campesinos the claim on resources they need to be productively employed while encouraging them to invest and increase their productivity. When there are idle or underutilized land resources—as there are in Chile—they must be made to contribute to overall development, defined broadly to include increased employment, more production, and a better distribution of income.

Using these criteria, the macro economic effects of the Chilean reform to date have not been significant. But micro studies of reform at the asentamiento level may give clues as to its probable impact in the future and to possible problems and bottlenecks as the reform becomes more widespread.

Micro Studies of the Reform

Meyer studied six asentamientos in the Central Zone that had been in operation for at least two full crop years.[14] He selected them to represent a wide range of resource endowment and profitability and found that net farm returns (gross farm returns minus cash operating expenses) and returns to capital and management (net farm returns minus labor payments and fixed costs) increased on all but one in 1967/68, the second year of operation, when compared to the first. If debt installments had been charged in 1966/67, three asentamientos could have met both land and working capital payments without reducing consumption. A fourth could have paid only one-half of its land installment; the two others could have paid neither. In 1967/68 five of the six could have paid the land debt installment, but two of these five could not have paid completely the working capital assessment.

To determine how this performance might be improved, Meyer paired each asentamiento with a nearby well-managed privately operated fundo of fairly similar physical resources and with a fairly long history of good management. With coefficients calculated from these data, he prepared enterprise budgets and used linear programming to analyze how output and efficiency of resource use on the asentamientos could be improved. The private farms used more fertilizer but had lower machinery costs and used less labor per hectare. Assuming improved management and selecting a farm income maximizing combination of enterprises based on the calculated input-output coefficients, he found that net farm income could be increased on all six asentaminetos, and that even the poorest one could almost pay the land installment. But maximizing net income with an optimum enterprise combination would have required a decline of 70 or 80 per cent of current labor use. When this labor is retained, net farm income declines, but five of the six could still pay all debt installments.

With capital investments in labor intensive enterprises, the poorest asentamiento still could not pay debt installments and retain the present labor force; on the other hand, three of them could increase farm employment while the remaining two could earn sufficient income to maintain present labor and pay all debts. If this latter alternative were selected, the area devoted to forage, beef cattle, poultry, sheep, fruit, and nuts would increase while that devoted to cereals, fallow land, and natural pasture would decline. Meyer's analysis indicates that in this case operating capital requirements would rise by 13 to 25 per cent (primarily in the form of such items as nursery stock and livestock and not machinery). Gross value of production would increase by more than 25 per cent over current levels.

A CORA study of 95 per cent of all 1966-67 asentamientos shows that most asentados made incomes between two and ten times the salario agrícola—the government-set minimum wage for an agricultural worker in Chile (see Table VII).

An FAO sample study in 1966/67 showed that the average income per asentado was between 2.8 and 4.6 times that of the agricultural minimum wage.[19] As a group, those who previously had administrative positions on the fundo do poorer after than before the reform. Apparently, within the beneficiary group the effect of reform on distribution of income is a downward shift of previous high-income earners and a shift upward for those workers who formerly received the lowest incomes.[11]

TABLE VII—Earnings of Asentados: 1966-67

Percent of Asentados	Number of Times the Salario Agrícola Earned
0.69	Negative Income
13.48	0-1
27.75	1-2
43.12	2-4
14.25	4-10
0.71	10-26

Source: Corporación de la Reforma Agraria (CORA). Unpublished data.

A CORA census of 226 settlements in 1967-68 showed per acre yields of the major crops grown to be somewhat above the national average despite the drought conditions (Table VIII).

TABLE VIII—Yields of Four Crops on 226 Asentamientos 1967-68

	National Average Yield in Quintales Per Hectare[a]	226 Asentamientos: Average Yield in Quintales Per Hectare[b]	Difference in Favor of the Asentamientos
Wheat	17.4	21.2	+3.8
Corn	36.2	37.8	+1.6
Barley	21.9	27.3	+5.4
Potatoes	90.6	127.8	+37.2

Source: E. Broughton, "Chile: Land Reform and Agricultural Development," Ph.D. dissertation, University of Liverpool, 1970.
[a]From Table 2.
[b]CORA

Jolly surveyed sixteen asentamientos in 1966-67, the harvest year before the passage of Law 16.640.[12] He found that when operating costs, settlers' advances, a 10 per cent interest on capital and credit, and an imputed value for land amortization were subtracted from total gross income on all the asentamientos taken as a group, the result was slightly negative. This, he claims, is not too unsatisfactory considering that most of these asentamientos were in their first year of operation. However, the interest rate he charged was negative (considering inflation), and he allowed only a minimum amount for cash advances. As one might suspect, these gross figures conceal a great deal of variability among asentamientos. Nine settlements produced a surplus after all the above subtractions were made while seven could not cover them. Four of these seven showed negative incomes even before land amortization was deducted.

In order to measure changes over a two-year period, a sub-sample of five settlements was chosen. These had been in operation the previous year and reflected the overall characteristics of the sixteen. This comparison showed that when the second year was compared to the first, there was: (1) an increase in total area devoted to crops (from 2.9 hectares per settler to 3.3 hectares per settler); (2) a 25 per cent increase in area directed to irrigated crops at the expense of grazing land and non-irrigated cropland; (3) more planting of crops with a higher value per hectare (total land in crops increased 14 per cent; less intensive crops increased by 9 per cent compared to a 17 per cent increase in more intensive crops); (4) a rise in real income from livestock although less area was devoted to pasture; (5) an increase in gross income on four of the five asentamientos; (6) an increase of labor use; (7) a rise in debt repayment capacity on only two settlements, indicating that operating costs ususally rose at a higher rate than gross income; (8) a continuing wide range of economic performance between the best and poorest asentamiento. The study further concluded that asentamientos with high operating costs do not necessarily receive the least net income; the crucial factor is the level and combination of inputs used to produce a high gross.

Implications for Policy

The data in most of the above-cited studies show that asentamientos exhibit a wide range of economic performance. This is hardly surprising: there are wide ranges in agricultural performance everywhere in the world. Besides, each asentamiento begins its history with a differing resource endowment. CORA and the campesinos must create viable, flexible "going concerns" in this pre-ownership period, and this is no easy job, but the overall task is even more complex and demanding. Each new firm attempts to act in its own self interest, and the sum of private interests may not be entirely congruent with the public interest. For example, under existing arrangements asentados may not want to provide employment to an extent that is socially desirable. CORA's policies—and those of other governmental agencies—must be designed to meet such national developmental priorities. Whether all of this can be done will depend on at least some of the following considerations.

First: The tendency toward use of more and more labor saving capital equipment on asentamientos—as well as in the private sector of agriculture—must be closely examined in terms of the pressing employment problems which confront the economy. Jolly found that rental of machinery (and some draft animals) made up 23.5 per cent of total operating costs of the asentamientos in his sample. One-third of a $23 million AID sector loan signed October 23, 1967, went into importing capital equipment, and three-quarters of that went to CORA. The projected expenditures for the 1969 sector loan likewise show capital equipment as a prominient expenditure, making up about 36 per cent of the $10 million. The government of Chile reports that there has, in partial consequence, been a 30 per cent price drop for tractors sold in Chile.

This emphasis on mechanization has serious employment repercussions in an economy where industry is not able to absorb those who must leave agriculture. In the Central Valley, where double-cropping is not a common practice, use of more capital equipment has little impact on increasing yields per hectare or on gross agricultural production. Meanwhile, improving irrigation works, use of more fertilizer, better management, and use of improved stock and seed could have a major impact. Jolly found that only 9 per cent of the operating expenses of the asentamientos he studied were for fertilizer purchases. Ten per cent of the 1969 sector loan is planned for fertilizer imports by CORA, a percentage very similar to that of the 1967 loan.

Second: The number of asentados needs to be carefully matched with the farm's carrying capacity. This is difficult because early in the process, when CORA has more prerogatives, CORA itself may be unable to calculate how many campesinos should be settled on a fundo; later (and sometimes even early in the process if campesinos are already organized) the campesinos themselves may be reluctant to take on new families as asentados: they see the land as creating a long run opportunity for their own families, and in the short run they cannot see the need for dividing profits among more people.

Jolly reports that the highest single operating cost on the asentamientos he studied was for hiring outside labor (28.7 per cent of total operating costs), and that many of the most successful asentamientos hired the most labor; meanwhile, the least successful asentamientos were probably overpopulated. While this does create employment opportunities, these are often seasonal. And such hired workers do not realize the benefits that would accrue to them as asentados. Yet estimates show that over 70 per cent more asentados could be accommodated on existing asentamientos in the southern part of the Central Valley than are actually settled there.

There are signs that in some cases the asentados themselves may be becoming a closed group with no more willingness to incorporate new labor and share more widely the wealth and opportunities than a latifundista. Of course, if this system results in more employment than would be the case in the absence of the asentamiento, the net social result may still be positive. However, even these gains may vanish if asentados become a progressively more privileged group and continue to substitute additional capital equipment for hired labor.

It may be possible to deal with problems of this kind through skillfully managed regional organizations in which all asentamientos participate along the lines attempted in the Talagante "area" in Santiago province (an "area" is a CORA-zone subdivision). The area chief (a CORA employee) together with each asentamiento president and one asentado elected at large from each settlement designed a joint cropping plan for the area that was labor intensive, involved high value crops, and was planned so that the harvest would reach the market at the time prices were most favorable. Tractors, when needed, were shared area-wide so each asentamiento did not need to have so many tractors and other pieces of equipment.

If similar institutional mechanisms were to become widespread and viable, settlers would realize that serving the broader public interests of the region is not inconsistent with their own self-interest. Asentados from underpopulated asentamientos might at least be willing to accept those from overpopulated ones within an area. Furthermore, this type of organization might provide incentives for the underpopulated settlements to take on additional landless laborers from the region as asentados. One advantage of the asentamiento form of land tenure is that it provides a good school for learning interpersonal cooperation after which inter-asentamiento cooperation should be easier. However, such developments may not materialize without strong leadership from CORA and general policy guidelines for moving in this direction.

Third: More attention must be given to the incorporation of younger-than-eighteen unmarried settlers who are now barred from becoming asentados. While the current method of settler selection provides community stability, it also means that most asentados are middle-aged. Because they are likely to have more schooling than their fathers, younger settlers may well add needed ingredients of flexibility and imagination to the asentamiento.

Fourth: Administration of the reform program and campesino skills must constantly be improved. Furthermore, incentives must be created to avoid the attitude, "If I don't work very hard, the job will be done by someone else anyhow."

CORA has attempted a mammoth task and in general has done an admirable job. But CORA technicians are under pressure to make certain management decisions centrally in order to assure that short-run production does not fall. Under these circumstances even a small mistake by a technician who is not completely familiar with local conditions—or an input delivered too late—can be serious. Even more important, campesinos—who may have merely taken orders from superiors prior to reform—must become entrepreneurs as quickly as possible. And if they are not permitted to become fairly skilled in decision-making, short-run gains in marketable surplus might be followed by long-run problems—reform does result in "independence" from CORA's tutelage at the end of three to five years.

An example of this problem (which has now been partially solved) is that, although CORA provides the inputs, it does not always inform the asentados why they are to use them and how much they cost. (In at least one case, however, there is an area-wide organization in which a representative of each asentamiento travels with a CORA official to the seed granaries to choose the variety best suited to conditions on each farm.) CORA may also have subsidized inputs and credit at too high a level. Delinquency on loans has been high. Furthermore, reports on the final accounting are often delayed—sometimes well into the next planting season. Entrepreneurs, whether working individually or as a group, must have continuous access to operating cost information (that reflects true market value) and price data if they are to make rational decisions.

Some of these problems remain; their resolution depends on increasingly decentralized administration but also on the personality of the technical and administrative personnel involved, many of whom find it difficult to overcome the paternalistic spirit which dominates labor relations on the private fundo.

The CORA administration has not been slow to learn; beginning in May 1968 it greatly reduced its own supervisory role on the settlements. It also placed more responsibility for keeping accounts with each asentamiento. As the program expands, it will be necessary to reduce CORA's role and decentralize its organization still further. The asentamiento period on exceptionally successful settlements should be shortened.

INDAP has proven very skillful in organizing some regional marketing cooperatives which also make bulk purchase of recommended inputs possible for small holders. The co-op grants credit; and since other members are responsible for repayment on loan defaults by individual recipients, each borrower is under pressure by his peers to increase his production. Under this form of technical assistance, paternalistic patterns are less likely to develop. CORA might well consider a similar arrangement during the asentamiento period on those settlements which show most promise. The technical assistance component is much larger in CORA than in INDAP programs. In many cases the CORA technical assistance component is vital since it works with farmers who are not as accustomed to decision making as the small independent holders who constitute INDAP's clientele.

Fifth: Complementary reforms must be made in secondary level institutions to prevent marketing agents from assuming the exploitive role of the old landlord. Some problems in the Chilean agricultural marketing system are well documented.[8] A regional organization of asentados together with INDAP cooperatives would help shape the market structure so that it lessens dependency on middlemen and on the monopolistic central market in Santiago. Such an organization might also be able to secure increased contracts on more favorable terms for such crops as sugarbeets, sunflowers, and barley. This type of contract farming is available to Chilean producers and usually includes credit, inputs, technical assistance, and purchase of the crop at a guaranteed price.

There also seems to be opportunities for asentados and their families to process more goods for the market—either on the farm or in nearby towns. In 1967 some asentamientos packaged potatoes and sold them directly to a Santiago supermarket. It was estimated that this reduced the usual marketing margin by 60 per cent—an amount which remained in the local community and provided employment for many who would otherwise have been jobless. This and similar partial processing could perhaps be extended to other vegetable crops, but it requires some coordination at the area or regional level: retailers need assurances of an adequate source of supply throughout the harvest season. Installation of processing plants for canning, dehydration, or even freeze drying fruits and vegetables would be another local-level possibility.

Sixth: Some infrastructural investments now being made might be postponed until later. Certainly new dwelling units, under construction on many asentamientos, could be delayed for a time while peasants live in the admittedly inadequate housing that exists. This would free funds for higher priority investments—fertilizers, hybrid seeds or education facilities—or even for more land expropriation to allow program expansion. Later campesinos could purchase construction materials cooperatively and build houses under a shared labor plan, which would lower costs.

Five years' experience in Chile has shown that reform is a difficult task. It is perhaps doubly so where institutions based on democratic principles prevail and are honored, where coalitions form and reshape themselves, where legalisms abound and strongman tactics are generally abhorred. Within the context of such political intricacies are the overall achievements sought—increasing production, training a new class of entrepreneurs, providing employment, stepping up economic growth of the economy as a whole, lessening dependence on the export sector, and devising a wholly new tenure form in agriculture. The problems that emerge are formidable. Still, in carrying out the agrarian reform, CORA's position has been generally open, pragmatic, and self-critical.

References

[1] Angell, Alan. "Chile: The Difficulties of Democratic Reform." *International Journal* 24 (1969): 515-528.

[2] ———. "Christian Democracy in Chile." *Current History* 58 (1970): 79-84.

[3] Arriaga, E. E. "Components of City Growth in Selected Latin American Countries." *Milbank Memorial Fund Quarterly* 46 (1968): 241-253.

[4] *Bank of London and South America Review* 3 (1969): 588-590.

[5] Broughton, F. "Chile: Land Reform and Agricultural Development." Ph.D. dissertation, University of Liverpool, 1970.

[6] Corporación de la Reforma Agraria (CORA). Unpublished data.

[7] Dirección de Estadística y Censos. *IV Censo Nacional Agropecuario, Año Agrícola,* 1964-1965. Santiago, 1966.

[8] Fletschner, Carlos. "Structural Patterns in the Marketing of Selected Agricultural Products in Chile: The Position of Small and Large Growers." Ph.D. dissertation, University of Wisconsin, 1969.

[9] Frei, Eduardo. "Fifth Annual Message to Congress, May 21, 1969."

[10] Herrick, B. H. *Urban Migration and Economic Development in Chile.* Cambridge, Mass.: MIT Press, 1965.

[11] Imable, Rogelio. "Asentamientos de Choapa: Cambios en la tenencia de la tierra y en los ingresos de los campesinos." *Economía* 25 (1967): 3-13.

[12] Jolly, A. L. "An Economic Evaluation of the Asentamientos of the Agrarian Reform." Preliminary draft. Santiago: Instituto de Capacitación e Investigación en Reforma Agraria (ICIRA), 1968.

[13] McBride, George McCutchen. *Chile: Land and Society.* New York: American Geographic Society, 1936.

[14] Meyer, Richard L. "Debt Repayment Capacity of the Chilean Agrarian Reform Beneficiaries." Ph.D. dissertation, Cornell University, 1970.

[15] Petras, James. *Politics and Social Forces in Chilean Development.* Berkeley: University of California Press, 1969.

[16] Rawlings, Steve W. *Population of Chile: Estimates and Projections, 1961-1991.* Bureau of the Census, U. S. Department of Commerce Series P-96, no. 1. Washington, D. C.: December 1969.

[17] Ringlein, Wayne. "Economic Effects of Chilean National Expropriation Policy on the Private Commercial Farm Sector, 1964-69." Ph.D. dissertation, University of Maryland, 1971.

[18] United Nations. *Populations and Vital Statistics Report.* Statistical papers, Series A, Vol. 20, no. 3. July 1968.

[19] United Nations. Food and Agricultural Organization and ICIRA. *Evaluación preliminar de los asentamientos de la reforma agraria en Chile.* Santiago: 1967.

[20] United States Agency for International Development. Unpublished memorandum. November 28, 1969, Santiago.

[21] Weeks, John R. "Urban and Rural Natural Increase in Chile." *The Milbank Memorial Fund Quarterly* 43 (1970): 71-89.

CHAPTER 7

Agrarian Reform: Boliva

RONALD J. CLARK

Assistant Professor of Agricultural Economics
and the Land Tenure Center
at the University of Wisconsin–Madison

CHAPTER 7

Agrarian Reform: Bolivia*

RONALD J. CLARK

The highlands and valleys, which together represent only about one-third of Bolivia's land area, contain nearly all the major mining and urban centers; in 1953, over 90 per cent of the population lived in the highlands and valleys. In these areas the work relations between large land owners and the indigenous population were traditionally organized so that landlord incomes were maximized and cash expenditures in the agricultural process were minimized. Particularly between 1860 and 1910, but continuing until the Revolution of 1952, the incorporation of more and more land into large private estates through purchase or usurpation of lands in Indian freeholding communities and the number of Indian families obligated to work for landlords grew along with the need for increased food production.

Bolivia's 1950 Agricultural Census [4, p. 2 ff.] reported a total of 82,598 private land holdings. Of these, 7,924 farms (approximately 9.6 per cent) of 200 hectares or more controlled 74 per cent of the total land area reported. These same large farms contained 62 per cent of the land cultivated. At the other extreme, 50,483 farms (61 per cent) had less than 5.0 hectares each and controlled only 0.28 per cent of the total area and 8.1 per cent of the cultivated lands. The 1950 Census recorded 3,783 Indian freeholding communities (communities where title to lands is held in the name of the community) but did not show the area occupied or cultivated by such communities.

On the highlands, an estimated 90 per cent of the owners of large holdings were absentee landlords. By way of contrast, about 50 per cent of the farms in the valley and subtropical areas were operated by their owners.

* This paper draws heavily upon parts of a past study—"An Evaluation of the Bolivian Land Reform"—undertaken during 1965-1968, and co-directed by Ing. Celso Reyes P. of the Bolivian National Agrarian Reform Service and the present author. That study was financed by the Land Tenure Center, University of Wisconsin; the Inter-American Committee for Agricultural Development (CIDA), Washington, D.C.; USAID/Bolivia; and the Bolivian Government. The more complete study is now in pre-publication revision by the National Agrarian Reform Service, La Paz, Bolivia.

The author wishes to express his gratitude to Miss Katherine Barnes, Lic. Hugo Romero, and Ing. Celso Reyes P., as well as to all other Bolivian personnel (especially Mr. Roberto Gumucio A.) who have made the writing of this chapter possible. Of course, he assumes full responsibility for conclusions reached and interpretations made.

On almost all of the larger holdings, the predominant tenure relation was the colonato system. The landlord granted usufruct rights to small parcels of land to the Indian families or colonos; in turn, each of these families was obligated to provide the landlords, without compensation, at least three and as many as twelve man-days of labor per week, depending on the quantity of land the colono family received. The colonos had to use their own tools and animals in working the landlord's lands, and had to provide additional labor services for such tasks as harvesting and transporting the landlord's produce to market. Colono families were also obligated to render personal and domestic services to the landlord and his family (in their homes both on the farm and in the towns). These same obligations pertained to work in the homes of the farm managers. All these services were unremunerated, except in terms of the opportunity costs of the parcel of land exchanged for them. This agricultural system minimized landlord investments but maximized their income flows, both in cash and in kind. This system generally precluded investments favoring the adoption of more productive inputs, as well as the adoption of different tenure relations with the Indian labor force. On most of the larger landholdings, the colono was virtually a slave. He was so tied to the land that even when properties were sold, they were listed as including "300 colonos." Also it was not uncommon for landlords to "rent" colonos for specified periods from other landlords.[1]

Landlords had little interest in and sometimes even prohibited schools in the rural areas; hence the country's high rate of illiteracy (estimated at 80 per cent before 1952). Similarly, colonos were not permitted to organize on the landholdings, even though national legislation allowed such organization. If organizations were discovered by landlords, peasant leaders, their families, and other organization members were usually forced to leave the landholding. And such evicted workers experienced great difficulty in finding work elsewhere. Literacy and property requirements kept the mass of the rural population from voting. Infant mortality was high and life expectancy low.

Nevertheless, some traditional landholdings were being broken up and sold to peasants before 1952, mostly in a few of the valleys (Cochabamba and Tarija) where landholdings were smaller and population pressure was high. Inheritance disputes and excessive inheritance fragmentation occasionally led to land sales. However, landlord associations usually exerted pressures on individual landlords to prevent selling or renting lands to peasants.

Despite the severely deprived social and economic position of the peasants, the thirty year period prior to the Revolution was definitely marked by a political movement in the rural sector. Sporadic uprisings occurred as early as 1921 and increased in frequency through the presidency of Gualberto

[1] These descriptions attempt to portray *general* conditions in Bolivia before 1952. There were of course many individuals, including some landlords, who realized the injustices of the prevailing tenure relations and the inefficiencies of the agricultural system. Also, a number of landlords were genuinely interested in improving farm operations by importing machinery, animals, and other inputs needed to increase both the quantity and quality of output per unit of land.

Villarroel (1943-46). By 1936 peasant unions (sindicatos) had formed on two haciendas in the Upper Valley of Cochabamba.[11, pp. 76 ff.] These developments can be attributed to several special circumstances in this area: (1) Cochabamba had long been an important producer of wheat and other produce for the mines and thus agriculture was more highly developed; (2) many young men from rural areas in Cochabamba went to work in the mines because no land was available, thus establishing contacts between local peasants and activist mine workers; (3) a higher level of social integration existed here than in other rural areas of Bolivia; and (4) public agencies and institutions (such as the Church and the City of Cochabamba) owned large holdings throughout Cochabamba.

The pre-1952 period was marked not only by uprisings and violence but also by farm workers' strikes and resistance in the form of work slowdowns. In 1945, after much conflict between peasant and landlord groups, the Primer Congreso Nacional Indigenal (First National Indian Congress) was called by President Villarroel. The result was the elimination of personal household services, though not of farm labor obligations; no steps were taken to distribute land. The years following the overthrow of the Villarroel government (1947-1952) were ones of repression of peasants who had taken part in the Congress, and personal service obligations were quickly reinstituted in those areas where they had earlier been abolished. However, in these same years peasant organizations in the rural sector grew in power and cohesiveness despite the fact that the principal peasant leaders from small rural towns often had to go into hiding.

Land invasions, strikes, and the measures taken by the Villarroel government resulted in an increasing polarization of opinion and positions among urban workers, intellectuals, and political groups. Increasingly, people had to choose between supporting the changes which peasants and some political leaders and authors proposed, including the expropriation and distribution of land to peasants, or the reinstatement of conditions existing before Villarroel. In the 1947-1952 period, those who favored a reinstatement of the previous rural conditions controlled the government. The opposing political and intellectual groups, and to some extent workers and peasants, decided to take the issues to the rural areas; there is no other explanation for the radical activity of peasants and their leaders once the MNR Party came to power in April 1952. The centers of this activity were the Upper Valley of Cochabamba, and Achacachi to the north of La Paz on the highlands. Both were strategic political centers, and it was in these areas that land invasions took place on a large scale between April 1952 and August 1953 when the Land Reform Law was finally decreed. In the interim, the revolutionary government directly aided the peasant movements.

The actual Revolution of 1952 was carried out by the National Revolutionary Movement (MNR) Party. The MNR was elected to office in 1951, but the results of the election were ignored and President Urriolagoitia turned the government over to a military junta (1951-1952). Only after parts of the armed forces rebelled in favor of the MNR did the new government take office on April 9, 1952. The masses of peasant families in the rural sector played no role in unseating the military junta or installing the newly-elected government.

The Land Reform Law of 1953

Whether or not the MNR Party was intent upon carrying out a radical land reform or merely intended to curb some of the more blatant abuses of the hacienda system has been questioned.[8; 9; 10] A period of sixteen months elapsed between the MNR's installation and its promulgation of the Land Reform Decree of August 3, 1953. During this period, however, land invasions occurred in the Upper Valley of Cochabamba and on the northern highlands, and the new government did directly aid the peasants. Emissaries of the government or regional leaders visited most of the large landholdings, urging the formation of peasant unions and promising land reform. Leaders and members of mining and urban workers' unions helped the government in this task.

After the Revolution, but not until after a number of land invasions by peasants, the government formed a commission to draw up a land reform decree. After long deliberations as well as marked differences of opinion between some members, the 1953 Land Reform Decree resulting from the Commission's work established a landmark, for it made a bold break with the past.[2] In this process the MNR Party was purposefully creating and relying

[2] The Commission which was to draw up the Bolivian Ley de Reforma Agraria began its work in April 1953, one year after the national Revolution. It was composed of numerous subcommittees such as History, Economics and Finance, Water Resources, Education, and Political Economy, with members drawn from most of the ministries and important sectors of society such as the peasantry, the Sociedad Rural (landlords), and the universities. In general, members were selected on the basis of their specific talent in certain fields and their diverse political opinions.

According to one member of the Subcommittee on Economics and Finance, the basic problem was that of time. The revolutionary government had committed itself to the agrarian reform and promised the peasants a land reform law by August 2, 1953–Día del Indio. Not only time but lack of important statistics and little knowledge of the national territory made the task more difficult.

Allegedly, it was the desire of most members of the Commission to create a law that was Bolivian, not one modeled after China, Russia or Mexico. Members were appointed by the new revolutionary government, and they were responsible to it. For this reason they did not have major disagreements with respect to overall policy. The Commission also kept in close touch with the new president, Paz Estenssoro. It appears that the particular personality of this leader tended to minimize discord within the Commission. The Commission visited the Presidential Palace every Wednesday for discussions with the President; during these periods the cabinet showed a united front, supporting Paz Estenssoro. Perhaps the most important factor in this relative harmony, despite varying opinions and backgrounds of members, was that the revolution itself was already a reality; it was backed by the new president with undeniable national support from the mining and peasant sectors. Even the most conservative members of the Commission found it difficult to muster any opposition.

In drawing up the Bolivian land reform law, many foreign laws were analyzed, and the experience of the Mexican ejido received special attention. However, the personality and ideas of Paz Estenssoro were of strategic importance.

upon the political support of the masses in the rural sector by giving peasants and their leaders in certain key areas what they wanted—access to and ownership of land.

In May 1952 the new MNR government created the Ministry of Asuntos Campesinos. This change not only recognized the socio-political and economic changes already under way in the rural sector, but also demonstrated the government's determination to support and enlarge upon these changes.

The promise of land reform, in combination with land invasions and arms to the peasants, was accompanied by a rapidly spreading national peasant union movement. Through these peasant unions—at the community, provincial, departmental, and national levels—the peasant sector expressed its voice. The peasants' interest were also expressed via: (1) the Ministerio de Asuntos Campesinos (Rural Affairs), which represents the peasants before the executive (sometimes this minister has been a national peasant leader or a member of the Confederación Nacional de Trabajadores Campesinos Bolivianos, CNTCB); (2) representatives of the peasantry as members of the legislative chambers; (3) the representative of the CNTCB in the National Agrarian Reform Service, which is empowered to expropriate and distribute land along with its other functions; and (4) the peasant union organization, which reaches directly to the level of the rural community.

The National Agrarian Reform Service was set up as an autonomous unit responsible directly to the President of Bolivia; it is empowered to interpret and to implement the land reform law. The Service holds a position within the government which is equivalent to that of the Ministry of Agriculture or the Ministry of Asuntos Campesinos. The Service has three divisions: the executive (Presidencia), the legislative (Asesoría General, or legal advisors), and the judicial (divided into three courts: Sala Primera, Sala Segunda, and Sala Plena). Besides the national office in La Paz, there are departmental offices, each of which has its set of judges and topographers. Additionally, there are offices in the provincial capitals.

The following additional areas of work were assigned to the Service at its inception: (a) national planning and integration concerning agrarian and peasant matters; (b) development of cooperatives and systems of agricultural credit; (c) organization of colonization projects; (d) provision of technical assistance to guarantee the rational utilization of soils and the eventual mechanization of the agrarian sector. [12, p. 22]

In practice, however, the Service has retained only its legal functions. All other complementary functions of the Service—extension, colonization, land reclamation, conservation of natural resources, community development, and economic planning—have been divided among various agencies. These agencies have their own policies and carry out independent programs with little or no coordination among them, and with no direct relation to the land expropriation and titling done by the Service. There is no national agrarian policy, nor is there an effective mechanism to coordinate the various functions and complementary services.[12]

The legal functions of the Service are to initiate expropriation decrees, to distribute land to peasant families, and to implement the legal aspects of title distribution for all landholders. Although the Service has legal powers to initiate independent suits, in practice it functions like a system of agrarian courts, before which are brought all cases dealing with land conflicts. The majority of the suits are initiated before an agrarian judge, with a judicial review held by the Sala Plena acting as the supreme court in all matters. The Service has jurisdiction over all rural lands in Bolivia, including those in the public domain.

Program Objectives

The basic objective of the land reform law was to transform the feudalistic land tenure system by promoting a more equitable distribution of land, raising productivity, and integrating the rural population into the national economy and society. More specifically, it was to:

a) give peasants that had little or no land adequate parcels with the condition that they work the land; expropriate underutilized lands, extremely extensive holdings (latifundio), and those lands not worked personally by the owner;

b) restore to the original freeholding communities all lands usurped since 1900;

c) change the predominant system of work relations;

d) stimulate the production and commercialization of agricultural products;

e) protect the nation's natural resources; and

f) encourage emigration from the densely populated highlands to the underpopulated tropical regions.

The Law made no more specific statement of objectives than the above, and no aspects were specifically quantified.

Implementation and Enforcement

Implementation of the law got off to a slow start because of the confusion existing in post-revolutionary Bolivia, not to mention the time necessary for setting up the National Agrarian Reform Service, recruiting personnel (topographers, lawyers, etc.), and getting peasants to present their cases for expropriation of the lands which they worked. Despite delays, no other Latin American country has expropriated and redistributed lands and land titles to peasant families on a similar scale.

Of approximately 15,332 expropriation cases initiated since 1953, 7,322 have been concluded at this time. Each expropriation case can affect from a few up to one hundred peasant families, sometimes more. The 8,000 cases still pending (1967) include some 165,000 families and about 5.3 million hectares. Many of these cases were begun eight, nine, or ten years ago. Although peasant families are in possession of the land, they remain in a precarious position until their legal rights are clearly defined. [12]

Many properties still have not been affected by any reform process. Using the only information available, the Census of 1950 (and without counting freeholding communities which are subject to a different process), one arrives at a figure of approximately 67,276 properties which remain to be processed by the Service. It is important to point out that these figures cover all rural Bolivian properties. According to the reform law, all rural property documents must be processed by the National Agrarian Reform Service in order to determine whether or not the property is subject to partial or full expropriation or, in the contrary case, to legal recognition of the property right and the issuance of a new title. [12, p. 3] Most properties not yet subjected to the land reform law of 1953 are either small holdings worked by their owners or larger holdings in the tropical lowlands where tenure relations and land problems are completely different from those in the old settled regions; in neither case is much expropriation likely to be carried out. [12]

Maximum legal sizes of landholdings were set by the land reform law; these were determined according to stated categories of geographic location and type of exploitation. For example, the maximum extension for a property along the shores of Lake Titicaca is only ten hectares, while that in the subtropical region of Santa Cruz is fifty hectares. Surplus land on such properties is subject to expropriation and redistribution.

In most cases the new owners (dotados) were ex-colono families who lived and worked on the former hacienda or relatives of these families. However, in many cases the final list of dotados is larger than the number of ex-colonos. This increase is due to some abuse in the application of the law; some who were not colonos on that landholding acquired a parcel for themselves. In some cases the parcel was a political payoff; also, some peasants from the highlands went into the more fertile, less populated subtropical areas such as Yungas, and were able to have their names entered on the lists of dotados. Moreover, colonos' sons, while they may have performed some work on the hacienda, many times did not figure as colonos with usufruct parcels, but when the reform came they too were entitled to receive lands.

The actual redistribution process, with all its abuses and legal intricacies, was highly complicated and varied from region to region. Its primary nature was political and many times it was determined in the provincial and departmental capitals rather than in La Paz and the reform tribunals. The redistribution process in its political context will be discussed later.

Table I shows the quantities of land distributed in Bolivia since the reform, and the number of families which have received land titles. As of 1969, land titles had been distributed to approximately 40 per cent of those who are entitled to receive them. However, the Bolivian government is now implementing a program to complete all titling by 1975.

The reform abruptly changed tenure relations between landlords and colono families. Even before expropriation procedures began, virtually all peasants became de facto owners of their usufruct parcels and no longer

TABLE I—Land Expropriated and Area and Titles
Distributed in Bolivia, 1953-1969

Total number of expropriated properties	11,971	
Total number of titles distributed	434,893	
A. Individual titles	228,201	
B. Collective titles	206,692	
Heads of families in receipt of titles	266,066	
Total land expropriated	12,037,722	(Hectares)
Total land distributed	11,671,874	(Hectares)
A. Cultivable land included in	3,039,911	(Hectares)
individual titles		
B. Land included in collective titles		
1. Cultivable land	1,180,345	(Hectares)
2. Pasture land	4,719,115	(Hectares)
3. Incultivable land	699,216	(Hectares)
4. School land	6,720	(Hectares)
5. Sports areas	610	(Hectares)
6. Land held in cooperatives	55,781	(Hectares)
7. Colonization areas	29,130	(Hectares)
8. Urban areas	9,849	(Hectares)
9. Land returned to the state	365,848	(Hectares)

Source: Consejo Nacional de Reforma Agraria, La Paz, Bolivia, unpublished data.

provided landlords unremunerated farm labor or personal services; the termination of these obligations was one of the provisions of the land reform law. Nevertheless, even in some of the more politicized zones, peasants continued to work for their ex-landlords for a wage. In a way, this appears to contradict the idea of a "revolution" in the rural areas, yet it is not so incongruent when one recalls that even the Minister of Asuntos Campesinos in 1953 was imploring the peasantry to tone down the land reform and to perform wage work for the landlords. The Ministry also tried to make the rural peasant unions responsible for keeping hacienda lands under cultivation and for marketing produce. This was an attempt to minimize the effects of land reform on production levels and on quantities of produce reaching consumption centers. This paradoxical situation—continued work for the landlord in the midst of political upheaval in the countryside, while many landowners and farm managers were seeking refuge in towns and cities— continued in many areas until 1957-58.

The settlement of virgin lands in the lowlands was also an integral part of the Bolivian land reform program. This idea was not new; at different times before and since the land reform, colonization has been regarded as the panacea for the ills of rural Bolivia. To date colonization has complemented the large scale reform carried out in the traditional highlands and valleys. With Point Four assistance, roads have been opened into the Caranavi-Alto Beni and Choquechaca zones close to La Paz, and these roads were later extended farther inland. Here, both planned and spontaneous colonies were established; most were settled by peasants from freeholding communities of dense population. Many ex-colonos from nearby Yungas took advantage of their proximity to the new lands and settled there. Other roads were also built or improved to open up additional areas to increased settlement.

During the decade 1962-1971, the government's objective was to settle 100,000 peasant families in areas of colonization. As of 1970, only about 30,000 families have actually been settled in these areas, and most are spontaneous settlers. This limited number of resettled families indicates that colonization programs have been unable to absorb the increase in the rural population; therefore the absolute number of peasant families in traditional areas of the highlands and valleys has undoubtedly increased substantially since the land reform.

The revolutionary government, as already mentioned, had very little information on which to base and to carry out a well planned land reform. There was a political need to fulfill peasant demands; each month the Land Reform Commission witnessed more land invasions and more de facto distribution of lands among peasants.

Immediately following April 1952, the Ministry of Agriculture asked its agronomists to develop some rational criteria for establishing parcel size. This they did for virtually all of Bolivia, coming to good theoretical conclusions as to ideal plot size for a peasant family of five according to geographical zone. In practice these criteria could not always be followed since often the hacienda contained insufficient land to accommodate all claimants with a plot of ideal size. The only recourse of the National Agrarian Reform Service was to divide the existing lands among all "rightful" claimants, and to recognize the de facto distribution which had already taken place elsewhere. It was neither physically possible nor politically expedient to meet the criteria of the law in terms of previously established minimum size of parcels in each geographical area. Furthermore, it was impossible financially to resettle many families on lands elsewhere, as colonization experience shows.

Though the Service had available the talent and training of some ex-military men employed by it, the Service could not build its capabilities rapidly enough. In the more distant provinces, mistakes resulting from inadequate training and abuse from political or monetary payoffs were common, and many of the present problems stem from this initial period. In some areas, the difficulties arising from the de facto vs. de jure distribution of land remain critical. For example, a peasant may farm a thirty hectare plot, but his title shows only fifteen hectares; other members of the community insist that he has encroached upon common pasture lands and want him to give up half his land. This problem, where peasant land titles show more or less land than the quantity actually received or entitled to under the law, is common in Bolivia. In these circumstances, peasants face continual disputes with their neighbors.[2]

Financial Aspects

The land reform law stipulated that compensation equal to five times the land values which owners declared for tax purposes in 1950 was to be paid for expropriated land. This was to be paid in twenty-five year bonds. Despite this provision, no official compensation has ever been paid; nor have agrarian bonds been issued. And the ex-landlords have never pressured government to get this provision enforced, probably because the compensation was to be computed on the basis of their past tax declarations of the properties' values. Since there were no suggested adjustments in bond values to protect landlords against inflation, this low basis together with the inflation from 1952-1956 would hardly have made compensation worth the effort.

Peasants receiving lands under the reform law were not obligated to assume part of the costs for compensating landlords since the government never acted on this matter. However, outside of official channels some peasants did pay landlords for their land; such payments, however, have not been general. Questions of landlord compensation and peasant payment for lands are at present relatively unimportant.

In the period 1953-1968, peasants usually assumed the direct costs associated with expropriation and topographic work. They sent representatives to the provincial or departmental capitals to begin expropriation procedures, to plead their case with lawyers, and to bring agrarian judges and topographers out to the property. In most cases this involved considerable expense, particularly when the case was contested by the landlord and a complicated legal battle resulted. Given the circumstances in Bolivia—poor roads and communications, underpaid civil servants, etc.—sustained efforts by the peasant union organization were essential for pushing the process from the level of the rural community. If each union member had not contributed time, produce, and cash, Bolivia's land reform could not have resulted in the accomplishments actually realized.

The budget of the National Agrarian Reform Service is one of the lowest among public agencies of the Bolivian government, representing only 0.6 per cent of the national budget. From 1960 to 1966, the budget approved for the Service was approximately U.S. $215,000 annually (from a minimum of U.S. $150,048 in 1960, to a maximum of U.S. $323,581 in 1965, making a total of U.S. $1,501,262 for this seven year period). But the funds actually received during this period were only U.S. $1,335,041, a reduction of U.S. $166,221 from the allotted total.[12] As usual, when funds received are less than budgeted totals, operating expenses suffer most since salaries cannot easily be lowered nor personnel levels reduced. The Institute of Colonization, for the same 1960-1966 period, received financing at about four times the annual level of the Service. It is ironical that an agency with duties not unlike those of the Service should fare so much better in the competition for national funds. Perhaps this is due in part to the influence of international agencies which lend large sums to support colonization, consequently motivating national governments to support the same programs.

Supplementary Measures

Some of the specific institutional measures effected by the revolutionary government to incorporate the peasant sector into the state and economy of the nation have been outlined. The major area in which very little was done was in providing new services and supply arrangements by which peasants could exploit their parcels of land more efficiently—e.g., extension and credit services, the provision of fertilizer, pesticides, and improved seeds, and the organization of irrigation and transport facilities. Also lacking were price stabilization policies and institutional arrangements for procuring and marketing surpluses.

The adequate provision by the central government of these supplementary measures during the period of most rapid land reform, 1953-1956, would have been difficult if not impossible. First, there was a general shortage of resources, and especially of foreign exchange following the decline in metal prices as the Korean War came to a close. The government could have financed these supplementary measures only by printing even more currency than it did during this inflationary period (1952-1956).

Second, conditions in the rural sector were generally chaotic and in some areas so explosive that it was almost impossible to establish new services and make them widely available to peasants. It is well to recall that peasants were armed and organized into peasant militias in some key political areas. In these areas the short run political objective was to defend newly won rights, and the more efficient exploitation of lands was of secondary importance.

Third, the few agricultural services that might have been available were made ineffective by these rural conditions. Many feared going to rural areas and technically qualified people often left the countryside.

Some cooperatives were organized after 1953, but generally these were not successful. The level of education, dedication, and instruction of members and leaders was too low. However, there were areas where peasants began self help programs on their own, acting through their peasant unions, without waiting for government aid or institutional services. The principal types of local rural community action were building and staffing community schools, building and/or maintaining access roads to the community and small irrigation facilities, allocating rights to irrigation waters, and resolving disputes arising over the use of land and water.

Mobilization of the Peasantry

In the period immediately following the 1952 revolution, the primary role of the peasant union organization in Bolivia was political. The MNR was able to exercise some degree of control over the socio-political process of change in the rural sector through adoption of a land reform policy in combination with the creation of party cells at the local level. These cells were given the task of controlling any peasant unions which did not wish to follow the MNR party line.[5, pp. 54-55]

There was an additional rural organization of a strictly military nature: the peasant regiments. These were initially created as a peasant-manned substitute for the old national army which had been disbanded. The largest and most loyal regiments, in the departments of Cochabamba and La Paz, constituted an armed force used by Paz Estenssoro to assure control over other sectors (miners and urban centers) and political parties. By threatening, at times with armed invasions, both the cities of Cochabamba and La Paz, and by economic and political reprisals against those not joining the MNR Party or at least refusing to cut old political ties, the MNR government assured its own continuation. Opposition political parties became powerless, but not until after two attempts at overthrowing the MNR government had failed.

Peasant unions provided an important organization for rural communities which, without a landlord or resident manager on the farm, would have been left in an organizational vacuum. These local unions also began processing the papers necessary for the expropriation of properties. Early in the reform process, the peasant union was made the legal representative of the community in its dealings with government, landlords, and others from outside the community. In fact, and particularly on expropriated landholdings, the peasant union is still the only local, community-wide organization in which frequently a majority of community members or at least family heads participate.

The Politics of Implementation

Much of the preceding discussion has already touched upon implementation of the Revolution of 1952 and the land reform of 1953. The influence of the Revolution varied by geographic area because of distance from political centers, poor roads, poor communications, and land use and tenure patterns. Much of the actual formation of peasant unions and the land reform process itself, postdating the Revolution but prior to the passage of the land reform law, was determined by such factors. For example, Otavi in Potosí was a focal point because it was the center of a region of large wheat-growing latifundia which were potentially expropriable; moreover, it was the center of a pre-Villarroel uprising. The organizers who visited the region in September 1952 were sent out by the MNR government—through the Ministry of Asuntos Campesinos—to form peasant unions. They came to Otavi by way of the easiest access route from Potosí, forming unions and telling the peasants to continue working the land because the reform was coming soon. Within a year such organizing teams were 600 miles to the south of La Paz in Nor Cinti, Chuquisaca. Other more isolated areas, such as most of Nor Chichas in Potosí were skipped, as were the Pampas of Lequezana.

Implementation required a cadre of experienced and committed workers. Accordingly, many peasant union organizers were miners experienced in union activity. There was also an immediate need for administrative skills, and virtually the only persons with such experience were the mestizos and the elite who had held posts in departmental and provincial administration. These people exercised a relatively conservative influence over the process of land reform implementation, especially in the more isolated departmental capitals. Thus, in some regions landlords were able to keep the peasants working on the haciendas for a wage and have the majority of properties declared medium-sized, a status which meant they would not be entirely expropriated.

Except in the Upper Valley of Cochabamba and a few other areas, there were virtually no pre-revolutionary peasant leaders who responded immediately to the news of revolution in April 1952. This is not to say that such leaders did not exist. Most of them simply adopted a wait-and-see attitude, which to them seemed politically astute. Even the rebellious few of Otavi (leaders of a pre-reform insurrection) admit that they feared continuing reprisals by landlords and the new government and thus would not risk immediately embracing the Revolution. They waited to see whether it would fail. When the organizers came, this risk seemed minimized, and peasants joined the union because every hacienda was being organized at the same time.

In Potosí, organizers combined haciendas into single unions, perhaps to give peasants some assurance that they were not alone. In Yungas—particularly Coroico—representatives from each hacienda were told that their haciendas would soon be organized individually. In both these regions one striking characteristic is the moderation which apparently prevailed among the organizers. In Yungas they called for the "oldest and most respected" members of the communities to become union leaders; in both Potosí and Yungas they told the peasants to continue working for the landlord because the reform would soon come. Even in the very politicized area of Ucureña (Cochabamba), where land invasions had been undertaken by peasants, the government feebly tried to preserve order. Understandably, the fringe areas and those harder to get into and communicate with were least affected by the early union organizing as well as by the subsequent reform.

Effects of the Land Reform

Land Tenure Structure

In Bolivia's present land ownership structure, the mass of peasants work their own land as individual owner-operators. This is true for both ex-colonos who received hacienda lands and for members of freeholding communities.

The number of peasants without access to land (or who are unlikely to inherit land from their parents) is insignificant in relation to the total number of peasants in Bolivia. However, the difference between minimum and maximum amounts of land received by peasants within a given area (where land quality is comparable) is impressive. This situation has arisen because differential access to land, based on work obligations, was customary before the 1952 Revolution. The land reform law, as well as the National Agrarian Reform Service, distributed lands to peasants based on the pre-reform, customary differences.

Despite the individual owner-operator status of most peasants, certain groups in areas of population pressure—especially the valleys and northern highlands—must gain access to land by largely customary means. For example, it is quite common for a peasant community to sub-divide land (usually pasture land) held in common by the community in order to provide at least a minimal customary access to land for newly created families. If a community does not have land for subdivision, a new family resides with parents and works the family land, supplementing its income, whenever possible, by seasonal off-farm employment in the cities or in other agricultural areas. This may eventually induce some of these younger families to migrate to the cities or to colonization areas. However, a peasant family without sufficient access to land will usually work out some kind of an arrangement with other peasant families in the same or in neighboring communities, i.e., peasants continue to rely upon age old customary arrangements. Thus the present land ownership structure and tenure system is a composite of the legally-prescribed and sanctioned landholding system based on the land reform law and the customary traditions of the people.

Agricultural Production and Productivity

The pre-reform rural economy of Bolivia had rather distinct landlord and peasant sectors. The former was primarily market-oriented and the latter subsistence-oriented. The peasant sector, in order to satisfy family consumption needs, was more diversified in its production. By way of contrast, landlords often specialized in the production of a single product (such as coca, wheat, coffee, meat) for the market. At the same time, some products were imported in large quantities; price policies and the prevailing land tenure system provided little incentive for farmers to increase output by improving their farming techniques. Uneven distribution of the agricultural population aggravated these conditions.

Within the context of the revolutionary situation after 1952, it would be erroneous to attribute agricultural production declines to land reform itself, i.e., to the subdivision of large farms. The popular revolution led to universal suffrage, to expropriation of the three larger mining concerns, to the creation of peasant unions and armed militias in the countryside, and to a land reform law which did indeed have immediate repercussions on the agricultural system, and possibly on the level of agricultural production—especially the quantities of produce delivered to urban centers. Altering the land tenure relations required the organization of peasant unions to undercut the power of the landlords and their efforts at counterrevolution; the temporary effects on agricultural production or on the movement of agricultural products to the cities were important although secondary considerations. This was part of the price that had to be paid for the possibility of creating a new agricultural system and a new popularly based government.

A study of fifty-one farms in the northern highlands [1] showed that seventeen were idled largely as a result of the political situation created by the Revolution. The lands of the landlords on these farms were left unworked for varying periods of time beginning in 1952 and 1953. Four of these farms were idle for two years, five for three years, four for four years, two for five years, one for seven years, and one for fourteen years. A total of seventy production years were lost. No subdivision of lands occurred on these farms in the periods during which they wery idle; the decline in agricultural production was therefore not a result of subdivision into small peasant holdings.

Many conflicting reasons were cited as to why these lands were left idle. In the one case where the land was not worked for fourteen years, the landlord, according to the people interviewed, was particularly abusive and still wanted the peasants to work his remaining land for him under the pre-reform system. In other cases peasants report that local or regional union leaders prohibited them from working the landlords' lands either because the owners had been very abusive or peasant leaders were trying to ensure that the landlords would not return. In some cases peasants did not work the lands "on orders from La Paz," without specifying the source of such orders. Peasants were also waiting to see the extent of expropriation; that is, they were awaiting official pronouncements from the National Agrarian Reform Service. These reasons and actions seem to contradict actual events on other farms immediately following the land reform, as well as to conflict with the policy of the Ministry of Asuntos Campesinos, as will be shown later. It seems that confusion within the ranks of the peasant unions on the one hand, and peasants who were unwilling to appropriate for themselves that which they assumed was not yet legally theirs on the other, resulted in these lands remaining unworked.

Of the fifty-one farms in the study, production continued without interruption on thirty-four of them. On two of these the landlords had extensive areas of pasture lands. The only cultivable areas were parcels worked for their benefit within the holdings of each peasant family. In these two cases the peasants simply worked the entire parcel for their own use, cultivating the same crops as before without leaving any lands idle. In a third case, the government immediately restored the peasants' lands which had been taken from them a few years before. Here too there were no measurable effects on production.

The work relations on seven of the thirty-four farms were adjusted very rapidly, in accordance with directives from the Ministry of Asuntos Campesinos. On these farms, as in the above cases, the lands were never left idle. Instead, the landlords agreed to share half of the agricultural produce from their lands with the peasants, with the other half to be delivered to the landlords in La Paz, as prescribed in a decree issued by the Ministry of Asuntos Campesinos. If the peasants did not sell all of their share, this could have been reflected in later marketing statistics and interpreted as a decline in agricultural production. These sharecropping arrangements lasted only two years on two farms and three years on the other five. In two cases peasants terminated the arrangements, claiming that they did not have the supervision needed to work the landlords' lands as a unit and therefore preferred to work them individually; in three cases the lands were declared latifundio, and the peasants assumed full rights to all the lands. These lands were divided among the peasant families after 1955 or 1956 to be worked individually.

On eight of the thirty-four farms where production was not interrupted, lands were subdivided (not always evenly) among the peasant families in 1953, with peasant unions usually playing an important role in the subdivision. These union leaders interpreted the Revolution and the talk of land reform as meaning that the peasants now had rights to all the lands. In this study, these were the only cases of large farms divided immediately after the Revolution.

In all these thirty-four cases lands were worked continually from 1952 to the present. On all these farms the peasants report that the same agricultural products were raised and sold after as before the Revolution. In all cases the peasants likewise report withholding a part of the products from the landlords' lands for their own consumption and selling the rest.

A decline in production of agricultural products could have taken place on all these thirty-four farms where lands were not idled. For example, the peasant family, no longer obligated to work a designated amount of time on the landlords' land, may have decided to work fewer hours. In the early years of the reform, peasants spent much time at local and regional peasant union meetings, perhaps at the expense of working landlords' lands as intensively as before. If peasants were unable or unwilling to work the lands as "efficiently" or as "labor intensively" as before, either individually or as a group, this would have reduced agricultural production.

The use of natural fertilizers on the landlords' lands probably also declined. This was the likely case especially on those farms where the landlord had sold some or all of his animals in anticipation of the land reform. In other cases before the reform peasants were obligated to work other of the landlords' properties or were loaned out to work for another landlord. This did not occur after the land reform, and indeed a labor shortage in some areas did not allow full utilization of the landlords' lands. In the northern highlands such adjustments probably affected agricultural production temporarily. This should be expected when land reform is undertaken rapidly and accompanied by major political changes.

There is evidence that the Bolivian government was aware of these effects and tried to avert a decrease in agricultural production and a disruption in the flow of agricultural produce to the cities. Peasant unions and inspectors from La Paz were asked to enforce Supreme Decree 03375 of April 30, 1953, which made the peasant unions and their leaders specifically responsible for the harvest (February through May) during that year, and for the planting and harvesting of lands in the succeeding years.[3] In nineteen of the thirty-four farms in the study not idled by the land reform, peasants did deliver the landlords' share of production (50 per cent) to the Ministry of Asuntos Campesinos in La Paz for varying periods of time after April 30, 1953. The government was trying to use the peasant unions as a channel of communication to assure that no farmlands would be idled. However, because of the political situation, the confusion, and the lack of communication during that period, it was surely very difficult to enforce this decree. Also, peasant unions were not organized equally as well in all areas at that time.

Another major problem facing peasants was marketing the increased quantity of agricultural produce at their disposal. After the Revolution, only a part of the pre-reform marketing structure remained—the weekly, subsistence-oriented fairs based on the exchange of small quantities of agricultural staples for other consumption items. Generally, landlords did not wish or were not permitted to return to their properties with trucks to bring agricultural produce to the city as they had done before 1952. Thus the large-volume cash sales made directly by landlords in La Paz or to the mines diminished. The stores of landlords ceased to function, and the major sources of supply of agricultural staples to La Paz markets and middlemen were reduced substantially.

Some middlemen were accustomed to bringing produce from the rural fairs, but they were too few to take over immediately the transportation and marketing functions which landlords had performed previously. Also, there were not enough vehicles available to persons other than the landlords which could have hauled commodities from the rural areas to La Paz. Landlords would risk neither their trucks nor their lives to the regional peasant union leaders.

Furthermore, the peasants had to become accustomed to dealing in larger quantities of produce and in cash on a regular basis at fairs. Most fairs were still distant and their numbers few. The only sales outlets the peasants had were the local fairs at the provincial and cantonal levels, and at La Paz. These were not sufficient to handle the increased volume of produce.

As a result of the land reform, the full burden of getting agricultural products to urban markets in sufficient quantities became the responsibility of the peasantry and buyers from the rural areas and the city. They were unable to meet the challenge rapidly enough to prevent disruption of the flow

3 It is important to note that this decree antedates the agrarian reform law of August 1953 by three months, showing once again that farms had been abandoned as a result of the Revolution. Also, the decree is ample recognition of the existence of peasant unions before the land reform law was passed.

of products to the city. Efforts were of course made to overcome these problems. Peasants came to the city more frequently than before; those with means of transport and others with funds combined to go to the countryside to buy from the peasants, not only in established fairs but also at roadsides wherever peasants brought their products for sale. This adjustment to a new marketing system, based on sales by peasants instead of by landlords, was one of the most important changes of the post-reform period, and one of the major reasons why agricultural produce marketed in La Paz decreased during the first three to five years after the 1952 Revolution.

It is an unfortunate misconception, yet rather widely held, that a decrease in agricultural production resulted from the land redistribution. Actually, such a decrease is not shown by Bolivian production indices. [6, pp. 10-11] This association between land reform and a decline in production can probably be attributed to three factors. One, some farms actually were idled and some lands underutilized because of the political situation after 1952 and the adjustments which peasants had to make. Two, products were scarce in urban centers. And three, in 1956 Bolivia had to import potatoes; other staples—especially wheat flour—also were imported in greater quantities after 1952.[7] All these could have resulted from marketing adjustments, as noted above, and from weather factors. In 1956 Bolivia experienced a severe drought, especially the region around La Paz; 1957 and 1958 were also dry years. These years correspond with those of potato imports (the increased imports of wheat flour after 1952 were in large part a substitution for wheat grain, which had been a major import long before 1952). The "apparent" decline in agricultural production after 1952, while true in part, is better explained by marketing adjustments, transportation bottlenecks, and weather phenomena, with the former two by far the more important factors during that period.

In response to the marketing and transportation bottleneck, peasants, unions, and middlemen have created many new fairs and markets and rapidly increased the number of trucks visiting these areas. Most new fairs started small, with only one or two trucks coming once a week to bring buyers from La Paz. In 1966, though, most fairs visited had five to nine trucks coming regularly. The agricultural produce sold in the new fairs (and in the older ones) consists mainly of agricultural staples destined for the La Paz market—the same products grown and sold directly in La Paz by the landlords before the reform. The cash income which landlords received from the sale of these products is now received by the peasantry. Ex-landlords generally play no part in these newly created fairs on the highlands.[1]

It is difficult to determine the effects of land reform on the productivity of either land or labor; there are no benchmark statistics which can be compared with more recent studies. Besides, too many changes have taken place in the interim to arrive at a clear conclusion. Many peasant families admit that productivity of land used exclusively by landlords before 1952 has diminished, either because the landlord is not using the land that still remains under his control as efficiently as previously, or because peasants are using less natural fertilizer on former landlord lands. At the same time, peasants are producing much more on their own parcels because they work more land and work it more intensively. These opposite changes stem from redistribution of land and the breaking of old tenure relations—the redistribution of peasants' time.

In several regions, agricultural production has been dramatically intensified through the increased use of fertilizers and pesticides. However, increased agricultural production has also resulted from substituting more labor intensive crops for less intensive ones. In all departmental and provincial capitals, as well as in most rural markets, there has been an increased supply of vegetables, fruits, and flowers. Especially in the case of vegetables and flowers, two or three crops a year can be grown and harvested in the temperate valleys and in some areas around Lake Titicaca. All these changes signify increased income for peasant families.

Rural Population, Employment, and Underemployment

In 1950 the estimated annual growth rate of Bolivia's population was 1.7 per cent, one of the lowest in Latin America. There are no available data showing pre-reform sectoral population or population growth rates, nor is there any specific information on rural employment and underemployment. However, some inferences can be drawn.

Only in areas where population density was relatively low did landlords find it necessary to make the colonato arrangement reasonably attractive to the Indian family. Probably little underemployment existed on the larger landholdings since colono family labor could be used throughout the year for constructing and maintaining roads, buildings, etc. At the same time there was a great deal of idle labor on the 50,483 farms (61 per cent of all farms reported in the 1950 census) smaller than five hectares. In the densely populated valleys where these small farms were concentrated, peasants would seek to work out arrangements with landlords and farm managers, offering a certain number of days' work per week in exchange for a parcel of land. Many peasants who were owner-operators of small plots also worked as colonos for landlords to gain access to more land.

Before the Revolution, rural-urban migration was minimal, not only because the peasant was virtually tied to his usufruct parcel and was occupied a good many days per week working for the hacienda, but also because the economy of Bolivia was so underdeveloped that it neither demanded nor absorbed rural workers in other occupations. However, those who did migrate to the larger cities (especially from free-holding communities during the Chaco War) usually did find work, primarily in construction.

Today, however, young people from some areas of Bolivia must seek other opportunities as a result of overpopulation in their home communities. These pressures are evident in the more diversified occupational structure in rural areas, the creation of new peasant towns, and the growth of the city of La Paz and other departmental capitals. Without doubt the reform provided the peasantry with a mobility and an increase in free time which it never had before. Yungas particularly has benefited from the increased migration of seasonal laborers from the highlands. Additionally, there has been a phenomenal increase in the activity of peasant traders, reflecting a basic change in the marketing system; a large segment of the rural labor force is accommodated in this new marketing structure.

Population pressure and new opportunities in both the rural and urban sectors, particularly in the northern highlands, are such that many leave the land—some temporarily and others permanently. The population of La Paz has grown from an estimated 300,000 in 1950 to over 600,000 in 1970.

Finally, there is some empirical evidence that the reform has been responsible for an increase in the population growth rate. From a 1950 low of 1.7 per cent, Bolivia's population growth rate is now estimated at 2.7 per cent. While the increase is more rapid in the urban centers as a result of migration, the overall growth rate reflects an improved diet and access to medical care, both lowering the previous high rate of infant mortality.

The estimated number of peasant families working in Bolivia's rural sector at present is at least 25 per cent greater than in 1952. There are no data on changes in underemployment or the landless agricultural labor force. In all areas, peasant families are being accommodated on the land by bringing new lands under cultivation, by a more intensive use of old lands, and by switching from production of traditional staples to more labor-intensive crops such as vegetables. In these ways the increasing rural population has been able not only to feed itself but also to meet the growing urban centers' needs for foodstuffs.

Income Distribution

No specific data on income distribution within the agricultural sector or between the agricultural and other sectors of the economy exist for the years before 1952. However, it is not difficult to draw some general inferences on the basis of the landholding structure and tenure relations existing at that time. A description of some of the actual differences in living conditions may be helpful.

The housing of colono families, substandard by any measure, was usually a one-room thatched roof dwelling with walls of earth or adobe construction. There were no windows or chimney; homes were constructed in this way to conserve heat. Few families were interested in investing much time and money in home construction because they were uncertain about the time they would remain on that site. The house was used for cooking, for storing belongings, for housing a few hamsters (for food), and for sleeping. A raised sleeping area was constructed from adobe, and sheep or llama hides and excess clothing were used for bedding.

Meat, cheese, eggs, and milk were seldom consumed. The daily diet consisted of cereals (barley, wheat, corn, quinoa), starches (potatoes, oca), and broadbeans, all of which were made into different kinds of soups. Pieces of dried mutton were at times used for seasoning.

Clothing and textiles for other uses were all made on the farm from homespun wool. Visits to doctors and education for children were almost unknown.

The world of the colono was largely confined to the landholding; here some of the major decisions affecting his life were made by the landlord—decisions concerning his schedule of work, how much land he was to have and where it was to be located, and questions of justice between him and other colonos and between him and the landlord. The major contacts that a colono family had with others off the farm were at the rural markets, usually held weekly. The colono and/or his wife carried agricultural produce to these markets for barter to obtain the weekly household needs of such items as condiments, grease or fat for cooking, wool, etc. Cash sales of agricultural produce such as meat, cheese, and eggs were infrequent; usually the cash from any such sales was accumulated for the purchase of farm animals, farm implements, and some articles of clothing.

Approximately 25 to 30 per cent of the rural families lived in freeholding communities where living conditions were generally better, especially where such communities were located near markets or transport routes. These peasants were free to come and go as they pleased, to sell and buy where they wanted, and to have a school in the community. However, most freeholding communities in Bolivia were isolated and hard to reach. Also, their land resources were generally poor, and often population pressure was very high. Because of past efforts by outsiders to usurp freeholding community lands, most were generally closed to outsiders; this closure was reinforced by very rigid organizational structures and rules in the communities. This combination of physical and social conditions tended to assure the continuance of the community.

It is difficult to generalize about the levels of living among the owners of large holdings worked by colono families. Owners who had holdings located near important consumption centers realized high profits from their farms. Such owners often lived and engaged in professional work in the city, and had the farm managed by an administrator. Among these landowners, trips abroad were frequent, and their children were often educated outside Bolivia.

However, many landholdings located in certain of the more remote departments were managed by their owners who suffered from a lack of market opportunities and poor transport and communication facilities. Relative to the absentee landlords mentioned above, many of these latter would have been considered poor. However, control over land resources, and especially over the labor time of colono families, provided even these landlords a lifestyle based on large homes, many servants, and an abundance of leisure time.

There are no quantitative data on post-reform income changes for Bolivian land reform beneficiaries. However, some idea of change can again be arrived at by inference.

The pre-1952 Bolivian peasant family had only the land parcel given by the landlord with which to sustain itself. The head of a peasant family devoted at least half of his labor time, and sometimes more, to the landlord. The redistribution of these two factors—land and labor—favored the peasants and shifted the relative opportunities for earning both cash and in-kind incomes from the production and marketing of agricultural produce away from the landlords. Many landlords (20 to 25 per cent) lost all their land resources to the peasants. On most other large landholdings (75 to 80 per cent), peasants acquired access to some additional pasture or cultivable land. In both cases, peasants had access to additional income earning opportunities. As a result, the rural sector was able to accommodate many additional peasant families at a higher level of living than before the reform.

By far the largest share of agricultural produce now comes from small peasant holdings, and there is no shortage of staples and other food commodities, signifying that peasants have taken advantage of the new income earning opportunities which the land reform presented. The real barrier is no longer on the supply side, but is more likely a function of the limited demand for agricultural produce in Bolivia.

For many peasant families cash transactions have practically displaced the former practice of bartering. This is especially the case for farms located near La Paz and other cities, particularly in the regions where vegetable production for urban markets is profitable. Generally, most other peasant families still barter at least some of the same products as before the land reform—agricultural staples in small quantities for other daily consumption items. In an agricultural economy such as that of the northern highlands, where peasants base most production decisions on subsistence criteria and where they do not need ready cash for day to day transactions, bartering has an important function and is still practiced. However, most peasants report that they now barter less frequently than before the land reform.

Tables II and III indicate the type of change which occurs when income earning opportunities are redistributed from landlords to peasants via the redistribution of land. These tables show the quantities and present values of goods which were bartered and purchased most frequently before 1952 and in 1966 for a family of five during a one-year period.

Table III shows that the total value of goods purchased for consumption on a regular basis for a family of five is U.S. $100.95, or three times more than the pre-1952 value shown in Table II. The quantity bartered is now only U.S. $5.05 of the total, while the participation of peasants in the money economy is over four times what it was before 1952. This change is a direct result of land reform and the concomitant redistribution of cash income earning opportunities in the rural sector.

Still, Tables II and III do not show the entire change that has taken place for they are based only upon transactions made on a regular or weekly basis in local markets or in La Paz. Besides the above, peasants also infrequently purchase certain items such as farm tools, implements, and work animals. These items have changed little in terms of quality or quantity, and are still acquired largely for cash. Some infrequent cash purchases which are

TABLE II—Articles, Quantities, and Values (1966 Prices) of Most Commonly Acquired Goods among the Bolivian Peasants in the Northern Highlands before 1952

Bartered Articles	Quantity	Present Value
Condiments	–	$ .65
Cooking grease	3 pounds	.60
Noodles, etc.	15 pounds	1.50
Pots for cooking	5	1.65
Salt	3 panes	.75
Wool	4 hides with wool	2.70
	Total value of goods acquired by barter during the year on a regular basis	$ 7.85

Purchased Articles	Quantity	Present Value
Alcohol	3 quarts	$ 3.50
Bread	30 pieces	1.25
Cigarettes	5 packages	.50
Coca	10 pounds	4.20
Dyes	2 pounds	.25
Hats	2	4.15
Kerosene	26 bottles	1.10
Matches	50 boxes (small)	.85
Pants	1 pair	1.50
Sugar	15 pounds	1.25
Tocuyo (cloth)	10 yards	4.25
	Total value of goods Acquired by cash during the year	$22.80
	Total value of all goods	$30.65

Source: Ronald J. Clark, "Land Reform and Peasant Market Participation on the Northern Highlands of Bolivia, "*Land Economics* 44 (May 1968): 153-172.

TABLE III—Articles, Quantities, and Values (1966 Prices) of Most Commonly Acquired Goods among the Bolivian Peasants in the Northern Highlands: 1966

Bartered Articles	Quantity	Present Value
Condiments	—	$ .65
Pots for cooking	5	1.65
Salt	3 panes	.75
Other food items in small quantities		2.00
Total value of goods acquired by barter during the year on a regular basis		$ 5.05

Purchased Articles	Quantity	Present Value
Alcohol	5 quarts	$ 3.50
Soft drinks	20 bottles	1.75
Beer	10 bottles	2.50
Cooking grease	3 pounds	.60
Cooking oil	3 bottles	1.25
Fruit and vegetables	various (in season)	2.50
Noodles	15 pounds	1.50
Bread	75 pieces	3.15
Flour (wheat and corn)	50 pounds	3.40
Rice	35 pounds	3.00
Sugar	25 pounds	2.10
Coca	5 pounds	2.10
Cigarettes	20 packages	2.00
Matches	60 boxes (small)	.95
Kerosene	26 bottles	1.10
Cloth of all kinds	15 yards	7.00
Dyes	—	.50
Shoes	2 pairs	12.50
Suits	1	12.50
Skirt	1	5.00
Sweaters	1	5.50
Pants	1	5.00
Shirts	2	2.00
Hats	2	8.00
Shawls	1	5.00
Soap	10 pieces	1.50
Total value of goods acquired by cash during the year		$ 95.90
Total value of all goods		$100.95

Source: Ronald J. Clark, "Land Reform and Peasant Market Participation on the Northern Highlands of Bolivia." *Land Economics* 44 (May 1968): 153-172.

now important and which hardly existed before 1952 are corrugated metal sheets for roofs, windows, cement, sewing machines, radios, and bicycles. Peasants are just beginning to purchase kerosene stoves and, most recently, records and record players.

To demonstrate the increasing frequency with which the above products are being purchased, one former large landholding, typical of most expropriated farms, can be analyzed. In this case there were approximately 200 families. In 1956 there was one house with a metal roof and one bicycle; in 1966 there were forty metal roofs and eighty bicycles. In 1952 there were 7 sewing machines; in 1966 there were 120. In 1959 there was 1 radio; in 1966 there were 100.[4] In most areas of Bolivia this great a change has not yet taken place, but in the northern highlands this is not an exceptional case.

The above does not include increased purchases of such items as chairs, tables, beds, plates, kitchen utensils, metal pots, etc., nor the construction of larger houses, many with two stories. All these types of commodities and more have been acquired by cash purchase during the years following the land reform. In terms of material comforts, the northern highland peasant is much better off than previously.

The items listed in Table III are usually acquired by peasants at the local fairs, whereas infrequent purchases are invariably made in La Paz. Peasants report that these higher valued items are purchased more cheaply there. When they go to make these purchases in La Paz, they usually take a large quantity of agricultural produce and sell it either to middlemen or directly to consumers. Although produce sold by peasants brings a better price in La Paz, except for the occasions when they travel to La Paz to make certain purchases, peasants sell little of their produce directly in La Paz unless they happen to be located near the city.

Even the new local fairs are beginning to reflect the peasant demands for items purchased infrequently. For example, at one fair created after the land reform and located on a major transportation route, now serviced once a week by some twenty trucks, one can find kerosene stoves, sewing machines, new and used bicycles, bicycle tires, parts, and accessories, as well as various radios and batteries. Besides these items, the fair has many stalls of ready-made clothing, plastic shoes, metal products (such as nails, hammers, and other carpentry tools), and factory made materials such as yardgoods and school supplies, in addition to the many small manufactured consumption articles and the food products which everyone now takes for granted. It is likely that the infrequent purchases of most of the more expensive items now purchased in La Paz will in the future be made with greater regularity at rural fairs as price differences between the rural markets and La Paz become smaller and as demand in the countryside grows.

4 It is fully realized that price changes and increased availability of many of these commodities, especially radios, sewing machines, and metal roofing, would have induced some of the above changes. However, it is the author's opinion that the most important factor determining increased consumption of these articles is the higher level of income realized by peasant families as a result of the land reform.

The peasants on the farms visited in the northern highlands area agree that the reform has had a greater impact on the market participation of women than of men. Men still deal in cash for the same products as before, although at a higher level. While women were largely confined to a barter economy prior to the reform, they are now not only learning to deal in cash, but they are gradually assuming a more important marketing role than men.

Women now participate more frequently on a cash basis in marketing eggs, cheese, and meat. Peasant men sometimes express the opinion that women are more adept at marketing activities, a judgment probably based on the increased number of women that come from La Paz to buy products from the regional fairs for the La Paz market. Without the land reform, or with a more gradual revision of tenure relations, the dramatic increase in participation of the peasantry, and especially of women, on a cash basis in many new markets would have been impossible.

One qualification should be added to the above description. All the conclusions are based on a study of fifty-one ex-haciendas and the peasants living on them in the northern highlands of Bolivia, a region where agricultural production is oriented toward both subsistence requirements and the market demands of La Paz and the mines. Therefore the conclusions are not indicative of changes throughout Bolivia. There are still many areas, isolated for want of better roads, communications, and transport links, where the effects of the land reform have not been so dramatic. In these areas peasants provide for their own subsistence needs and sell very little for cash since they lack markets for their produce; they continue to wear mostly homespun clothing, and purchase few consumer durable goods. However, they no longer work for a landlord, but work on their own account as individual owner-operators.

Supplementary Services and Supplies

Before the reform, research on local crops and livestock, extension services, producer associations, available agricultural credit, improved seeds, fertilizers, machinery, and irrigation and transport services were almost exclusively designed to serve the large landholdings. Any new or expanded opportunities arising from such services and supplies primarily benefited landlords by reducing costs of production or by increasing output. The increased income flows to landlords widened the income differences between them and their colonos.

There were only sporadic and isolated agricultural research efforts on local crops and livestock in Bolivia before 1952. Research requires a heavy input of public resources over a long period to get worthwhile results. The research that was carried out was undertaken by the Ministry of Agriculture. Approximately thirty extension agents were responsible for nearly one million square kilometers, a circumstance which indicates a relatively weak commitment of public assistance to the rural sector.

Before 1952 most landlords did not ordinarily regard farming as mainly a business enterprise. Land served as prestige capital which secured proper social standing and leisure to the proprietor and his family. Investments in agriculture were low; agricultural credit was scarce and expensive. Even the few progressive farmers who produced for the market did not reinvest their profits in their farms, but often invested in other sectors of the economy instead.

Improved seeds, fertilizers, pesticides, and farm machinery were not in wide use before 1952, though there were exceptions in some relatively important areas of commercial agriculture. There were also instances of landowner cooperatives organized by the Ministry of Agriculture, but no specific data are available.

An increased availability of services and supplies of agricultural inputs in rural Bolivia has come about as a result of, rather than as a part of, the land reform. In 1953 the Bolivian government was able to enact and implement only the land reform, which did not include technical services, increased supplies of credit or agricultural inputs. But by restructuring the agricultural system, the foundation was laid for greater success with technical assistance programs, especially from 1956 onward.

Since 1952 Bolivia has been the recipient of relatively large amounts of aid, loans, and technical assistance from the United States, as well as from other governments and various international agencies. One result has been the creation of a much better system of roads throughout Bolivia, and the construction of the roads necessary for opening the lowlands to colonization. There have also been loans and grants for specific colonization projects. Likewise Bolivia negotiated loans and grants for improving and expanding the extension service, the research service, and the agricultural credit bank.

Technicians have been employed for the improvement of rice production and storage, and wheat and wool production and marketing. For a time efforts were also directed at increasing the production and improving the transport and marketing of tropical fruits for export. One of the largest community development programs in Latin America, including an estimated 40 per cent of rural families in Bolivia, has been set up. More recently, the land reform program has been aided by both loans and grants for the more rapid distribution of land titles to peasants. All these programs were initiated because of bottlenecks and development problems in the rural sector. International assistance was sought because local resources were insufficient to deal with these problems.

What chances would any of these programs have had in Bolivia before 1952, with their objectives to increase peasant incomes, to involve peasants in voluntary community development organizations, to involve them to a greater extent in a market economy, and to increase output of the staple agricultural commodities through the greater use of fertilizers and other inputs? The landholding structure and predominant tenure relations would have precluded peasants receiving any substantial benefit from such programs. But it is precisely toward these masses that all the above programs are presently oriented.

Peasant Participation in Decisions

A good example of the political activity of the peasantry and their degree of influence on an issue of national concern is the fate of a central government-proposed tax on all rural lands. This proposal was introduced and explained by government and ministry officials at the "First Economic Conference of the Bolivian Peasantry" held in La Paz in December 1968. The peasant leadership "chosen" to attend the conference came only from national, departmental, and provincial levels; the central government thought that it could count on these leaders to approve the tax. There was no direct representation from local rural communities.

These peasant leaders however, felt their economic and political interests were being threatened by the proposal. Nevertheless, with some changes in the text and a reduction in the tax rates to be levied, the delegates approved the first draft of the government's land tax proposal.

But outside the conference, the proposal lacked support in two important areas—Oruro and La Paz—at the local community level among members of freeholding communities. This discontent was voiced to the government by certain peasant leaders who subsequently formed the Bloque Campesino Independiente (the Independent Peasant Block). This group in turn signed a pact with university students in La Paz. These political machinations, in combination with the articulated discontent of peasants in rural communities, obliged the government to give up the tax proposal, even though it had been "officially" approved at the economic conference held in La Paz.

One example does not prove a point, but in Bolivia peasants and their spokesmen are integrated into the government. This is shown by the extent to which *every* government since 1952 has relied on the rural sector by actively seeking peasant support.

Character of Rural Society

For purposes of analysis it is important to focus attention on three major components of the rural scene: (1) the traditional provincial towns, (2) the new (since 1952) primarily peasant towns, and (3) the rural ex-haciendas and freeholding communities where agriculture is the primary source of income. These three components represent respectively: (1) the pre-1952 social and political structure, with some cases in which pre-1952 economic relations between peasants and townsmen still exist; (2) the post-1952 material, political, and psychological changes which have taken place among the peasantry; and (3) the changes in the ex-haciendas and freeholding communities since 1952—and their relations to and interactions with the rural towns. Around these three focal points in the rural sector the peasants today organize their lives, earn a living, and come into contact with development programs and new values from outside their communities. At these three levels peasants establish relationships with people of nonpeasant backgrounds and/or nonagricultural occupations.

Because of the revolution and subsequent reform, groups in rural areas have become polarized. There are encounters and outbursts between the old elite of the provincial capitals and the newly vociferous and organized peasantry. For example, on the provincial level, when the peasant goes to town for services not available in rural areas (hospitals, police, courts, market, high schools, etc.) he is still treated as a second-class citizen. The ex-landlords or traditional groups not of peasant extraction who administer these services take advantage of the peasants and continue to treat them according to the old patron-client relationship. The older peasants, as well as the ex-landlords, have not been able to change their own attitudes and ways of behavior toward one another sufficiently to obviate the above problems. As a new generation assumes more importance, relations between the provincial town and the surrounding peasant communities should improve. But at present, the change which most clearly illustrates the degree of integration of peasants into the society and economy of Bolivia, as well as into its political-administrative structure, is the rapid formation in some regions of new peasant towns.

Basic to new town development, of course, are favorable conditions with respect to geography and population. Most new town sites are located at the intersection of ex-hacienda or freeholding community boundaries, which allows for increased intercommunity cooperation and organization. Such sites were frequently utilized by landlords before 1953 as loading points for hacienda produce; since 1953 truck stops and marketing centers have developed at these same locations. The formation of new towns is the result not only of restructured marketing opportunities, but also of new socio-political peasant aspirations fostered and encouraged by the revolutionary government.

A fundamental motive of peasant leaders in establishing the new markets and towns was raising the area to the administrative level of canton. Within the national government system, the canton is entitled to a slate of officials—a corregidor, a civil register, a judge, and a policeman. Also, the sooner a site gains such offices, the more influence it has in specifying its market day, which in turn is important for attracting more peasants, merchants, and truckers.

Most new peasant town formation has taken place on the northern highlands because of its proximity to the city of La Paz, its government agencies, and its marketing opportunities. However, other areas have also benefited from contact with government officials and union organizers who infused the peasantry with the revolutionary ideology and established peasant unions which then provided an important link between the local communities and the national government. Such new groups on the local level were valuable to the MNR Party for carrying out its programs. Peasants began to work through their newly organized unions to expropriate the landholdings on which they lived, to build schools and market places, and to organize development projects such as the construction of health stations, access roads, dams, and wells. Because the unions were able to amass power on an intermediate level, some of the most important ideological aims of the

Revolution were translated into reality.

Many of these changes in rural society have significant implications. The organization of peasants at the local level around market and school districts, accompanied by political pressure for the administrative elevation of such units to canton level, led to the ascendence of some peasant-dominated regions around provincial towns. In many cases, new towns have gradually come to dominate the old towns. In some of the more politicized areas, the new towns even supply alcaldes for the provincial capitals. Even today, peasants sometimes show a threatening force which is sufficient to intimidate the provincial town dwellers.[5]

In order for such changes in power relations to occur in the rural sector, peasant organizations in the new outlying towns had to become more sophisticated and consolidated. Neither was possible without the support of the central government and the revolutionary changes effected by it. The motive for new towns, partially eclipsing traditional towns and sometimes even intimidating them, did not so much reflect a negative orientation among the peasants as it did a desire for services which were previously unavailable to them.

Through the electoral process, the more aggressive peasant leaders frequently move into the political structures of the traditional provincial towns—where election to mayor or other official posts has sometimes led to success in elections at the national level as representatives to parliament. Such leaders no longer rely on naked power and threat to achieve their objectives; instead, they rely on their constituencies and allies in provincial towns and outlying rural areas to attain the same ends. Gradually, the post-1952 revolutionary political changes at the national level have been reflected at the local and intermediate administrative levels.

The point to be emphasized is that a segment of the population heretofore isolated from the mainstream of national events has become restructured into functioning political units. Influence spreads not only downward to the surrounding rural peasant communities but also upward within the formal structure of provincial and departmental government. The fact that primarily peasant-dominated, peasant-organized and peasant-run towns are now accepted as part of this formal structure indicates the type of change which has occurred in the rural sector.

Critique and Evaluation

The Bolivian land reform of 1953 was just one part of the national revolution begun in 1952. As such, the effects of the land reform on the nation as a whole cannot be separated from the total effect of the Revolution. A great deal of evaluation of the changes in Bolivian society, economy, and polity is implied in the above description and analysis; this

[5] Specifically, in January 1968 the sedate, aristocratic city of Sucre was temporarily invaded by hundreds of peasants from Tarabuco. This move was sufficient to unseat the abusive alcalde and avoid similar abuses against peasants in other traditional towns.

final section will focus on some of the more important features of the Bolivian experience.

(1) Current land disputes between peasants and landholders in Bolivia illustrate the type of problems which arise when the rate of land redistribution to peasants exceeds the capacity of the government to officially sanction such redistribution by delineating boundaries and by distributing and enforcing land titles.[2] Two general types of conflict have resulted from the delay in granting legal title to peasant holdings. The first is between displaced landlords and the new owners. Problems of this type occur: (a) when landlords intimidate peasants in order to retain title to, obtain payment for, or reassert traditional labor arrangements on part or all of their former holdings; (b) when peasant unions employ pressure tactics to intimidate landlords and force them to abandon or sell their lands; (c) when peasants and landlords attempt to work out compromise arrangements; and (d) when peasants use existing agrarian legislation to try to obtain unused lands still belonging to landlords.

The second general type of conflict arises between new peasant owners, including such problems as: (a) land-grabbing by more powerful peasants; (b) competing claims to the land of deceased peasants, often based on emotional ties to the land; (c) disputes involving subdivision of individual and common lands; (d) competition between claims based on tradition and legal title; and (e) intimidation by peasant leaders and government officials.

Finally, various other tenure problems remain or have newly emerged: (a) the continuance, in some areas, of the pre-reform colono system; (b) some loss of community lands to outsiders; (c) problems surrounding work contracts between landlords and peasants; (d) the institution of a neo-colonato system in some areas, allowing peasants the usufruct rights to lands still belonging to landlords in exchange for stipulated labor obligations; (e) conflicts and problems over water rights; and (f) marketing and credit problems.

(2) The Bolivian revolution, the land reform, and the peasant organizations led to a considerable degree of integration of the masses of peasants into the national economy, society, and polity. In general, peasants have had to make astute adjustments—other than political—to counteract traditional forces in the rural areas and to take full advantage of the new opportunities offered by the Revolution and the reform. To date the peasantry has usually chosen to avoid confrontation on the provincial level. Three important inferences can be drawn from this: (a) peasants still feel unsure of themselves when facing the provincial situation in contexts other than political ones based upon group action; (b) they not only have new channels (markets, transport, education, new towns) at their disposal but they are aware of and utilize these new channels; finally, (c) whether consciously avoiding contact with the provincial society or not, the fact remains that in isolating the old town and its traditional functions, the peasantry has in some areas restructured the rural scene, creating new lines of communication with the national government and forcing concessions from the traditional rural towns.

(3) As a result of rapid institutional modification and the creation of new ones, considerable jurisdictional confusion exists between pre-reform and post-reform authorities and institutions. While problems of jurisdictional confusion and nondefinition of official roles have long been typical, these problems take on additional complexity in post-reform Bolivia. With the entrance of the peasant sector into the national society there is effective but personalistic communication at the national level, despite the absence of direct, de jure voice via local rural units or unions. The substantial power wielded by peasants in the parliament, and well-placed spokesmen such as in Asuntos Campesinos and the Peasant Block, assures the peasantry a voice in national affairs.

(4) There is a tendency in Bolivia (and elsewhere) to expect too much from land reform alone. As a policy instrument, the redistribution of property rights in land can only break down societal rigidities and lay the basis for a different organization in the agricultural sector. Land reform does not automatically make peasants market-oriented entrepreneurs, and it does not make them more literate or more willing to give up traditional values and ways of doing things. These latter changes are all inherent in the efforts to create new income earning opportunities (that is, economic development) and they usually require many years.

(5) When a massive land reform is part of an overall revolution, as was the case in Bolivia, it should be expected that some of the existing technical and managerial capacity in the rural sector will be lost as people move to the cities or leave the country; also, a period of adjustment is to be expected during which agricultural production may decrease and/or quantities of agricultural produce reaching urban centers may decline.

(6) When most rural lands are redistributed to peasant families, one should expect a considerable readjustment in marketing channels and relations. Landlord-dominated functions will be taken over by peasant families, leading to a greater involvement of these families in a cash economy. Another inpact will be on the increased national markets for light consumer goods as well as for consumer durables.[1]

(7) The Bolivian government has not been able to meet the service needs of the rural sector since the land reform. This failure has been due largely to a lack of resources. Based on this experience, international agencies should be prepared to make resources available for these purposes, providing the situation is sufficiently settled so that program implementation is not entirely precluded.

(8) At certain points in the development of a country, it is impossible to settle all peasant families on quantities of land necessary for the creation of "economically viable" units. It is possible to do so in certain regions, defining "economically viable" as the quantity of land and other agricultural inputs and services necessary to reach a predefined family income target. However, this is often not possible for the country as a whole. There may be limitations on aggregate demand for farm produce; alternatives may not exist for all the excess families that have to move elsewhere; government may not be able to

organize to provide the needed services; etc. This was indeed the case in much of Bolivia, therefore many peasant families received parcels of less than five hectares. Nevertheless, these small parcels provide at least a subsistence base.

(9) To carry out a massive land reform requires peasant organizations with direct access to government. Without such organizations at the local as well as the regional and national level, even a government with a strong commitment to land reform will find it difficult to reach the masses and to involve them in the process. In the case of Bolivia, the very success of this aspect of the Revolution did at times lead to political excesses and abuses.

(10) In the case of Bolivia, colonization programs have not been able to resettle the natural increase in population in the traditional highland and valley areas. It would probably be wrong to expect such accomplishments from resettlement in any country where the agricultural sector still employs over 50 per cent of the working population.

(11) Despite far-reaching land reform, as in Bolivia, it is difficult to eradicate many of the work relations of the pre-reform period. Even today some traditional tenure relations persist.

(12) It can be assumed that the results of a land reform will be partially negated and the social aims undermined if ex-landlords are permitted access to their previously-held lands and if they continue to hold influence in the provincial towns.

References Cited

[1] Clark, Ronald J. "Land Reform and Peasant Market Participation on the Northern Highlands of Bolivia." *Land Economics* 44 (May 1968): 153-172.
[2] ———. "Problems and Conflicts over Land Ownership in Bolivia." *Inter-American Economic Affairs* 22, no. 4 (1969): 3-18.
[3] Consejo Nacional de Reforma Agraria, La Paz, Bolivia. Unpublished data.
[4] Dirección Nacional de Estadística y Censos, Ministerio de Hacienda. Bolivian Agricultural Census of 1950.
[5] "Estatuto Orgánico–MNR." 1954.
[6] *Indices of Agricultural Production for the 20 Latin American Countries.* ERS-Foreign 44, Economic Research Service. Washington, D.C.: U.S. Department of Agriculture, 1966.
[7] Ministerio de Hacienda, Sección General de Estadística y Censos. La Paz, unpublished data.
[8] Patch, Richard W. "Bolivia: U.S. Assistance in a Revolutionary Setting." In *Social Change in Latin America Today*. Richard N. Adams, et al. New York: Harper and Brothers, 1960.
[9] ———. "Bolivia: The Restrained Revolution." *The Annals of the American Academy of Political and Social Sciences* 334 (1961): 123-132.
[10] ———. "Peasantry and National Revolution: Bolivia." In *Expectant Peoples*. K. H. Silvert, ed. New York: Random House, 1963.
[11] Romero, Hugo, "Integración y politización de una sociedad compuesta: Primeros sindicatos agrarios, huelgas de brazos caídos y el Primer Congresso Indigenal en Bolivia." *Temas sociales*, no. 4(1970).
[12] Thome, Joseph R. "Problems Which Obstruct the Process of Title Distribution under the Bolivian Agrarian Reform." Report to USAID/Bolivia, 1967.

Bibliography

Alexander, Robert J. *The Bolivian National Revolution.* New Brunswick, New Jersey: Rutgers University Press, 1958.

Andrews, Stanley; D. C. Myrick; and Glen R. Sasom. *Bolivian Agriculture: Its Problems, Programs, Priorities, and Possibilities.* Washington, D. C.: Economic Research Service, United State Department of Agriculture, 1962.

Antezana, Luis. "Centenario de la reforma agraria del General Mariano Melgarejo." *Presencia.* September 29, 1969.

―――."Bibliografía anotado de carácter selectivo sobre tenecia de la tierra y reforma agraria en Bolivia." La Paz: Land Tenure Center/Bolivia, 1969.

Arnade, Charles W. *The Emergence of the Republic of Bolivia.* Gainesville: University of Florida Press, 1957.

Barcelli, Agustín. *Medio siglo de luchas sindicales revolucionarias en Bolivia.* La Paz: Editorial del Estado, 1957.

Barnes, Katherine. "Revolution and Land Reform in Chuquisaca and Potosí." La Paz: Comité Interamericano de Desarrollo Agrícola: Land Tenure Center/Bolivia, 1968.

―――. "Land Reform in Yungas: Case Study of Five Ex-haciendas." La Paz: Land Tenure Center/Bolivia, 1967.

―――. "La formación de nuevos pueblos en Bolivia: Proceso e implicaciones." *Estudios andinos* 1, no. 3 (1970): 23-37.

Burke, Melvin. "An Analysis of the Bolivian Land Reform by Means of a Comparison between Peruvian Haciendas and Bolivian Ex-haciendas." Ph.D. dissertation, University of Pittsburgh, 1967.

Camacho Saa, Carlos. "Minifundio, Productivity, and Land Reform in Cochabamba." Ph.D. dissertation, University of Wisconsin, 1966.

Carter, William E. *Aymara Communities and the Bolivian Agrarian Reform.* Gainesville: University of Florida Press, 1964.

Cespedes, Augusto. *El dictador suicida: cuarenta años de historia de Bolivia.* Santiago: Editorial Universitaria, 1956.

―――. *El Presidente colgado.* Buenos Aires: Editorial Jorge Alvarez, 1967.

Clark, Evelyn K. "Agrarian Reform and Developmental Change in Parotani, Bolivia." Ph.D. dissertation, Indiana University, 1970.

Clark, Ronald J. "Land Reform and Peasant Market Participation on the Northern Highlands of Bolivia." *Land Economics* 44 (1968): 153-172.

―――. "Problems and Conflicts over Land Ownership in Bolivia." *Inter-American Economic Affairs* 22, no. 4 (1969): 3-18.

―――. "Reforma agraria e integración campesina en la economía boliviana." *Estudios andinos* 1, no. 3 (1970): 5-22.

Comitas, Lambros. "Educación y estraficación social en Bolivia." *America Indigena* 28, no. 3 (1968).

Condarco Morales, Ramiro. *Zárate, el "Temible" Wilka: Historia de la rebelión indígena de 1899.* La Paz: Talleres Gráficos Bolivianos, 1965.

Daza Barrenechea, Oscar. *Sistematización armada de la revolución nacional.* La Paz, 1959.

Erasmus, Charles, Jr. "Upper Limits of Peasantry and Agrarian Reform: Bolivia, Venezuela, and Mexico Compared." *Ethnology* 6, no. 4 (1967).

Estudio de la estructura agraria en Bolivia. *Reforma agraria en Bolivia: Titulación.* La Paz, 1967.

Flores, Edmundo. "Land Reform in Bolivia." *Land Economics* 30 (1954): 112-124.

Garcia, Antonio. "La reforma agraria y el desarrollo social de Bolivia." In *Reformas agrarias en América Latina: Procesos y perspectivas.* Oscar Delgado, ed. México: Fondo de Cultura Económica, 1965.

Goins, John Francis. *Huayculi: Los indios quechua del Valle de Cochabamba, Bolivia.* Mexico City: Instituto Indigenista Interamericano, 1967.

Heath, Dwight B. "Commercial Agriculture and Land Reform in the Bolivian Oriente." *Inter-American Economic Affairs* 13, no. 2 (1959): 34-45.

———. "Land Reform in Bolivia." *Inter-American Economic Affairs* 12, no. 4 (1959): 3-27.

———. "Land Tenure and Social Organization." *Inter-American Economic Affairs* 13, no. 4 (1960): 46-66.

———; Charles J. Erasmus; and Hans C. Buechler. *Land Reform and Social Revolution in Bolivia.* New York: Praeger, 1969.

James, Preston E. *Latin America.* New York: The Odyssey Press, 1959.

Junta Nacional de Planeamiento. *Plan de desarrollo económico y social de Bolivia 1962-1971.* La Paz, 1961.

Klein, Herbert S. *Origenes de la revolución nacional boliviana: La crisis de la generación del Chaco (1920-1943).* La Paz: Librería y Editorial Juventud, 1968.

Land Tenure Center/Comité Interamericano de Desarrollo Agrícola/Bolivia. "An Evaluation of the Bolivian Land Reform." Preliminary Report. La Paz, 1969-70, Chapters 8, 9, 10.

Leonard, Olen E. *Bolivia: Land, People and Institutions.* Washington, D. C.: The Scarecrow Press, 1952.

———. *El cambio económico y social en cuatro comunidades del Altiplano de Bolivia.* México: Instituto Indigenista Interamericano, 1966.

Leons, Madeline Barbara. "Changing Patterns of Stratification in an Emergent Bolivian Community: Arapata, Sud Yungas." Ph.D. dissertation, University of California at Los Angeles, 1966.

Lora, Guillermo. *La revolución boliviana.* La Paz: Difusión S. R. L., 1964.

Lynch, John V., and Paul J. Ferree. *The Agricultural Economy of Bolivia.* Washington. D. C.: ERS, U.S. Department of Agriculture, 1961.

Malloy, James M. "Bolivia: A Study of Political Change." Ph.D. dissertation, University of Pittsburgh, 1967.

Maroff, Tristan. *La ciudad ilustre.* La Paz, 1956.

McEwen, William. *Changing Rural Bolivia.* Research Institute for the Study of Man for Peace Corps/Bolivia. New York, 1969.

Ministerio de Agricultura, Ganadería y Colonización (MAGC). *Estudio socio-económico de las provincias Ingavi, Los Andes y Omasuyos del departamento de La Paz.* La Paz, 1946.

Muratoria, Blanca. "Changing Bases of Social Stratification in a Bolivian Community." Paper presented to American Anthropological Association, Denver, 1966.

Osborne, Harold. *Bolivia: A Land Divided.* 3d ed. London: Royal Institute of International Affairs, 1962.

Otero, Gustavo Adolfo. *Figura y carácter del indio: Los andobolivianos.* La Paz: Editorial Juventud, 1954.

Patch, Richard W. "Bolivia: U. S. Assistance in a Revolutionary Setting." In *Social Change in Latin America Today.* Richard N. Adams; Oscar Lewis; John P. Gillin; R. W. Patch; Allan R. Holmberg. New York: Harper and Brothers, 1960.

———. "Bolivia: The Restrained Revolution." *The Annals of the American Academy of Political and Social Sciences* 334 (1961): 123-132.

———. "Peasantry and National Revolution: Bolivia." In *Expectant Peoples.* K. H. Silvert, ed. New York: Random House, 1963.

Peinado Sotomayor, Marcelo. "Land Reform in Three Communities of Cochabamba, Bolivia." Ph. D. dissertation, University of Wisconsin, 1969.

Peñaloza, Luis. *Historia económica de Bolivia.* 2 vols. La Paz: Talleres Gráficos Bolivianos y Editorial Fenix, 1953-54.

Pérez, Elizardo. *Warisata, la escuela Ayllu.* La Paz: Gráfica E. Burillo, 1963.

Reyeros, Rafael. *El pongueaje: La servidumbre personal de los indios bolivianos.* La Paz: Empresa, 1963.

Romero, Hugo. "Integración y politización de una sociedad compuesta: Primeros sindicatos agrarios, huelgas de brazos caídos y el Primer Congreso Nactional Indigenal en Bolivia." *Temas sociales,* no. 4 (1970).

–––. and Luis Antezana. "Origen, desarrollo y situación actual del sindicalismo campesino en Bolivia." Estudio de la Estructura Agraria en Bolivia, Comité Interamericano de Desarrollo Agraria/University of Wisconsin/Government of Bolivia, 1968.

Sanjinés, Alfredo. *La reforma agraria en Bolivia.* 2d ed. La Paz: Editorial Universo, 1945.

Saavedra, Bautista. *El Ayllu.* 2d ed. La Paz: Gisbert y Cia, 1955.

Taboada Teran, Nestor. *Indios en rebelión: hechos de la revolución boliviana.* La Paz: Editorial Amigos del Libro, 1968.

The American University, Foreign Areas Studies Division, Special Operations Research Office. *U. S. Army Area Handbook for Bolivia.* Washington, D. C., 1963.

Thome, Joseph R. "Problems Which Obstruct the Process of Title Distribution under the Bolivian Agrarian Reform." Report to USAID/Bolivia, 1967.

United Nations, Technical Assistance Administration. *Report of the Technical Assistance Mission to Bolivia.* New York, 1951.

United States Operations Mission to Bolivia. *Point Four in Bolivia: 1942-1960.* La Paz, 1960.

Urquidi, Arturo. *El feudalismo en América y la reforma agraria boliviana.* Cochabamba: Imprenta Universitaria, 1966.

–––. *Bolivia y su reforma agraria.* Cochabamba: Editorial Universitaria, 1969.

Valencia Vega, Alipio. *Desarrollo del pensamiento político en Bolivia: Bosquejo.* La Paz, 1953.

Warriner, Doreen. *Land Reform in Principle and Practice.* Oxford: Clarendon Press, 1969.

Zondag, Cornelius H. *La economía boliviana 1952-65: la revolución y sus consecuencias.* Cochabamba: Los Amigos del Libro, 1968.

CHAPTER 8

Agrarian Reform: Colombia

HERMAN FELSTEHAUSEN

Associate Professor of Agricultural Journalism
and the Land Tenure Center
at the University of Wisconsin-Madison

CHAPTER 8

Agrarian Reform: Colombia

HERMAN FELSTEHAUSEN

The Colombian government has approved a variety of agrarian reform measures during the past thirty-five years; yet, despite broad legal changes, very little land redistribution has thus far been accomplished. When the Colombian Congress passed Law 135 in 1961, many throughout the hemisphere hailed the new legislation as a prelude to genuine and sweeping reform. The record of the past decade is now being written with much of the early optimism tempered by reports of only modest accomplishments.

The 1961 agrarian reform law provided for land titling, colonization, and rural services and included specific provisions for expropriating and dividing private land. The law created a single land reform agency—the Instituto Colombiano de la Reforma Agraria (INCORA)—to administer all public land and resettlement programs, specifically excluding only forests and watersheds already under government control. A farm credit program was added later to complement the legal and technical services to new land owners.

Agrarian Reform Procedures and Results

INCORA used its authority to grant land titles to settlers already establsihed on public lands, to create new irrigation districts and facilities, and to provide credit to small- and medium-sized farmers in both new and establsihed farming regions. By July 1, 1969 the Colombian government had titled 88,200 farm parcels comprising 2.8 million hectares of land. Nearly 96 per cent of the land and 96 per cent of the titles were assigned to settlers who were already living on or had recently moved onto public land.[11] Attempts at acquiring private land through expropriation, however, were thwarted by persistent resistance from land owners. By the end of 1969, 115 expropriation cases had been initiated by INCORA attorneys; 23 cases were won, 13 were lost, and the rest were blocked or withdrawn in favor of "friendly settlements."[31] [1] The successful expropriation cases netted the government 4,194 hectares of land, while the friendly settlements yielded about 120,000

---

[1] Friendly settlements are made by bargaining with the owners; they often result in the government paying above the appraised price to meet seller demands.

hectares more.[11; 31] INCORA projects have increased the irrigated land area for eventual transfer to private farmers by 11,000 hectares as of 1969, but so far these lands are managed by INCORA with potential beneficiaries farming them under rental contracts.

Colombian agrarian reform legislation has been enacted in an atmosphere of heated political debate and often on the heels of civil strife or economic crisis.[15, p. 17; 20, p. 53] The comprehensive reform program of 1961 was based on the assumption of a country already developed, rich in natural resources and sophisticated in the use of legal, administrative and fiscal procedures for transforming and modernizing society.[15, p. 61; 26, pp. 134-213; 12, p. 192-202] The legislation did not adequately reflect Colombia's limited administrative and legal capabilities, while the assumptions about the availability of fertile land resources was probably overly optimistic since Colombia has less available farm land than is commonly supposed.

In 1960 Colombia had 1.2 million farms with 27.3 million hectares under private ownership (of its total land area of 113 million hectares).[10] Subtracting land in farms, roads, and towns, more than two-thirds of the total area of Colombia—about 80 million hectares—is still in the public domain. This seeming abundance of public lands, however, must be evaluated in terms of the location and quality of those lands as well as the restrictions on their settlement posed by customary practices and recent legislation.

The government's Instituto de Desarrollo de los Recursos Naturales Renovables (INDERENA) is charged with managing national forests and claims about 50 million hectares.[32] Much of the 30 million hectares of public lands theoretically remaining for private acquisition, like much of the forest reserve land, is either unsuited for agriculture or unavailable for colonization in any practical sense. First, these lands include mountains, deserts and swamps. Second, much of this land is located in low fertility, low access areas of the Eastern Plains (Llanos Orientales). Agricultural scientists are currently compiling data on this vast region of 67 million hectares—59 per cent of the territory of Colombia.[34]

Much of the soil in the Llanos is highly weathered and low in natural fertility. There are wide expanses of savannah which are used mainly for livestock grazing. Subsistence colonization and cropping have been tried repeatedly without much success, suggesting that the region would require regular and substantial additions of commercial fertilizers and other inputs in order to make it economically suitable for intensive agriculture. The region is also characterized by an extended annual dry season, although this may not have serious consequences for a well planned agriculture. The northern areas flood extensively during the wet period.[22, p. 248]

An estimated 3 million hectares of well-drained, level savannahs are potentially suitable for agriculture, but many of these lands are already claimed and used by private ranchers. Technical observers report that since "land has long been available for the taking, ranches are expensive. Ranch sizes varies from 500 to 50,000 hectares or more...." [34] This statement suggests the problem associated with figures used to show the theoretical availability of land in Colombia. Much of the land listed as available is already in farms and ranches but is not included in statistical reports because it is not titled or recorded. Such lands are often held under informal possession and use arrangements. Occupation rights, in turn, are bought, sold and exchanged outside the recorded land transfer system.[2]

This problem—the lack of a reliable system of land measurement and registration—has hampered every agrarian reform program instituted including that of the 1960s. There are no systematic records to facilitate precise identification of either private or public property.[2] Farms, even when titled, are only generally described. The size of farm units is often estimated; thus figures reporting land in farms are subject to large errors.

The rural population is highly concentrated on the naturally fertile mountain soils in the Andean Region. Slightly more than one-half (53 per cent) of Colombia's rural population lives in 429 mountainous municipalities which comprise 8 per cent of the national territory.[8][2] In the 200 most densely populated of these 429 municipalities there are only 1.3 hectares of land per rural inhabitant including forest areas, towns and roads, and wastelands.

In 1960, more than 70 per cent of Colombia's rural families either lived on sub-family sized farms (farms of less than 5 hectares employing two persons or less) or were headed by farm workers without land. Although sub-family and family farms utilize less than one-third of Colombia's agricultural land, they account for about two-thirds of the value of agricultural output.[6] The basic misallocation of land and labor resources under these conditions is evident—too much land and too little labor on the large farms and too little land and too much labor on the small farms, as illustrated by Tables I and II.

The 1960 figures in Table I show the extremely large number of small farms of less than five hectares. The number of small farms today is even higher since a common pattern of rural labor absorption on minifundios is to divide farm land among family members.[24] Increased population pressures on the land resources in minifundia areas has been accompanied by a major destruction of soil resources due to intensive cropping with poor soil management practices. Some of the surplus population of course continues to move onto public lands hoping to find more productive soils and new ownership opportunities. And, as in most Latin American countries, large numbers are moving to the cities.

INCORA administers three basic titling processes which increase privately owned land and constitute the main land reform activity. Under the principal procedure, INCORA grants title to settlers who have established farms on unclaimed public land. This procedure accounted for 95.9 per cent of all land titled by the Colombian government between 1961 and 1969.[11]

---

2 Tabulations of population density were made by the author based on census figures of population and total land area in each municipality.

TABLE I—Number of Farms, Land in Farms and Percent of Arable Land under Cultivation in Colombia: 1960

Size category in hectares	Number of farms	% of total farms	Hectares occupied	% of total area in farms	Approximate % arable land under cultivation
0 to 4.9	756,605	62.6	1,238,976	4.5	75
5 to 29.9	327,425	27.1	3,780,379	13.8	65
30 to 99.9	82,730	6.8	4,275,618	15.6	48
100 or more	42,912	3.5	18,042,654	66.1	36
Totals	1,209,672	100.0	27,337,827	100.0	

Source: DANE, 1964 [10, pp. 39-45]

TABLE II—Percentages of Farms, Work Force, Agricultural Land and Value of Production by Farm Size Groupings in Colombia: 1960

Percent of Total	Farm Size Grouping				
	Sub-Family a	Family b	Multi-Family Medium c	Multi-Family Large d	Total
Farms	64	30	5	1	100.0
Agricultural Work Force	58	31	7	4	100.0
Agricultural Land e	6	23	21	50	100.0
Value of Production	21	45	19	15	100.0

Source: CIDA, 1966 [6]

aSub-Family: Farms large enough to provide employment for less than two persons with the typical incomes, markets and levels of technology and capital now prevailing in each region.

bFamily: Farms large enough to provide employment for 2 to 3.9 persons on the assumption that most of the farm work is being carried out by the members of the farm family.

cMulti-Family Medium: Farms large enough to provide employment for 4 to 12 persons.

dMulti-Family Large: Farms large enough to provide employment for over 12 persons.

eCultivated and pasture land: same as the definition of land in farms.

Any person may settle on unclaimed land[3] after using it for at least five years and installing capital improvements, the claimant can initiate a title request. INCORA sends a survey team to the farm to establish boundaries, measure the parcel and assist the claimant in drafting a title application.

The Services of INCORA are free, although the farmer must pay the costs of notarizing and filing his new title. An individual can claim up to 200 hectares, or up to 450 hectares in certain parts of the country by paying survey and mapping costs. Under this procedure there is a practical minimum size of 25 hectares to prevent formation of new minifundios; however, parcels as small as one hectare can be titled if completely surrounded by other parcels.

In a second process, INCORA grants title for land claims privately initiated and sponsored. Before consolidation of titling work under INCORA, land titles were applied for through the mayor's office and approved at the level of state governments. This alternative procedure still exists, but applications now go to INCORA for final approval. This method is frequently used for titling large farms and ranches or lands for speculative purposes in development zones. An interested party who, through a variety of ways, can show at least five years' use rights on public land may register with the local mayor his intention to have this land titled. The claimant must hire his own surveyor and legal counsel to map the land and draft a title. If there are squatters on the land, the claimant can remove them through friendly settlement by paying them for improvements. Sometimes most or all of the land for a new farm or ranch will be assembled by buying squatters' rights rather than waiting five years to fulfill the occupation and capital improvement requirements applicable to unsettled land.[21] When preliminary documents are ready, the claimant must pay the cost of having the mayor make a personal inspection visit to the property. A claimant may title up to 450, 1,000, or 3,000 hectares of land by this method depending on the region.

Data released by INCORA do not specify the number of parcels titled in this way, but subtracting other subtotals from total titles granted in the 1961-1969 period yields a figure of 11,619 titles under this procedure.

Finally, INCORA may title land acquired from private owners through purchase, gift, or expropriation. This third procedure was to have been the principal feature of the 1961 agrarian law. Since public lands are often

3 It is not always clear whether settlers are claiming public land or land previously allocated by early land grants and since abandoned. In cases of conflict, INCORA follows an intermediate procedure to clear previous claims. Such steps are frequently required since land records are vague and poorly kept, boundaries are crudely marked, and many lands have a history of previous use. The 1961 agrarian law allows the government to initiate action to redefine the public domain. If the government is not opposed in court by a private party, it will issue a decree to redeclare the land in question part of the public domain. This action is often followed by immediate titling of the land to established settlers. Much of the titling work of INCORA is concerned with the legalities necessary for clarifying the status of the public domain.

inaccessible or poorly suited for intensive agriculture, the intent of the law was to provide peasants with more of the land already under cultivation. Detailed mechanisms for expropriation and government purchase were written into Law 135, but expropriation attempts have been unsuccessful. Legal procedures are complex, slow, and cumbersome.[43] Usually landowners are able to stall government attorneys in the courts or to negotiate a sale to INCORA outside of court at the owner's price.

Much of the expropriated and purchased land obtained by INCORA was used for reclamation and public works projects, not for retitling to farmers. Through mid-1969 INCORA had titled 1,194 parcels of purchased and expropriated lands, distributing to private owners 13,600 of the 124,000 hectares acquired. These titles represent 1.3 per cent of all those granted in the past nine years.

The number of titles distributed under the three procedures are often quoted in statistical reports to illustrate the success of the Colombian agrarian reform program. However, titling activities which could have an impact on Colombia's land tenure structure are covered only in the third procedure and constitute a small fraction of INCORA's land titling work. Meanwhile, neither agricultural production nor land ownership patterns have been transformed by the two principal procedures.

TABLE III—Summary of INCORA'S Land Titling and Credit Activities in Relation to the total Number of Farms and Farm Land: As of June 1969

	National Total	INCORA Activity	INCORA Activity As a Per cent of National Total
Land in Farms in relation to land added to farms by INCORA (thousands of has.)	27,372	2,833	10.3
"Available public land" in relation to land titled by INCORA (thousands of has.)	29,488	2,833	9.6
Number of farms in 1960 in relation to farms titled by INCORA	1,209,672	88,200	7.3
Number of farms in Colombia in relation to number receiving INCORA credit	1,209,672	29,849	2.5

Sources: [6; 10; 11]

Recent evidence shows that the unequal ownership distribution of farm land has been extended to new settlement regions by the titling program. In 1968, the only year for which data are available, 64 applicants received parcels of more than 200 hectares each while 7,037 applicants received less than 10 hectares each. Another 7,125 settlers received between 10 and 50 hectares and 906 received between 50 and 200 hectares. All were cases of settlements on public lands.[29] [4]

In terms of numbers of new or previously landless families seeking land, the titling programs have been only a partial remedy while the redistribution aspects have been insignificant. When INCORA began operations, there were an estimated 350,000 tenant and landless farmers in Colombia.[6] Rural population has grown at an estimated 2 per cent annually despite large numbers migrating to the cities. The net increase in adults in rural areas between 1951 and 1964 was 554,395 persons.[8; 9] Allowing for rural to urban migration and, assuming each two remaining adults formed a new family, more than 21,000 new rural families were added to agricultural regions each year. The Colombian land titling programs, as pointed out, established only 88,200 titled parcels during 1961-1969, an average of about 11,000 per year.

INCORA's largest capital expenditures have been for construction of irrigation and drainage projects. Such projects received 40 per cent of budgeted funds in the mid-1960s while only 4 per cent was spent on land purchases and expropriations.[33] INCORA has planned and constructed irrigation works on about 11,000 hectares. It also administers two districts established earlier by the Agricultural Credit Bank consisting of about 30,000 irrigated hectares. By the end of 1968, crops were being grown in seven irrigation districts, including those taken over from other agencies. INCORA has announced long-term plans to build irrigation facilities in twelve more districts to bring a total of 450,000 hectares under irrigation.[11; 28]

Land improvement projects are costly and the distribution of benefits to farmers is still largely undetermined. Roger Soles suggests that land purchases and titling activities result in a near-doubling of income for the small farmers benefitting from such programs while small farmers operating in the irrigation projects realize an increase in incomes of about three times their former level. At the same time, however, irrigation projects are developed at many times the cost per farmer of the land purchase and titling efforts.[39] Productivity advantages of the irrigation projects may be overstated by technicians anxious to see the projects approved. Present procedures often prove inadequate for the management of farms on these projects. As Soles points out: "Farming decisions are too numerous, too urgent and too specific to be shunted up and down bureaucracies, initialed a dozen times, requisitioned, okeyed and filed, because meanwhile the insects are eating up the crop!"[40]

---

4 Some argue that the wide differences in size are due to differences in land quality. Yet the report shows the same skewed distribution of parcel sizes among departments regardless of land quality.

When INCORA builds new irrigation districts, it does not grant immediate title to farmers who move onto the completed projects. Instead, the farmers are assigned a parcel under contract with INCORA. This provides a trial period to test farmers' interests and skills. As nearly as can be determined from INCORA records and reports, the agency has not yet given final title to new farmers in any of its irrigation districts.

The latest statistical report indicates that 4,153 farmers are operating under parcel contracts [11], but this figure too is subject to various interpretations. In one project near the Atlantic Coast, parcels are assigned on a crop-season basis. Since some crops can be grown in four months, a farmer may obtain several contracts within one year. Contracts are renegotiated for each crop; and farmers move from place to place within the irrigation district depending on season, rotation plans, and availability of irrigation water. The projects are managed by INCORA technicians, with very little participation by farmers in the planning. Some contract farmers view the program as a substitute for similar share-cropping arrangements formerly held with ranchers and plantation owners.[19]

A supervised credit program is another major feature of Colombia's agrarian reform program. When INCORA was organized, agricultural technicians argued that small farmers could not modernize production without additional sources of credit and that, to maximize the effectiveness of credit use, trained agricultural technicians were needed to supervise the lending program.[1] The Agency for International Development (AID) concluded that "a program of supervised agricultural credit was a key element of, and crucial to, agrarian reform in Colombia." [46, p. 120] AID thus provided INCORA with an initial 10-million-dollar loan in June 1963 and increased the amount by 8.5 million plus the equivalent of 20.6 million dollars of counterpart pesos in March 1966.

By 1964, 2,556 farmers were receiving agricultural credit under this program. The number increased to 11,570 by 1966 and to 29,849 in 1969. INCORA's supervised credit is a supplement to and in some cases a substitute for other credit sources—especially the Agricultural Credit Bank (Caja Agraria).[1; 23] Meanwhile, the high cost of supervising these loans has prompted INCORA to shift the credit gradually to larger and larger borrowers. The average size loan increased from about $800 in 1965 to more than $1,500 in 1968. INCORA reports that the average gross farm income for farmers in the credit program is now double that of several years ago [35], but at least a part of this increase may be due to allocating more of the credit units which started with higher gross incomes.

In 1967 the total amount of credit available in Colombia was $774.7 million with $137.5 million lent for agricultural crops, $140 million for livestock and $17 million for specialized enterprises.[36] Industry received the next largest share, $180.5 million, followed by commerce with $120 million. About three-fourths of all the credit used for agricultural and livestock purposes is lent through government agencies and banks, the other one-fourth through commercial banks. Between 1960 and 1967 foreign loans were used increasingly as a source of capital for Colombian agriculture; these were mainly from the United States and totaled $92.2 million for the eight-year period.

A new program was added to the national agrarian reform package by Law 1 of 1968.[27] This law gives tenants and sharecroppers, if they operate a unit of less than 15 hectares (about 25 per cent of all farmers in Colombia in 1960), the opportunity to purchase the land they rent or work. The government first acquires the property by purchase or expropriation if necessary and then sells it to the small farmer on favorable terms.

It is too early to evaluate the effects of this program, but it has encountered difficulties and fallen far short of its goal—ownership status for 100,000 families during the first two years. Under these provisions, as of October 1969, INCORA had taken over only 29 large farms totaling 21,380 hectares for resale to fewer than 2,000 tenants and share-croppers. [30]

In addition to the programs already described, INCORA operates a number of directed colonization projects. Government colonization projects were consolidated under INCORA by the 1961 agrarian reform law. Settlers moving into remote areas usually do not have access to regular markets and

TABLE IV—Volume of Agricultural Lending by Colombian Agencies: 1967

Lending agency	Millions U.S. dollars	Percent of total ag. credit
Commercial banks including the Livestock Bank (Banco Ganadero)	130.0	44.1
Agricultural Bank of Colombia (Caja Agraria)	111.0	37.6
National Livestock Fund (Fondo Ganadero)	25.0	8.5
Colombian Agrarian Reform Institute (INCORA)	15.0	5.1
Regional Finance Corporation (this figure is for 1966)	8.0	3.0
National Coffee Bank (Fondo Rotatorio, Federación Cafeteros)	5.0	1.7
Total	294.0	100.0

Source: Latin American Seminar on Rural Credit, 1968 [36, p. 131].

conditions are further complicated since the settlers incur substantial clearing and maintenance costs before the first crop is harvested. The idea underlying directed settlement is to ease these adjustments through advance planning and prior investments in infrastructure—especially roads, schools, clinics, and marketing and credit facilities. In some areas, housing is also provided.

Directed settlements on new land have been costly. At least two general problems arise. Tinnermeier, in an evaluation of new settlements in the rain forests of Caquetá, found that individual settlers often had to assume large debts resulting from the public investments made in the projects.[42] These debt obligations, though long term, required annual payments from the settlers before they were fully established and before productivity potentials and natural uncertainties could be fully assessed. Private settlers who at their own expense moved onto public lands in the surrounding areas often had higher incomes, a lower abandonment rate, and made larger investments in their farms.

A second problem has been the inability of government agencies to prevent exploitation of new settlers. Infrastructural improvements and services provided by the government—roads, market places, river ports, storage warehouses, and agronomic services—also attracted livestock and grain buyers, truckers, river haulers, money lenders, land speculators, bus companies, and other commercial interests. With inadequate regulation, these groups are able to further their own interests at the expense of the new settlers. Furthermore, since the volume of business transactions in new, isolated regions is generally quite small, at least initially, there is little competition, and single firms monopolize the market. Once establsihed, they are able to maintain a monopoly position through a variety of noneconomic actions. [48]

Agrarian Reform and the Agricultural Economy

Colombia's attempts at agrarian reform have been limited both in scope and application. New agricultural programs may have helped to maintain the level of agricultural output, but they were not sufficiently general to increase agricultural productivity on the majority of farms. Total agricultural output during the past twenty years increased at about the same rate as population growth. Most of the expansion in crop production came from larger plantings and higher yields of cotton, sugar cane, and rice—crops produced with relatively modern technology and grown on farms that are large in relation to peasant holdings.[3]

Part of the emphasis on large scale production of cash crops resulted from the need to find substitute export products to compensate for the relative decline in earnings from coffee, the source of more than three-fourths of the total value of exports until the early 1960s. Colombia still depends primarily on agriculture for foreign exchange earnings. Cotton, bananas, and sugar, the three main agricultural export products besides coffee, together generated about 8 per cent of the value of total exports in 1967, but their importance rose sharply in 1968 when coffee's percentage of total export earnings dropped to 53 per cent.[41]

Attempts to produce rapid and substantial increases in agricultural exports shifted agricultural program emphases to mechanized field cropping and extensive livestock enterprises. Consequently, employment opportunities in agriculture may have been affected negatively on both large farms and in frontier areas. When trouble arose recently between large producers and cotton workers in Cesar, the first mechanical cotton picker was imported with the expectation that the machine could replace 200 seasonal workers.[17]

Livestock production, also low in labor requirements, is likewise being promoted to generate additional exports. The program faces marketing difficulties—problems of entry and competition in the world meat trade.[5]

Agriculture provides about 30 per cent of the gross domestic product and employs 47 per cent of the economically active labor force.[4; 8] Migration out of agriculture is heavy but manufacturing yields few jobs—employment there grew at a rate of only 2.2 per cent annually between 1951 and 1964 while urban population in the sixteen largest cities (each with a population of over 100,000) increased by 5.6 per cent annually.[44; 37, pp. 5-6] Bogotá's population during this period grew by 6.8 per cent per year. Many workers had to seek employment in personal services and other low skill, low productivity jobs; recorded employment in this tertiary sector grew proportionately faster than the total nonagricultural labor force. As a result, income distribution among urban workers also became more skewed.[38]

Modern manufacturing currently provides about 10,000 new jobs per year, compared with an annual increase in the total labor force, including agriculture, of an estimated 168,000 to 200,000 workers per year. Manufacturing's inability to keep up with the growing labor force will likely become even more serious. Estimates of current unemployment rates in Colombia range as high as 20 per cent of the total labor force, and some studies project even higher rates of unemployed in the future.[46] With manufacturing unable to absorb large numbers of additional workers, it becomes imperative to find employment for them in the countryside, even at low levels of productivity.

Yet farmers, especially small operators, even if accommodated on the land, face many structural limitations to increasing production. Grunig concludes from a study of small farms that "Colombian rural conditions and public programs are such that very few campesinos can become entrepreneurs. The large majority are blocked from access to resources, markets, and education necessary to allow entrepreneurial development." [23, p. 19]

The physical isolation of many Colombian farm families limits their market alternatives as well as their opportunities for education and other services. Colombia produces more than 21 million metric tons of agricultural products annually, more than half of which moves off the farm on the backs of pack animals.[18]⁵

Rural communities also face serious shortages in such services as education, health, information, and public utilities because of many fiscal and administrative limitations. The majority of rural youth in Colombia receive less than three years of education. The value of education received must be further discounted because of the low quality of rural schools and teachers, and because of the traditional practice of separating children in school on the basis of sex, providing for attendance during only one-half of the day or half of the days per week for each sex group.[25]

Public investments in rural areas are very low. A land tax provides municipal revenue but the tax rate is so low that the income it produces is used almost entirely to maintain local bureaucracies.[7] At the same time, control over rates and tax structures rests with the national government which generally has blocked local tax reform.

Because of the poor record by the municipalities and the nation in providing public services, many rural communities have begun using informal procedures for raising local funds. This practice was partly formalized in 1958 when locally organized and already operating community action boards called "Juntas de Acción Comunal" were given legal status. The enabling legislation provides that local groups may assume and share responsibility for certain public works, especially schools, health centers, roads and bridges, recreation and cultural centers, and activities to improve agriculture and cooperatives.[16]

Attempts at reorganizing farm markets through the formation of cooperatives have not met with much success in Colombia. Cooperatives face the same structural problems which often limit individual producers—they find it difficult to maintain a democratic structure and to compete with monopolistic enterprises, especially under conditions of widely fluctuating product prices. Private dealers, on the other hand, are often able to set prices for the produce farmers have to sell. They may provide credit and other services, which obligates the farmer to sell his produce to them.[48]

For similar reasons, rural union movements have not been particularly strong in Colombia. Attempts at obtaining land have provided the impetus to organize some rural peasant unions. Urrutia says agrarian unions can sometimes force landowners "to sell land to the peasants on credit; in other cases the Land Reform Institute intervenes and declares the invaded land a 'land reform' area; and in other cases, the peasants keep their land through force." [47, p. 133]

Collective action by peasants leading to land invasions appears to be partially effective in keeping the government active in land reform work. Urrutia cites Enrique Peñalosa, the first director of INCORA, as saying that

⁵ In 1968 there were only 4,000 kilometers of rural access roads, 18,000 kilometers of national highways of which about 4,000 were paved, and 16,000 kilometers of departmental (state) roads. The nationally owned railway has 3,436 kilometers of track connecting the main cities and sea ports. In practice only about one-fourth of the farms are accessible by motor vehicle.

178

very few land reform projects have been started in areas that have had no serious social conflicts.[47, p. 134]

Policy Implications

The rural economy of Colombia is faced with two overwhelming policy problems. One is to find ways of allocating land, capital and technology in a manner that will productively employ the still growing numbers of people who remain in agriculture. The second, closely related to the first, is to develop means for reducing the direct competition between small and large farmers for resources and services while improving the productivity of both groups. Accomplishing these policy objectives could have a number of beneficial effects: (a) increased employment and incomes in agriculture; (b) increased productivity of the rural labor force; and (c) increased demand for consumer goods.

The number of Colombians directly dependent on agriculture for a living is likely to increase for many more years. This is true even if migration to urban areas continues at a high rate. In absolute numbers, the rural population increased by one-quarter million adults (persons 15 years of age and older) in the thirteen-year period 1938-51, and increased by one-half million adults in the next thirteen-year period, 1951-64.[8; 9][6]

Future increases in demand for farm products must come largely from the domestic market because export markets simply are not available. Unless a large increase in the size of that market can be generated by a better distribution of incomes (a corollary of a more equitable distribution of productive opportunities among the farm population), the increase in effective demand will probably be insufficient to justify continued future investments in large farms and capital-intensive enterprises. Likewise, the demand for manufactured goods will continue to have a narrow base, and problems of unemployment and underemployment will become even more serious.[13]

Colombia's remaining public domain must provide some of the additional land needed to employ the growing agricultural population without further subdividing existing small holdings. However, some land must also come from existing large holdings if increasing numbers are to be accommodated within the agricultural sector.

An active agrarian reform program which includes land redistribution can, of course, be expected to meet strong political opposition. Based on the experience of the past ten years, governments of both the liberal and conservative parties lack the support to press forward with a massive land reform program. But while direct approaches have been blocked, many of the intermediate strategies have also been neglected. These areas require renewed

---

6 Calculations are based on rural population figures and include small towns and villages but exclude all county seat towns regardless of size. This treatment was necessary because of the way population figures are reported.

attention. Programs need to take into account the disadvantaged position of the majority of farmers who operate small holdings or receive all or part of their income through wages, share-cropping or tenancy arrangements. As shown in Table II, these categories account for 64 per cent of all farms and 58 per cent of the agricultural work force.

Elsewhere we have suggested a policy of "dualism" [14] which would establish separate programs and services favoring small farmers in order to keep large operators from monopolizing resources and services to the virtual exclusion of the smaller ones. After a time, such a policy would tend to shift resources and power to the side of the peasants, resulting in greater equality in income and resource control.

Even without a land reform, it is shortsighted for Colombia to plan its development without an overall public lands policy. The government has recently taken over much of the remaining unoccupied land through forest reserve and watershed programs. But traditional practices of settlement and use still prevail. The law allows a person to settle anywhere he can physically gain access; and, depending on his ability to obtain legal assistance, he can establish his property rights expostfacto. Since public forest lands are not clearly identified, colonists continue to occupy these reserves along with other unclaimed lands.[21] The result is a haphazard and often destructive use of resources, abusive practices, and endless conflicts over boundaries and possession rights.

Various measures would be required to formulate a public lands policy which is integrated with the development plans of the country. Simplified and low-cost survey and boundary identification procedures are needed to replace the present archaic methods. Improved title transfer and registry procedures would have to be part of such a program. The technology and administrative machinery have already been suggested and are within the financial and technical capabilities of the country.[2]

Once boundaries can be easily identified, the way is opened for other measures needed to increase investments and services in agriculture. The obvious case is to increase the use of the land tax. There is at present an agricultural land tax, but rates and collections are low and most of the revenue is used for local administrative purposes.[7]

A critical requirement for the success of these development strategies is for farm people to gain increased control over public as well as private resource allocations. It is not sufficient simply to increase revenues. Rural road planning and construction provide an illustration of this point. The need for expanding access to rural roads is widely recognized. Highway construction revenues are becoming available from a newly established gasoline tax. Yet rural road improvements have been virtually at a standstill; resources for transportation are allocated primarily for national highways.[18]

Local road building is the responsibility of the municipalities working in collaboration with departmental committees. Local committees are composed of a representative from the state office, plus the local mayor and priest. Most have vested interests in using funds for purposes other than roads or for giving priority to urban projects. The record shows that in fact little rural road construction has taken place.

Planning and investment policies in other areas which recognize explicitly the needs of the peasant subsector are also required. The development of new technology and the allocation of capital to agriculture are currently heavily biased to benefit large operators. Agricultural research and demonstration projects have given overwhelming emphasis to large farm, mechanized field cropping or large scale ranching as opposed to practices applicable to small farms.[14] Administrative procedures for capital and credit programs need to be changed so that each farm size group can be assured of receiving assistance appropriate to its needs. More than half of the institutionalized credit currently goes to fewer than 10 per cent of the borrowers.[36] Many producer associations and public assistance agencies direct their services only to commercial producers. A long history of these practices has given large farmers a disproportionate voice in setting the terms and conditions for borrowing, leaving peasant farmers in insecure and vulnerable positions where they are easily exploited by other groups such as landlords and middlemen.

Additional rural infrastructural investments could also be expected to speed the development process. The small farm subsector is the main client for rural schooling and health facilities, collective forms of transportation and communication, and local product handling and marketing facilities. Large farmers, on the other hand, frequently send their children to urban schools, have their own transportation and storage facilities, and bypass local markets.

Increased average incomes for the large number of small farmers would provide the small farm subsector with more economic and political leverage with which to influence decision making bodies on the questions of improved rural services. Higher incomes would also strengthen the demand of the small farm subsector for nonfarm inputs and consumer goods, attracting additional commercial services into the countryside and thereby creating more employment opportunities.

References

[1]   Adams, Dale W.; Antonio Giles: and Rodrigo Peña. *Supervised Credit in Colombia's Agrarian Reform: An Evaluative Study.* Bogotá: Centro Interamericano de Reforma Agraria, 1966.

[2]   Arévalo, Luís. "The Legal Insecurity of Rural Property in Colombia: A Case Study of the Notarial and Registry Systems." Ph.D. dissertation, University of Wisconsin, 1970.

[3]   Atkinson, L. Jay. *Changes in Agricultural Production and Technology in Colombia.*   Foreign Agricultural Economic Report, no. 52.   Washington, D. C.: U. S. Department of Agriculture, June 1969.

[4]   Banco de la República. *Cuentas Nactionales.* Cuadros 99-101. Bogotá, 1951-67.

[5] Bleidner, James O. *La situación económica de la ganadería*. Bogotá: Instituto Colombiano Agropecuario, 1969.

[6] Comité Interamericano de Desarrollo Agrícola (CIDA). *Tenecia de la tierra y desarrollo socio-económico del sector agrícola: Colombia.* Washington, D.C.: Unión Panamericana, 1966.

[7] Davis, L. Harlan. "Economics of the Property Tax in Rural Areas of Colombia." Ph. D. dissertation, University of Wisconsin, 1968.

[8] Departmento Administrativo Nacional Estadístico (DANE) *Censo nacional de población: 1964.* Bogotá, 1967.

[9] ———.*Censo nacional de población:* 1951. Bogotá, 1954.

[10] ———. *Directorio nacional de explotaciones agropecuarias: censo agropecuario, 1960, resumen nacional.* Bogotá, 1964.

[11] ———. "La reforma agraria en cifras." *Boletín mensual de estadistíca,* no. 222 (1970).

[12] Dix, Robert H. *Colombia: The Political Dimensions of Change.* New Haven: Yale University Press, 1967.

[13] Dorner, Peter. "Needed Redirections in Economic Analysis for Agricultural Development Policy." *American Journal of Agricultural Economics.* 53 (1971): 8-16.

[14] ———, and Herman Felstehausen. "Agrarian Reform and Employment: The Colombian Case." *International Labour Review* 102 (1970): 221-240.

[15] Duff, Ernest A. *Agrarian Reform in Colombia.* New York: Frederick A. Praeger, 1968.

[16] Edel, Matthew D. "The Colombian Community Action Program: An Economic Evaluation." Ph. D. dissertation, Yale University, 1967.

[17] *El Espectador* (Bogotá), January 25, 1970.

[18] Felstehausen, Herman. "Planning Problems in Improving Colombian Roads and Highways." *Land Economics* 47 (1971): 1-13.

[19] ———, and Roger Soles. Unpublished notes on a trip to the Lower Magdalena region. Land Tenure Center, Madison, Wis., 1969.

[20] Fluharty, Vernon Lee. *Dance of the Millions: Military Rule and the Social Revolution in Colombia, 1930-1956.* Pittsburgh: University of Pittsburgh Press, 1957.

[21] Geographic Institute, Agustín Codazzi, Interview with the legal staff. Bogotá, January 1970.

[22] Guhl, Ernesto. *Colombia: bosquejo de su geografía tropical.* Rio de Janeiro: Instituto Panamericano de Geografía e Historia, 1967.

[23] Grunig, James. "The Minifundio Problem in Colombia: Development Alternatives." *Inter-American Economic Affairs* 12, no. 3 (1969): 3-23

[24] Haney, Emil B., Jr. "The Economic Reorganization of Minifundia in a Highland Community of Colombia." Ph. D. dissertation, University of Wisconsin, 1969.

[25] Havens, A. Eugene. *Education in Rural Colombia: An Investment in Human Resources.* Land Tenure Center Research Paper, no. 8. Madison, Wis.: University of Wisconsin, 1965.

[26] Hirschman, Albert O. *Journeys toward Progress.* New York: Twentieth Century Fund, 1963.

[27] Instituto Colombiano de Reforma Agraria (INCORA). "Ley Uno de 1968: Adiciona a la Ley 135 de 1961." Bogotá: Asesoria Jurídica, Agosto 1968.

[28] ———.*Plan Quinquenal 1969-1973.* Vol. I and II. Bogotá: Oficina de Planeación, Mayo de 1969.

[29] ———."Adjudicaciones en tierras baldías durante 1968 clasificadas por extensión y ubicación." Bogotá: División de Adjudicaciones, September 1969.

[30] ———"Principales actividades realizadas, 1969." Unpublished tables. Bogotá, 1970.

[31] ———. Resumen de expropriaciones, 1962 a deciembre 31, 1969." Unpublished manuscript. Bogotá: División de Tenencia de Tierras, 1970.

[32] Instituto de Desarrollo de los Recursos Naturales Renovables (INDERENA). *Estatuto forestal,* acuerdo número 3. Bogotá 1969.

[33] International Bank for Reconstruction and Development and the International Development Association. *A Review of INCORA and Its Program in Colombia.* Bogotá, October 1967.

[34] Mullenax, Charles H.; James S. Plaxico; and James M. Spain. *Alternative Beef Production Systems for the Eastern Plains of Colombia.* Cali: Centro Internacional de Agricultura Tropical, 1969.

[35] Purcell, Carl, and Carol Steele. "INCORA Fulfills Dreams in Colombia." *War on Hunger* 4 (1970): 9-12.

[36] República de Colombia. "Los problemas del crédito agropecuario y el desarrollo económico en Colombia." Working papers, Latin American Seminar on Rural Credit. El Salvador, October 1968.

[37] Schultz, T. Paul. *Population Growth and Internal Migration in Colombia.* Memorandum RM-5765-RC/AID. Santa Monica, Calif.: The Rand Corporation, 1969.

[38] Slighton, Robert L. *Relative Wages, Skill Shortages, and Changes in Income Distribution in Colombia.* Memorandum RM-5651-RC/AID. Santa Monica, Calif.: The Rand Corporation, 1968.

[39] Soles, Roger. "Rural Land Invasions in Colombia." Ph. D. dissertation, University of Wisconsin, in process.

[40] ———."Comments on Planning Future Irrigation Projects in the Rio César Region of Colombia." Unpublished paper. Madison, Wis.: Land Tenure Center, October 1970.

[41] Superintendencia de Comercio Exterior. *Análisis del comercio exterior colombiano 1957-1967,* Bogotá: Imprenta Nactional, 1968.

[42] Tinnermeier, Ronald L. "New Land Settlement in the Eastern Lowlands of Colombia." Ph. D. dissertation, University of Wisconsin, 1964.

[43] Thome, Joseph R. "Title Problems in Rural Areas of Colombia: A Colonization Example." *Inter-American Economic Affairs* 19, no. 3 (1965): 81-97.

[44] United Nations, Economic and Social Council. *El desarrollo industrial de Colombia.* Santiago, Chile: Economic Commission for Latin America, 1966.

[45] United States Embassy in Bogotá. Agricultural Attaché. "Monthly Reports." Various dates.

[46] United States, Senate, Committee on Foreign Relations. "Colombia: A Case History of U. S. Aid Together with a Report of the Comptroller General." In *Survey of the Alliance for Progress,* Document No. 91-17, 91st Cong., 1st sess., 1969.

[47] Urrutia, Miguel. *The Development of the Colombian Labor Movement.* New Haven: Yale University Press, 1969.

[48] Wierer, Karl. *Economics of Improving Marketing Organization and Facilities to Accelerate Agricultural Development in Land Settlement Projects.* Bogotá: Instituto Latinoamericano de Mercadeo Agrícola, 1967.

PART IV
SUPPLEMENTARY REFORM
MEASURES

CHAPTER 9

Peasant Organizations as Vehicles of Reform

MARION BROWN

Associate Professor of Agricultural Journalism
and the Land Tenure Center
at the University of Wisconsin-Madison

CHAPTER 9

Peasant Organizations as Vehicles of Reform

MARION BROWN

If there is one thing about which reactionaries, reformists, and revolutionaries seem to agree, it is that peasants are stubbornly passive people who must be persuaded to act in their own interest. Some writers place so much emphasis on the attitudinal backwardness of the peasant that they seem by implication to define rural underdevelopment as a state of mind. To the conventional capitalist observer the problem lies in the peasant's inability to recognize and exploit economic opportunity—to make the "new factor combinations" which can turn a vicious circle of poverty into an upward spiral of sustained growth. To some Latin American revolutionaries the peasant's cognitive deficiency—a consequence of capitalist socialization—consists of insensitivity to his own relatively deprived status and ignorance of his own class interests and enemies. Conservatives, liberals and radicals all tend to see the problem as one of traditional attitudes which stubbornly resist change. The nonrevolutionary view has been summarized by Rogers, who describes what he believes to be an almost universal "subculture of peasantry," characterized by such nonadaptive attitudes as "(1) mutual distrust; ... (2) perceived limited good; (3) dependence on and hostility toward government authority; (4) familialism; (5) lack of innovativeness; (6) fatalism; (7) limited aspiration; (8) lack of deferred gratification; (9) limited view of the world; and (10) low empathy." [46, p. 40] Intellectuals to the left of Rogers are sometimes even less flattering.

For example, Brazil's Julião complained that the typical peasant does "not act like a human being, but like a vegetable. ..." [28, p.9] Hugo Blanco characterized his campesino followers in Peru's Valle de la Convención as too petits bourgeois. [12, p. 292; 24, p. 419] Chaplin cites Peruvian revolutionaries who view highland peasant society as a "*Lumpenproletariat* dominated by a false consciousness," [10, p. 413] blinded by "the veil of deceit, dread and skepticism," [16, p. 25] exhibiting "the vain cretinism of the enslaved," [32, p. 35] and evidencing personality and character traits that make the peasant "in many respects his own worst enemy." [10, p. 413] In advocating guerrilla warfare, Luis de la Puente wrote: "Armed action radicalizes the masses and the same applies to the repression which it evokes," [16, pp. 25-26] which comes close to "admitting the tactic of provoking brutal reprisals by the army in order to stir up the 'vain cretinism of the enslaved.' . . ." [10, p. 415] A somewhat different, but still condescending tone is found in Regis Debray's advocacy of a military vanguard which carries out the revolution for the peasants rather than with them.[15, pp. 41-45 and 55-56]

Observers on both ends of the political spectrum also tend to propose solutions that are similar in form if not in substance. One would "educate" or "modernize" the peasant so that he gains traction within the established order. The other would "radicalize" him so that he becomes an instrument for changing the system. In both cases the aim is to resocialize the peasantry—to literally "change men's minds." Yet the question remains whether the peasant's attitudes really distinguish him from other people; Rogers himself raises this issue when he suggests that the subculture of peasantry "may even be valid to describe most types of traditional people, whether they be peasants or not."[46, p. 41] Somewhat differently, studies of peasant mentality and "consciousness" fail to show that self-reported traditional attitudes bear an important relation to the way peasants behave—specifically to their propensity to perceive and exploit opportunities to change the quality of their lives.

If there is anything like a universal subculture of peasantry, it presumably must include such diverse groups as the Mexican revolutionaries of 1910 and the "passive" ejiditarios of 1971; the peasant supporters of Castro and the Bolivian campesinos who were reluctant to help Che Guevara; the Cuban workers who readily accepted collectivization of the island's sugar plantations and the individualistic Russian peasants; Central America's tenaciously traditional penny capitalists and the Asian smallholders and share-tenants who have so quickly adopted the technology of the "green revolution." It must also encompass peasants the world over who leave their rural homes to search for work in the cities. Why is it that generalized fatalism and limited world view do not inhibit such a radical innovation as rural-urban migration?

The view taken in the present chapter de-emphasizes psychological variables and seeks the origins of peasant activism not so much in the campesino's mind as in the changing situational realities with which his mind must deal. The peasant is assumed to be naturally active and adaptive. He perceives his situation fairly accurately—probably as accurately as his urban counterpart. He is rational in the sense that he formulates feasible ends-in-view and seeks realistic means to those ends. He seizes opportunities for both individual advancement and mutually advantageous collective action about as readily as other people—only he does it less often because he seldom gets the chance. It is probably safe to assume that organizational skills are scarce, but present, in all segments of society, and that the peasant stratum has its share. It is not necessary for every peasant to be a profit maximizer or a skilled organizer. If the productive ingenuity and organizational talent that already exists in the peasant sector can be mobilized, less innovative people will adapt.

This is not to say that peasant attitudes, values, or "cognitive-motivational states" are irrelevant. Seen within the institutional and situational settings of which they are a part, attitudes can help to explain the pace and direction of change. Peasant mentalities are consequences of existing social structures, and as such, antecedents of new structures. They are not, however, universal causal factors which determine peasant behavior at large. Overemphasis on the mental and cultural deficiencies of the peasantry has, I believe, obscured far more important structural and situational causes of peasant "backwardness," and heightened the campesinos' vulnerability to repression and co-optation. Furthermore, when one looks at what Latin American campesinos do rather than merely what they say, one sees little evidence of apathy or passivity. Indeed, there seems to be considerable generalized readiness to engage in radical collective action. In Bolivia between 1861 and 1944, there were more than 2,000 peasant rebellions or movements related to land rights or labor disputes [4, p. 16], and rural syndicalism grew gradually throughout the thirties and forties, despite overt attempts to repress it.[11, p. 10] Nearly twenty thousand peasants fought and died in the Salvadorian uprisings of 1932.[6, p. 3] Colombia only recently emerged from two decades of rural upheaval, with at least a hundred thousand violent deaths.[6, p. 4] In Brazil, more than 2,000 peasant unions were organized in less than a year after passage of the Rural Labor Statute of 1963.[6, p. 4] Similarly, in Chile the number of de facto unions increased sharply, and grievance petitions trebled in a matter of months after President Frei announced his intention to liberalize the rural labor law.[2, p. 25] A few years earlier, a sweeping electoral reform which made it much more difficult for employers to control laborers' ballots had been followed almost immediately by a sharp drop in the rightist vote in rural Chile.[40, p. 5] In Venezuela the number of sindicatos increased rapidly during the revolution of 1945-48, dropped off sharply (at least in terms of their visibility) during the ten years of "counter revolution" from 1948 to 1958, and immediately soared again when Betancourt took office in 1958.[41, pp. 14-155] All of these events unfolded with a rapidity which belies the notion of a passive peasantry which must be coaxed and persuaded to try anything new or radical.

Structural Obstacles to Organization

The pace of peasant unionization in Latin America is undoubtedly much more affected by a "culture of repression" than by a "subculture of peasantry." In fact, the latter—to the extent that it exists at all—is probably a consequence of the former.[1] This view is, of course, directly opposed to landowners' claims that the traditional patrón-peón relationship is mutually beneficial and harmonious. The myth of benevolent paternalism has been an extremely useful one for the landed elite. It has done much to legitimize both direct and indirect repression of peasant movements and to shift the blame for violence and unrest to "malevolent outside agitators." Erasmus reports

---

[1] Gerrit Huizer presents an interesting discussion of this point.[24, pp. 13-46]

that in post-reform Bolivia landowners complained that "the reform had created a lucha de clases (class struggle). 'Before the reform, . . . the peón had cariño al trabajo y al patrón (love for work and patrón). Now the laborers sabotage their work for us, and there is not the same fondness between peón and patrón.' "[19, p. 366]

Clearly, landed oligarchies have frequently exerted strong pressures to maintain this "fondness." In northwestern Mexico, landowners employed a debt slavery system to control scarce labor. Hacienda stores gave credit, and once in debt, few peasants were able to gain enough freedom even to leave, let alone to organize. If indebted peones escaped, they were pursued by hacienda policemen and punished.[19] The hacienda system in Venezuela was very similar; haciendas had "company" stores and policemen, and workers were sought out if they did not appear for morning chores. Capangas (hacienda police) are still very much a part of rural culture in northeast Brazil [20, p. 440], and arbitrary firing and other sanctions against peasant union leaders continue to be common in much of Latin America. In a 1968 study of peasant leadership in Chile, Affonso reports that more than two-thirds of the regional leaders, and 40 per cent of the local leaders, had been threatened with dismissal, docked, or fired. [3, p. 184]

Feder characterizes the traditional hacienda structure as "not unlike a military organization" in which a complex administrative hierarchy acts as a "sponge" to absorb the immediate resentment of workers.[20, p. 406] This hierarchy also minimizes and distorts patrón-peón interaction and provides a modicum of social mobility which the landowner can manipulate to reward loyalty. Feder argues that landowners suppress peasant "organizability" by keeping incomes at or near the hunger level, promulgating and enforcing "an iron law of subsistence wages," often in violation of labor and other social welfare legislation.[20, p. 410]

Landowners have often been able to count on government support in their antiunion efforts.[38] In Mexico, Bolivia, and Venezuela municipal jails were often used to hold runaways, and government authorities legitimized and institutionalized the control of workers.[19, p. 368] In Chile a vigorous peasant organizational movement which started in 1938 was quickly curtailed when landowners succeeded in striking a bargain with the ruling coalition, giving rise to a prohibitive order from the labor ministry. Eight years later a new political bargain produced the "Ley de trabas" (Law of Obstacles). This was Law No. 8811, which confined unions to farms with more than twenty adult workers, all of whom had been on the farm for a full year, and half of whom could read and write. It also prohibited any participation by outsiders and made it illegal for unions to extend beyond the boundaries of a single farm unit.[2, p. 49] The law continued in force until 1967.

How Movements Begin

Where peasant organizations have managed to emerge and survive, their development has coincided with a gradual, and sometimes temporary, erosion of the traditional land-based power structure. Urbanization, industrialization, population growth, shifts in world markets and international political crises, have been cited as causes of a general decline in the power of the hacendado class.[30, pp. 23-28] As Landsberger puts it, peasant movements start when "traditional elites objectively weakened and weakening also in the 'will to govern' . . . permit some peasants to improve some aspects of their status." [30, p. 25; see also 1, p. 199] This apparently happened in La Convención Valley of Peru when the traditional hacendado class lost ground relative to the new entrepreneurs of the coastal plantations and industry.[12, p. 292]

The same was true of northeast Brazil. Julião's famous Ligas Camponesas and other organizations in Pernambuco grew up while the traditional sugar growers were feeling the effects of strong competition from the new, more modern plantations and mills of São Paulo.[22, p. 383] The fact that the hacendados have been able to curtail and control the movement, at least for the time being, speaks again of the enormous political power they continue to enjoy, despite some loss of economic dominance.

Mexico's landed oligarchy lost ground under Díaz, who played off one elite faction against another to gain support for his industrialization policies. The economic boom at the turn of the century tended to favor the emerging urban-industrial elite and tempted many hacendados into the cities, with correspondingly less attention to their haciendas. But even the traditional hacendados participated in the new prosperity, and Díaz courted them by keeping wages low, opening up what remained of the public domain, legitimizing the takeover of communal lands, and allowing villagers to be pressed into forced labor. By 1910 Díaz was old and his regime was weak with inefficiency and corruption, which was especially rife in the army.[48, p. 138] The landowners could not depend on traditional agencies of social control, as they had during two civil wars and scores of peasant uprisings during the previous century. The general weakness of the Díaz government plus the distraction of Madero's national movement, made it possible for the Zapatistas and other agrarian radicals to get under way.[48, p. 104]

Bolivia's elite was bled by a series of disastrous wars which stripped the nation of her rubber plantations, her sea coast and her Chaco claims. When the last war ended in defeat in 1935, the establishment was discredited, demoralized and barely able to govern. The result was a power vacuum in which peasant unions and other new interest groups began to thrive and compete for national prominence. As Patch puts it, "The old regime no longer existed as a group with faith in itself and the power to enforce its beliefs; it was a shattered conglomerate of special interests without the force or the talent to impose the principles which supported their privilege." [35, p. 127; see also 36, pp. 108-176]

According to Powell, the hegemony of Venezuela's rural oligarchy began to erode with the loss of German coffee markets during the World War I blockade. At about the same time the infant oil industry began to compete for available credits, driving up the costs of production. The Great Depression, and World War II brought new shifts in foreign markets, and new disequilibria. "The erosion of the rural economy from 1920 onward was accompanied by a certain amount of rural unrest and occasionally violent outbursts." [43, p. 64] By 1936 the declining power of the landed elite was being further challenged by the famous "Generation of '28," especially Rómulo Betancourt who was "particularly committed to the syndicalization of the peasantry." [43, p. 65]

In Chile, landowner resistance to peasant unions has been strong, and until recently, very effective thanks in part to timely alliances with emerging urban elites. Even after Arturo Alessandri liberalized the labor laws in the 1920s, giving rise to vigorous industrial unions, peasant organizations were systematically suppressed. The only rural unions with long and relatively successful histories are found in isolated areas where the traditional hacienda structure was never dominant. A notable example is the sheep ranching area of the Far South where most of the labor force is seasonal and migratory and therefore somewhat less dependent than the resident laborers on the haciendas of the central valleys. The first successful unions appeared on the sheep ranches in 1927. Another cradle of peasant unionism in Chile is the Choapa Valley, north of Santiago. Here most of the lands (eleven haciendas belonging to a single family) were willed to charity sometime soon after Chile gained independence. This abdication by a local oligarch greatly altered power relations in the valley, making it possible for the workers to organize. These farms and a few others in different parts of the country were administered by the National Health Service which tolerated, and depending on the regime in power, sometimes encouraged peasant unionism within their boundaries. [2, p. 152] This was especially true during the administration of Pedro Aguirre Cerda (1938-1941) when Chile's current president, Dr. Salvador Allende G. served as Minister of Health.

The Mapuche Indians in Chile's mid-South have also been able to maintain viable communal organizations based somewhat on their traditional tribal structure. These have sometimes acted as pressure groups despite steady and occasionally violent opposition. [2, pp. 26-30; 47, pp. 19-28] The very survival of these organizations is remarkable, however it cannot be said that they have been notably successful in counteracting the power of the local landed elite which has managed to take over a major share of the communal lands ceded to the Mapuches when the Indian Wars ended late in the last century.

All of the above examples argue that the take off point for peasant unionism in Latin America is usually some kind of shift in traditional power relations rather than a mere change of attitude or outlook. It would seem that the mental and emotional stuff of which movements are born is abundant. There is probably enough despair, anger, perceived relative deprivation and "consciousness" to start an uprising in most any traditional rural community in Latin America on any given day. The traditional patrón-peón relations of the hacienda system simply cannot exist without systematic and effective suppression of peasant organizations. Thus whenever the local landed elite begins to lose its grip, usually because of larger economic or political circumstances, peasant activism springs up rather quickly, often with little or no initial debt to outside agitation. This is not to say that urban intellectuals and representatives of political parties and governments have no significant role in peasant movements. However, as we shall attempt to show in the next section, their principal contribution is, in spite of what they themselves may believe, one of tactical planning and organization more than persuasion. As Julião told his friend Antonio Callado in 1963: "Oh Callado! Agitating is a joy. It's organizing that's so difficult." [9, p. 58]

Rural-Urban Interaction

Some analysts say that among the more successful peasant movements in Latin America are those which have been largely instigated and fostered by campesinos themselves; others maintain that they were primarily the creations of urban intellectuals and politicians. Bolivia's sweeping land reform of 1953 seems to lend itself to both interpretations. Reading Patch, one would conclude that the reform was imposed by the peasant unions and that the government decree which made it official was primarily an emergency response to their demands.[13, p. 17] Heath, on the other hand, says this analysis gives too much emphasis to peasant initiative and too little to the organizational activity of the National Revolutionary Movement Party (MNR). [13, p. 17] He points out that peasant leaders had nonpeasant allies as early as 1936, when the movement started in Ucureña. In the first months after the 1952 revolution, some of the more radical MNR leaders collaborated actively with the head of the Cochabamba syndicates, José Rojas. Thus Heath contends the agrarian reform was effectively imposed by the government; peasants in the areas he studied apparently did not act until after the decree was signed.

Patch acknowledges that agents of the Ministry of Peasant Affairs and university students worked with Rojas in October and November of 1952 and that Rojas himself joined the MNR at that time. However, as the sindicatos of the high valley organized under Rojas, "the whole movement released itself from the control of the national government and of the leaders of the MNR."[37, p. 56] Dandler also refutes the simplification that campesino leadership was an improvised creation from above after April 1952.[13, p. 23] His analysis shows that the unions emerged in a post-war context of complex and changing socio-political relations between urban groups, workers, and intellectuals.[13, p. 23] Edmundo Flores, who served as a U.N. advisor to the Bolivian land reformers, described the role of the MNR leaders as "more that of channelizers and interpreters of the public's will and less that of policy makers. It is to their credit, however, that they have given evidence of shrewd political sense that has enabled them to keep several steps ahead of popular demands." [21, p. 117]

In summary, it seems safe to say that the reform was greatly influenced by the initiative of the strong peasant unions in Cochabamba, but it is equally clear that neither the peasant union movement nor the land reform could have developed rapidly on a national scale without the active support of the MNR government.

In the early years of the Mexican Revolution, local peasant initiative was undeniably of crucial importance. Zapata's militia was certainly not the invention of urban intellectuals, and except for a brief alliance with Madero, it enjoyed little early support from any urban-based groups. Far from yielding to urban manipulation, Zapata's agraristas waged a nine year war with three successive governments.[23, pp. 16-24; 48, pp. 101-169] During these years of conflict, the agrarian radicals succeeded in gaining official acceptance of Zapata's land reform program (the Plan de Ayala), but even then lands were actually redistributed only in those areas where the peasants were strongly organized and armed. The pace of implementation of the reform in Mexico has continued to fluctuate with the strength of peasant movements. At one point during the Cárdenas regime, the armed peasant militia numbered 60,000 men who defended not only their land, but also the government, which was under strong pressure from conservative forces.[34, p. 99] Working closely with peasant organizations during his six year term, Cárdenas redistributed 18 million hectares, far more than any administration before or since. Militant direct action by peasant groups (UGDCM) in northern Mexico led to another spurt of reform activity in the late fifties under President López Mateos.[6, p. 8]

The importance of urban-rural interaction in peasant movements and land reform can be seen by comparing Bolivia and Mexico. Zapata's initial de facto redistribution of land in Morelos was as significant as the Cochabamba land invasions that triggered Bolivia's reform in 1953. However, in the early days of the revolution in Mexico, there was no strong, cohesive counterpart to the Bolivian MNR to support the movement and help it spread to other parts of the country. Such support came after nearly three decades of struggle, but even then it was shortlived. By and large the Mexican peasants have had to rely on their own initiative and resources to pressure first for the promulgation of reform legislation and then, over a fifty-year period, for enforcement of the law. Local movements as vigorous as those that began in Cochabamba and Morelos have also occurred in isolated regions of other countries, notably Peru and Colombia, but these efforts succumbed, partly for want of support from strong, urban-based political movements.[10, p. 415]

Craig describes the peasant movement in Peru's Valle de la Convención as "an unusual Latin American phenomenon of a rural union organizing itself from the bottom up—rather than being organized and directed from outside." Even so, Craig cites important contributions by non campesinos, especially lawyers (who were paid for their services), labor leaders from Cuzco, and Hugo Blanco who assumed an important leadership role in 1962, some ten years after the movement began.[12, pp. 284-292]

Modern peasant movements in Venezuela, Brazil and Chile have apparently been greatly influenced by non campesino organizers almost from their inception.

The Venezuelan peasant culture of the 1930s could hardly be characterized as passive or submissive, but neither was it organized. The period was marked by "scattered land invasions and even isolated attempts at guerrilla warfare,"[43, p. 64] but there was no cohesive movement until 1936 when Betancourt's organizers began to recruit peasant influentials to form sindicatos. According to Martz, Betancourt mobilized some 200 full time peasant union organizers during the 1936-39 period.[33] As president of the revolutionary junta (1945-47) Betancourt greatly accelerated the pace of peasant organization, revamped the electoral system, and carried out a "highly significant but little known de facto agrarian reform" which greatly increased the power of peasant leaders.[43, p. 66]

Heavy repression was reinstated by a military coup in 1948. The peasants' material gains were quickly wiped out, and leaders were subjected to ten years of "assassination, torture, imprisonment and exile." Even so, the organization survived and contributed to the overthrow of the Pérez Jiménez dictatorship.[43, p. 69] When Betancourt came to power again in 1958, these unions became the major instruments and beneficiaries of his agrarian policies.

Together with the AD government the Federación de Campesinos de Venezuela (FCV) represented for a time what Powell called a "rural problem-solving system," with transactional flows of information, demands, voting support, and goods and services. This alliance produced an agrarian reform program providing more than 5 million acres to over one hundred thousand peasant families.[43, p. 71] At one point it seemed as if the alliance was "self sustained, dynamic, adaptable,"[43, p. 87] and destined to bring about "the incorporation of the peasantry into the political process."[43, p. 63]

In recent years, however, it has become apparent that the peasant movement never really achieved its avowed goal of representing and benefitting the mass of the peasantry. Rather it seems to be creating a new "Kulak" class which is decreasingly inclined to press the interests of the peasant masses.

In a recent article Powell modifies his earlier optimistic assessment of Venezuela's peasant movement, citing the rural-to-urban population shift as a major cause of the FCV's declining influence.[42, pp. 12-15] He might have added that this massive migration is also an index of the movement's earlier failures—its inability to protect and expand rural employment opportunities rapidly enough to absorb a larger share of population growth. Although the number of direct land recipients in Venezuela is high in comparison to nonrevolutionary reforms in other countries, it represents only about a third of the legally eligible campesino families. Many of these, while undoubtedly better off, have not succeeded in breaking out of poverty. Most of the country's credit and other services still go to the remaining large landowners and to a small rural middle class, made up of the more successful entrepreneurs created by the reform. As Barraclough puts it, "In Venezuela, peasant organizations enjoyed a brief period of relatively strong power when the Pérez Jiménez dictatorship was overthrown, but they soon became mere instruments for carrying out government agrarian policy rather than for shaping it, much in the same way as had happened earlier with the CNC. in Mexico."[6, p. 12]

The peasant organizations of Pernambuco, Brazil, represent an even clearer case of urban influence and intervention. Almost all of the major leaders of the ligas were nonpeasants, and the rhetoric of Communist and Catholic, as well as liga organizers emphasized the movement's psychological and cultural goals, i.e., "to awaken" the peasant and make him "live life like a human being." [28, p. 9]

With this strong top-down focus it is not surprising that some observers report difficulty detecting campesino participation in the formulation of programs and demands, or campesino understanding of the movement's various ideological trends.[22, p. 386] As one liga member put it, "we don't know what to do. One becomes crazy: one [person] says [we] must pay the landlord, the other [says we] must pay the judge, the third [says] not to pay it at all because land reform is coming and everyone will have some land. . . ." [25, p. 240]

The movement was characterized by competition, conflict and unsteady alliances between Julião, the Catholic Church, Moscow communists, Peking communists, trotskyites, organizers mobilized by Pernambuco's governor, Miguel Arraes, and representatives of João Goulart's national administration. According to Hewitt, "a very large part of the resources of each faction . . . had to be devoted to maintaining that faction against attacks by other groups of organizers."[22, p. 395]

By 1964, just before the military coup, a Goulart-communist alliance had succeeded in gaining control of most of the unions by virtue of the fact that "Goulart . . . commanded both the monetary and legal resources to inhibit independent action . . . and force unions into a national confederation fully controlled by the government."[22, pp. 395-96]

After the coup in 1964 the peasants quickly lost their gains. Many peasant leaders suffered vengeful reprisals, minimum wage laws were again ignored, and on some plantations, cash wages were suddenly replaced by vales (I.O.U.'s).[22, p. 398] Only the Church unions have survived, and their leaders have been replaced by government appointees.

The mobilization of peasant unions in Chile has also been characterized as largely a "top-down phenomenon."[2, p. 235] Socialist and Communist party organizers have been sporadically active in the countryside since the 1920s, with major lapses during the regimes of Pedro Aguirre Cerda and Gabriel González Videla when, paradoxically, one or both formed a part of the ruling coalition and presumably could have accelerated the movement.

Since the early 1950s, and especially after electoral reforms greatly increased campesino voting autonomy in 1958, several Christian-oriented groups, including the Catholic Church, the Instituto de Educación Rural (IER), and the Partido Demócrata Cristiano (PDC) have been organizing unions and competing for peasant loyalty.[2]

The election, in 1964, of reformist Christian Democrat Eduardo Frei M. on a platform which emphasized mass participation, marked a major increment in what had been a slow decline in the hegemony of the landed class. After 1965 peasant organization accelerated rapidly under the partial protection of Frei's reform-oriented regime, especially during the first half of his term. The prohibitive rural labor law was first ignored (1965) and later repealed (1967). In 1965 the Instituto de Desarrollo Agropecuario (INDAP) had nearly 500 functionarios engaged fulltime in promoting campesino labor unions and smallholder cooperatives. [3, p. 138] Stripped of ready access to the repressive machinery of government, the hacendados could resort only to harrassment and punitive firing, and these tactics became less effective as the unions grew strong enough to protect the members' jobs and incomes through strikes and "tomas" (invasions). [39, p. 26]

The latter tactic, however, was not acceptable to the government and Frei's relations with the movement deteriorated markedly with the intervention of the rural Grupo Móvil, a special "mobile squad" whose job was to put an end to illegal strikes and tomas. One confrontation involving a suburban invasion reportedly resulted in eight deaths and twenty-seven injuries. [14, p. 50]

Despite setbacks, and some quarrelling among rival organizations [3, p. 237], the movement has continued to grow. Official figures reported in August of 1970 listed some 130,000 workers in more than 500 rural labor unions grouped into three major national confederations: "Ranquil" (Marxist, 48,000), "Libertad" (Christian, 25,000), and "Triunfo" (INDAP, 57,000). By April of 1971, Ranquil President, Enrique Avendaño, estimated that his organization had increased its membership to more than 70,000, including newly organized workers and converts from Libertad and Triunfo. He also claimed that the three organizations were working much more closely together than in the past. [5] In addition to the unions there are about 3,000 smallholder committees claiming over 100,000 members, a national federation of cooperatives with about 10,000, and a national confederation of some 25,000 land reform beneficiaries. Together these organizations incorporate more than half of Chile's campesinos. [6, p. 6]

Since his election in September of 1970, Allende has promised greater support for rural organizations and more campesino participation in government. One of his first acts as President was to dissolve the Grupo Móvil.

While Chile's rural organizations have lately enjoyed considerable support from the government, political parties and other urban groups, they also seem to enjoy a good deal of independence. The militancy of the Christian and INDAP unions, which supposedly owed some allegiance to Frei, contributed to a split in the PDC, giving rise to the Movimiento de Acción Popular Unida (MAPU), which now supports the ruling Marxist coalition; and

---

2 For a detailed account of the early Christian-oriented unions, see [31].

the repeated intervention of the Grupo Móvil made it clear that the unions reserved the right to oppose government policies.

If Frei did not control the movement, neither is it dominated by Allende or the parties of the Unidad Popular (Popular Union). With the demise of the Grupo Móvil, illegal land invasions began to accelerate. Concerned that this would lend credence to rightist charges of anarchy and erode the legitimacy of his new government, perhaps even provoking a military coup, Allende has sought to calm the more radical elements in the movement. As of this writing (early April 1971) he appears to be having at least partial success. The Mapuches have stopped (or at least postponed) their "corridas de cerco" (fence moving invasions), a brief flurry of "sit-in" demonstrations at CORA offices has ended amicably [44, p. 2], and the Movimiento Campesino Revolucionario (MCR) has agreed to turn several occupied haciendas back to their owners. [26, p. 37; 27, p. 23; 17, p. 21; 18, p. 23]

These concessions by militant campesino groups do not appear to reflect government coercion or control of the unions, but rather a growing confidence that Allende will indeed carry out a profound agrarian reform. Allende's promise in this regard represents a very serious commitment and keeping it will severly test his equally strong committment to legal and constitutional means. It remains to be seen, of course, whether such confidence will continue, but for the time being, Allende seems to have reinforced it by greatly stepping up the pace of the reform, expropriating 328 large farms in the first five months of his term—more than a third of the number taken during the six years of the Frei regime. [45, p. 4]

As the above examples from Bolivia, Mexico, Peru, Venezuela, Brazil and Chile show, urban influence on peasant movements is a complex phenomenon about which it is difficult to generalize. The Patch-Heath controversy cited earlier, and some other discussions of rural-urban interaction in campesino movements seem at times to pose a false dichotomy: either the movements are spontaneous through and through, or they are manipulated by outsiders.[3] Since some cosmopolitan influence can be found in virtually all peasant movements, these discussions soon turn to questions of timing (did the agitators arrive before or after the movement started) and regional variations (were outsiders less active in some areas than in others). One difficulty with such arguments is that they dwell on the mere presence or absence of urban influence, more than on its function and consequences. The outsider's presence has been abundantly documented, but what is his primary role? If it is to talk the campesino out of foolish submissiveness—to "modernize" or "radicalize" his "cognitive-motivational state"—then an essentially elitist persuasion model would seem to apply. If urban intellectuals were absent or completely ineffective, one could argue that a purely spontaneous, grassroots model would be more fitting. What

[3] See for example [49].

more often appears to occur, however, is a very complex interaction which includes elements of both spontaneity and persuasion, but which more importantly often includes genuine dialogue between what are essentially emerging pressure groups in search of political alliances. It is not as if the peasants have a problem and the urban intellectuals a solution. Both have problems, and they attempt to work out a strategy, and most importantly, an organizational structure, designed to yield a mutually advantageous solution. Of course this does not always work the way either party wants it to. In some cases the appearance of "change agents" in the countryside may do little more than signal perceptive campesino leaders, or potential leaders, that the times and the power structure are changing. The very fact that reformers and revolutionaries are allowed to speak and move more or less freely about in rural areas without themselves being immediately repressed may tell the campesino that traditional forces of repression are weakening and direct radical action has a better chance of success. Even moderate modernizing policies of essentially conservative governments are usually accompanied by the rhetoric of social change. Such liberal posturing may be ficticious, but it can be a useful fiction for peasant leaders if it undermines the legitimacy of strong, overt repressive measures.

In many cases, however, urban influence has undeniably been strong and direct. Even so, rural-urban alliances are characterized more by their differences than their similarities. The allies may work together very closely (as in Cárdenas' Mexico) or merely use each other from time to time (as in Paz Estenssoro's Bolivia), and the urban element may indeed gain dominance and control (as in Venezuela and Brazil). And of course the relationship is bound to change over time. In Mexico, Madero's national movement probably did little more for Zapata than open the door by distracting and dispersing the already weakened forces of social control. On the other hand, the alliances forged during the regimes of Cárdenas in Mexico and Betancourt in Venezuela did much to elevate local agrarista movements (albeit temporarily) to national prominence.

Tactics and Accomplishments

Tactics employed by peasant groups in pressing their interests range from gentlemen's agreements through guerrilla warfare. Typically, conflicts have begun with modest demands (such as compliance with minimum wage legislation), and moderate tactics (such as grievance petitions). Almost as typically, they have culminated in strikes or land invasions with a parallel escalation of demands (such as expropriation). Strikes and tomas have been very effective in generating immediate concessions. Indeed they are probably directly responsible for much of the land redistribution that has occurred to date.

Strikes and land occupation have been instrumental in every active phase of the Mexican reform. The Bolivian reform, both before and after the decree, consisted almost exclusively of direct, immediate peasant occupancy of the large estates. The strikes and demonstrations in La Convención, Peru, brought ruthless reprisals, but they also prompted a decree which broke up the large estates in the valley, stimulated new land reform legislation [6, p. 12], and influenced the policies of the military government which took over in 1968. Chile's reform to date has been concentrated in areas where peasant groups were most militant [2, p. 137; 47, pp. 19-28], and Powell concludes that the Venezuelan reform "has been characterized by compromise, modifying its objectives as the intense pressures and land invasions of 1959 and 1960 subsided." [42, p. 11]

In addition to influencing reform plans, peasant organizations have been instrumental in carrying them out, especially in Bolivia, Mexico and Venezuela. In Bolivia and in Zapata's Mexico, the peasants themselves were the reformers. Cárdenas relied heavily on the Confederación Nacional de Campesinos to implement his agrarian policies. Betancourt and the FCV established an elaborate working arrangement in which many program and project decisions were made by peasant leaders.[43, pp. 84-87] However, none of these peasant organizations was able to maintain strong influence for very long. Zapata was murdered and his armies were eventually defeated; Cárdenas' powerful CNC was gradually co-opted and neutralized; Bolivian peasants have been largely ignored since the early days of the revolution, and Venezuela's once influential FCV has won few gains in recent years.

In all of these countries reform and related programs have slowed markedly or stopped altogether, and investment funds have been shifted away from the peasant sector. Therein lies an apparent dilemma for peasant leaders: without strong allies they are restricted to local influence and vulnerable to repression; with an institutionalized role in government programs they seem to become vulnerable to co-optation. To date few if any movements have been able to forge strong alliances without sacrificing some independence, although such a feat is still theoretically possible.

Just as peasant organizations have not fared well over the long run as political forces, neither have they enjoyed great success as collective or cooperative owners and managers of redistributed land. The former problem undoubtedly has contributed to the latter. Reform beneficiary cooperatives or collectives have made promising starts in some cases, but they have tended to fade with the waning of peasant political influence. The transition from pressure group to production cooperative is difficult at best, and probably impossible without continuing public support. Working with the CNC, Cárdenas established apparently viable collective ejidos in the Laguna area, supported by peasant owned and managed service and marketing facilities. He also set up the Banco Ejidal to nurture the growing ejido sector.[6, p. 7] However, the collectives lost out to the private sector after 1940 as urban middleclass groups gained dominance in the ruling party.[6, p. 15] As was seen earlier, a similar shift in priorities has occurred in Venezuela, and while there are some successful cooperatives associated with the reform, the tendency is toward individually owned and managed units. Similarly, many agricultural cooperatives have been legally recognized in Bolivia, but most are cooperatives in name only, and they have received very little government support.

So far, Chile's coop-like asentamientos seem to be relatively more successful than reform-created producer organizations in neighboring countries. The asentamiento is a transitional arrangement by which CORA and a peasant committee jointly manage expropriated properties during a three to five year training period. The asentamiento concept represents an interesting case of campesino union influence on reform policy. It is largely a product of struggle, dialogue and negotiation between CORA and the strong Marxist unions of the Health Service haciendas in the Choapa Valley. Since these farms were state owned, they were among the first to be reformed. The unions went on strike to oppose CORA's original plan, put forth in the final months of Alessandri's regime, which called for individual plots first rented and later purchased by selected families. It would have meant the immediate loss of social security benefits, the end of the unions, and a mass exodus from the valley since there would not be enough parcels to go around. The strike blocked Alessandri's reform and the unions struck again in opposition to the first proposal of the Frei administration. In this context of strikes, marches, demonstrations, and rightist accusations of "communist subversion and sabotage," a commission was established with representatives of CORA and the unions. The outcome was a "working association" which set the pattern for the Frei reform.

According to the present law, the peasants on each asentamiento (which now averages about 30 families) decide at the end of this period whether to continue with cooperative ownership and management, to divide the land into individual units, or some combination of the two. The Frei government encouraged cooperative and mixed options and nearly all of the asentamientos which matured during his term have chosen accordingly. Allende's planned "reform by areas" will bring together more families into larger units, and will undoubtedly accentuate the tendency toward cooperative ownership and management.

Compared with the haciendas they replaced, most asentamientos have been quite productive, and they have succeeded in raising members' incomes. However, seen as part of the larger campesino movement, they are not without some of the same flaws that have plagued reform-created cooperatives in other countries. Campesino participation in decisions and management activities (especially cost accounting) has been minimal on many units, especially those on which workers were not organized prior to expropriation. Little has been done to develop a cooperative marketing structure, leaving the new units dependent on CORA and traditional input and product markets. More importantly, the asentamientos have tended to create a new subsidized and privileged minority which continues to benefit from the labor of landless workers. More than a third of the campesinos who work on the asentamientos are not members, and therefore do not participate in profits or decisions.[7, p. 55]

The Allende government is, of course, well aware of these and other difficulties with the reform, including the high cost per family benefitted. His projected "empresas campesinas" developed on an area basis rather than estate by estate, will presumably be open to a greater proportion of Chile's landless peasants. These area cooperatives, if successful, will give a strong impetus to the emerging cooperative marketing and processing structure, and could, at best, develop into an integrated national campesino-producer cooperative sector encompassing virtually the entire rural population. Realizing this "dream" will require profound structural changes throughout Chilean society, but most of all it will require vigorous and organized action by the campesinos themselves. If the Chilean movement can sustain its present semi-independent course, it will establish an important new model for reform and development in Latin America. It will also do much to correct the "urban bias": the widespread tendency to exaggerate the supposedly nonadaptive nature of the peasant mentality. As I have tried to show in this chapter, such overemphases has worked against peasant movements in two ways: 1) by distracting attention from the profoundly repressive nature of the hacienda structure; and 2) infecting rural-urban political interaction with variously disguised elitist vanguard strategies which put the peasant down as an exotic, childlike creature, to be protected, patronized, agitated, manipulated or simply used by an urban "benefactor." At its worst this bias subverts the independence of peasant movements and gives rise to a new form of repression not essentially different from the old.

References

[1]   Alberti, Georgio. "Los movimientos campesinos." In *La hacienda, la comunidad y el campesino en el Perú.* Robert G. Keith, Hernán Fuenzalida, José Matos Mar, Julio Colter, and Georgio Alberti. Lima: Instituto de Estudios Peruanos, 1970.

[2]   Affonso, Almino; Sergio Gomez; Emilio Klein; and Pablo Ramírez. *Movimiento campesino chileno.* Vol. 1. Santiago: Instituto de Capacitación e Investigación en Reforma Agraria (ICIRA), 1970.

[3]   ———, et al. *Movimiento campesino chileno.* Vol. 2. Santiago: ICIRA, 1970.

[4]   Antezana E., Luis. *El movimiento obrero boliviano.* La Paz: Comité Interamericano de Desarrollo Agrícola (CIDA), 1966.

[5]   Avendaño, Enrique. Personal communication with as president of Ranquil. Santiago, April 14, 1971.

[6]   Barraclough, Solon. "Farmers' Organizations in Planning and Implementing Rural Development Programs." In *Rural Development in a Changing World.* Edited by Reanan Weitz. Cambridge, Mass.: MIT Press, forthcoming.

[7]   ———. "Reforma agraria: Historia y perspectivas." *Cuadernos de la realidad nacional,* no. 7 (1971): 51-83.

[8]   ———, and Arthur Domike. "Agrarian Structure in Seven Latin American Countries." *Land Economics* 42 (1966): 391-424.

[9]   Callado, Antonio, *Tempo de Arraes.* Rio de Janeiro: José Alvaro, 1965.

[10] Chaplin, David. "Peru's Postponed Revolution." *World Politics* 20 (1968): 393-426.

[11] Clark, Ronald J. "Agrarian Reform: Bolivia." Chapter 7 of this book.

[12] Craig, Wesley W. Jr. "Peru: The Peasant Movement of La Convención." In *Latin American Peasant Movements.* Edited by Henry A. Landsberger. Ithaca: Cornell University Press, 1969.

[13] Dandler, Jorge. *El sindicalismo campesino en Bolivia: Los cambios estructurales en Ucureña.* Mexico City: Instituto Indigenista Interamericano, 1969.

[14] Debray, Regis. "Allende habla con Debray." *Punto Final* (Santiago), March 16, 1971.

[15] ———. "Revolution in the Revolution? Armed Struggle and Political Struggle in Latin America." *Monthly Review,* special edition, (1967).

[16] De la Puente Uceda, Luis. "The Peruvian Revolution: Concepts and Perspectives." *Monthly Review* 17 (1965): 2-28.

[17] *El Mercurio.* "Campesinos revolucionarios firman acta con intendente." Santiago, April 1, 1971.

[18] ———. "Ocupantes ilegales de predios participan en actas de acuerdo." Santiago, April 2, 1971.

[19] Erasmus, Charles. "Upper Limits of Peasantry and Agrarian Reform: Bolivia, Venezuela, and Mexico Compared." *Ethnology* 6 (1967): 349-380.

[20] Feder, Ernest. "Societal Opposition to Peasant Movements and Its Effects on Farm People in Latin America." In *Latin American Peasant Movements.* Edited by Henry A. Landsberger. Ithaca: Cornell University Press, 1969.

[21] Flores, Edmundo. "Land Reform in Bolivia." *Land Economics* 30 (1954): 112-124.

[22] Hewitt, Cynthia N. "Brazil: The Peasant Movement of Pernambuco 1961-1964." In *Latin American Peasant Movements.* Edited by Henry A. Landsberger. Ithaca: Cornell University Press, 1969.

[23] Huizer, Gerrit. *Los movimientos campesinos en México.* Mexico City: Centro de Investigaciones Agrarias, 1968.

[24] ———. "The Role of Peasant Organizations in the Process of Agrarian Reform in Latin America." Mimeographed. Geneva: International Labour Organization and Inter-American Committee for Agricultural Development (CIDA), 1969.

[25] Inter-American Committee for Agricultural Development (CIDA). *Land Tenure Conditions and Socio-Economic Development of the Agricultural Sector: Brazil.* Washington, D. C.: Pan American Union, 1966.

[26] Jorquera, Ricardo. "Expropian fundos tomados in Parral." *El Mercurio* (Santiago), March 28, 1971.

[27] ———. "MCR asegura misión complida en Zona de Parral." *El Mercurio* (Santiago), March 29, 1971.

[28] Julião, Francisco. *Qué son las Ligas Campesinas?* Montevideo, Uruguay: Ediciones ARCA, 1962.

[29] Landsberger, Henry A., ed. *Latin American Peasant Movements.* Ithaca: Cornell University Press, 1969.

[30] ———. "The Role of Peasant Movements and Revolts in Development." In *Latin American Peasant Movements.* Edited by Henry A. Landsberger. Ithaca: Cornell University Press, 1969.

[31] ———. "Chile: A Vineyard Workers' Strike–A Case Study of the Relationship between Church, Intellectuals and Peasants." In *Latin American Peasant Movements.* Edited by Henry A. Landsberger. Ithaca: Cornell University Press, 1969.

[32] Martínez de la Torre, Ricardo. *Apuntes para una interpretación marxista de la historia social del Perú.* Vol. 1. Lima: Empresa Editorial Peruana, 1947.

[33] Martz, John D. III. *Acción Democratica: Evolution of a Modern Political Party.* Princeton, N. J.: Princeton University Press, 1966.

[34] Nathan, Paul. "México en la época de Cárdenas." *Problemas agrícolas e industriales de México* 7, no. 3 (1955): 17-176.

[35] Patch, Richard W. "Bolivia: The Restrained Revolution." *The Annals of the American Academy of Political and Social Sciences* 334 (1961): 123-132.

[36] ———. "Bolivia: U.S. Assistance in a Revolutionary Setting." In *Social Change in Latin America Today: Its Implication for U.S. Policy.* Council on Foreign Relations. New York: Random House, 1960.

[37] ———. "Social Implications of the Bolivian Agrarian Reform." Ph.D. dissertation, Cornell University, 1956.

[38] Petras, James. "Book Reviews and Notes." *The American Political Science Review* 64 (1970): 1319-1320.

[39] ———. "Christian Peasant Unions in Chile." *Land Tenure Center Newsletter* (Madison), no. 23 (1966).

[40] ———, and Maurice Zeitlin. "Agrarian Radicalism in Chile." *British Journal of Sociology* 19 (1968): 254-270.

[41] Powell, John D. "The Politics of Agrarian Reform in Venezuela." Ph.D. dissertation, University of Wisconsin, 1966.

[42] ———. "Venezuelan Agrarian Problems in Comparative Perspective." Mimeographed. Cambridge, Mass.: Center for International Studies, 1970.

[43] ———. "Venezuela: The Peasant Union Movement." In *Latin American Peasant Movements.* Edited by Henry A. Landsberger. Ithaca: Cornell University Press, 1969.

[44] *Puro Chile.* "El PDC sabotea reforma agraria y desata plan provocador." Santiago, March 30, 1971.

[45] ———. March 31, 1971.

[46] Rogers, Everett M. *Modernization among Peasants: The Impact of Communication.* New York: Holt, Rinehart and Winston, 1969.

[47] Thiesenhusen, William C. "Grassroots Economic Pressures in Chile: An Enigma for Development Planners." Land Tenure Center Paper, no. 28. Madison: Land Tenure Center, 1966.

[48] White, Robert A. "Mexico: The Zapata Movement and the Revolution." In *Latin American Peasant Movements.* Edited by Henry A. Landsberger. Ithaca: Cornell University Press, 1969.

[49] Whyte, William F. "El mito del campesino pasivo: La dinámica del cambio en el Perú rural." *Estudios Andinos 1,* no. 1 (1970): 2-28.

CHAPTER 10

Colonization: Alternative or Supplement to Agrarian Reform

WILLIAM C. THIESENHUSEN

Associate Professor of Agricultural Economics,
Agricultural Journalism, and the Land Tenure Center
at the University of Wisconsin–Madison

CHAPTER 10

Colonization: Alternative or Supplement to Agrarian Reform

WILLIAM C. THIESENHUSEN

In the United States, the concept of "settlement" is used to describe the westward movement of population across the Appalachians in the 1800s; the participants were searching for new opportunities on the land and were called settlers, immigrants, or pioneers. For a similar phenomenon in Latin America the best Spanish term is colonización. And in many countries the process can be referred to in the present tense. Accompanying high rates of population growth and increased rural-to-urban migration, rural people in Latin America are today moving to other rural areas, especially from the crowded highland plateaus to the tropical lowlands and from some coastal areas to the less populated interior.

As used here, and in keeping with the broader connotation of the Spanish term, colonización will not only mean settlement on virgin or empty lands, often in the public domain, but also establishment of peasants on heretofore idle tracts made arable through investments—such as irrigation works. It also includes token agrarian reforms—ad hoc and occasional establishment of campesinos on haciendas which were either state or privately owned. Colonization encompasses not only government sponsored settlement but that of private institutions, like religious organizations, or of foreign agencies which operate with host-country permission. It includes directed settlement and spontaneous settlement which may later be legitimitized by varying degrees of public aid. Furthermore, it encompasses spontaneous settlement that is government instigated—or at least sanctioned—in its initial stages. [4, pp. 1-2; see also 18] [1]

Spontaneous colonization would probably occur in any country with a frontier. But as population grows, as farming in settled areas becomes more mechanized and enterprise patterns change, increasing numbers of campesinos seek new economic opportunities for themselves and their families. In the absence of agrarian reform, which would make available substantial areas of

[1] We include in our concept of colonization those governmental efforts which provide new opportunities for small numbers of campesinos but do not make available substantial areas of land in presently farmed areas. Also, in order to gain perspective, since detailed studies are scarce, we will at times include comparisons with land reforms which are more than ad hoc efforts of governments to establish campesinos on farms of their own.

land in presently farmed areas, movement to cities or to the frontier may offer the best possibilities.

Government sponsored colonization may be consciously pursued as a policy in the hope that this may divert campesino pressure for agrarian reform. If some peasants can be encouraged to move as pioneers to the tropical jungles (even though the capacity of resources may be poor or at least unknown, and infrastructure may be minimal), there are fewer to exert pressure on the existing social structure in areas dominated by latifundios. Colonization efforts may be widely publicized in an attempt to satisfy demands for land reform that come from various groups within the society, or to comply with international promises to carry out reforms as a precondition for aid.

In fact, colonization rather than land reform more nearly describes the activity undertaken as a result of most (though not all) agrarian reform laws passed in Central and South America in the last decade or so, with the obvious exception of Cuba. Venezuela under Betancourt, agrarian policies which accelerated reform in Chile from 1964 to 1970, and the military-imposed changes in Peru which began in 1969 suggest that the relationship between colonization and reform is a subtle one. It is possible to transform programs which began as colonization into genuine land reforms. In Mexico, agrarian development policies consist of both colonization and reform. Mexico, usually considered to exemplify thoroughgoing reform, has also had a parallel colonization program and "spent a major part of its public investment budget since the 1940s in a massive campaign to expand its cultivated land base. The expenditures went fundamentally into new irrigation works. . . . In the Papaloápan Basin and other parts of Mexico's tropical frontier. . . more than 60,000 families have been resettled. . . . " [4, pp. 11-12]

In most countries it is difficult to separate directed colonization from reform, and the distinction finally made often depends on the political orientation of the observer. One appropriate distinction is scope: successful reform includes a higher percentage of the country's agricultural land and rural labor force. Costs per settler are usually smaller in land reform than in directed colonization. For example, Parsons notes that in land reform, project participants usually live in the same houses and cultivate the same land as before, while in colonization projects the visible changes are normally great. [13] More importantly, land reform usually connotes a drastic change in ownership patterns in the established private sector. On the other hand directed colonization on state lands or on a small number of formerly private farms frequently has little to do with making overall resource or income distribution more egalitarian: only a few settlers benefit.

Yet directed and spontaneous colonization may be important in the Latin American context. A rigid social structure may be made somewhat more flexible if possibilities exist and colonization occurs. And by a systematic study of colonization projects one can learn how they may be improved and even make some extrapolations for a more general reform. Furthermore, colonization may be a useful supplement to an agrarian development policy provided it does not divert too many funds from more basic redistributive reforms.

But some countries have used colonization as a surrogate for agrarian reform: a few showpiece projects may be offered as a substitute for institutional change in the countryside. What travelling official, interested in progress in the rural areas, has not been shown some neat settlement project where a few lucky farmers have tripled or quadrupled their incomes? The peripatetic visitor may take little notice of (a) the exhorbitant per settler cost; (b) the fact that land grantees may have been very carefully selected from among the best workers on a number of haciendas—or may not be campesinos at all, but former hacienda foremen (a number of professional people or businessmen may have received generous plots for one reason or another);[2] (c) a lack of community cohesiveness and sense of self-help because of the heterogeneous backgrounds of the settlers and/or because authority often tends to flow from the top down so that grassroots organization is neither fostered nor encouraged. Since government interest and funds are its lifeblood, the community may well be thrown into complete disarray when another regime takes office, for new governments often do not show the slightest interest toward colonies established under their predecessors. The observation of Wilkening and Iutaka about Brazil probably has fairly general application in Latin America: "With each change of government, colonies established by the previous government tended to be neglected and a new group of colonies was established." [28, p. 5]

Aside from "showcase colonization" one must be aware of another type of project with very limited applicability to wider reforms. Colonizing frontier areas may merely be a very efficient means of exploiting the landless. In some instances land is cleared by squatters, but since no credit is available to those without land title and since access to market is tenuous, they are often forced to abandon their holdings or transfer them to more prosperous neighbors. They clear the land, but benefits are reaped by others who can afford a more long-term investment. And the net result is that colonized areas become latifundios.[24] Taylor reports on another variant of this problem:

A common practice for persons going into livestock farming in [central] Nicaragua . . . is to lease woodland out to landless campesinos. These in turn

2 One study in Chile investigated twelve randomly selected colonies established by the government colonization agency that operated between 1929 and 1962 and found that "a percentage breakdown of owners' former occupations reveals additionally that: 4.6 per cent were professionals; 10.8 per cent had worked for the Caja de Colonización Agrícola; 9.9 per cent had worked for another government agency; 8.4 per cent were engaged in some sort of business; 10.7 per cent had been fundo employees; 16.7 per cent had been engaged in some other form of agriculture (owner of another parcel elsewhere, a fundo owner, or Ingeniero Agrónomo, for example); and 9.9 per cent of the colonists were remember by our informants simply as 'they came from elsewhere,' or 'they had never worked in agriculture,' but were neither inquilinos nor medieros. Ther percentage of parcels reserved for community use was 9.2." p. 175]

clear the forest with axe and machete, plant an annual cultivated crop (usually rice, corn, or beans), and simultaneously with the cultivated crop, pasture, which takes over once the crop has been harvested. The land then rarely reverts to being used for cultivated crops. . . . Once an area has been so converted to pasture, renters and laborers seeking employment in agriculture have to move on to new lands . . . which may also be in the process of preparation for livestock grazing. [19, p. 29]

Within the general concept of colonization in Latin America as used here, several important questions will be discussed:

(1) How may settlement cost be minimized? How, that is, may the largest group be benefitted given limited government funds?

(2) How may a spirit of community be fostered such that when public expenditure ends the community will perpetuate itself as a "going concern?"

(3) What institutional innovations have proved successful in past colonization projects?

(4) What besides land is necessary to make colonization programs successful?

(5) What effects have colonization programs had on such key economic indicators as productivity and employment?

Financing Problems. The distinction between colonization and reform, as noted, is usually somewhat obscure. Yet it is essential that domestic policymakers within Latin American countries distinguish between the two concepts. If they regard the latter as merely a quantitative extension of the former, they are likely to be saddled with such expensive "reform" that it cannot go far in alleviating the pressing needs of the countryside—simply because there aren't enough funds. There is an obvious danger of stifling reform when a country's leaders assume that they can accomplish it by merely continuing colonization on a larger scale. Sometimes this assumption is conscious and has political overtones: elected leaders have no intention of pushing for wider reforms. If scarce public funds are expended on a few settlers, budgetary deficits will soon set an outer limit on the effort, especially under conditions of inflation, which places a squeeze on the purchasing power of the urban middle classes.

Carroll estimates that if land were to be provided for half of the low income families in Latin American rural areas over the next decade, between 600 and 700 thousand families would have to be involved each year. If 90 per cent of them were included in colonization type programs and the remainder in confirmation and legalization of titles, unit costs for the former group would probably be in the $2,000 to $2,500 range while those for the latter group would be in the neighborhood of $1,200. Carroll claims "these figures are based on actual experience with low-cost programmes and represent . . . averages for the region." If these figures are used, "the range of annual total financial requirements for [such programs] . . . is between $1,350 million and $1,550 million." [3, p. 38]

Carroll's settlement figures may be high for an average, but on balance they do not appear too extravagant. A recent U.S. Department of Agriculture publication claims that there have been cases of settler programs in Latin America with a per family cost of between $10,000 and $20,000. [10, p. 58] During the presidency of Betancourt the average cost for each family participating in the Venezuelan reform was about $2,000, while land improvements for those settled on public lands amounted to about $750 per family. In Chile the government reform agency's expenditures for infrastructure (well over half of which was financed with foreign loans) likewise ran about $2,000 per family during the pre-Frei government. [22] One costly item in the Chilean case was redesigning irrigation systems to fit the needs of small family farms. Even when some cooperative labor projects were organized, modifying the irrigation system on one farm to settle seventy-nine households cost nearly $21,000—a per family average of about $265. [5]

On balance, most progress under recent agrarian reform laws falls far short of previously announced plans, and accomplishments resemble colonization more than reform. Under the center-right coalition governing Chile until late 1964, projections called for the establishment of from 10,000 to 12,500 families on their own farms. But in the two years of their "reform" (1963 and 1964) only about 1,100 families were settled. The Instituto de Promoción Agraria (INPROA), a private foundation colonizing Church lands, hoped to settle at least 1,000 families, but funds ran out after about one-fifth of that number were settled. [21] Frei's ambitious projection of 100,000 families in six years was thwarted, and only about 20,000 were settled when he left office. [20, p. 2] In Colombia only about 1,200 families were settled on parcels of expropriated and purchased land between 1961, when the agrarian reform law was passed, and mid-1969, by which time emphasis had shifted almost entirely from parcelization to settlement on the frontier. [6]

The records of such countries as Panama, Nicaragua, and Brazil are even less impressive. In Venezuela oil resources made high settlement costs easier to finance and land of the former dictator and his allies became available for resettlement purposes. The long-term target was to settle 400,000 families in a decade; the short-term goal was 100,000 families by March 1964. Even here, however, projection overshot progress. The short-term goal was not quite reached because of financial stringency during 1963 and a decision to devote more resources to the consolidation of old settlements, rather than to the establishment of new ones. By the end of 1963 some 33,000 families had been settled on land expropriated from private haciendas and another 34,000 had been settled on public land. By 1968 about 96,000 were permanently settled [29, p. 39], although some published sources claim that a larger number actually received parcels. The Inter-American Development Bank reported approximately 115,000 grantees by 1966 [12, p. 381], and in 1968 the government was using a figure of 154,000. These are probably overstatements; at the least they do not make allowance for what appears to have been a high rate of abandonment after settlement.

Politics is certainly responsible for a great deal of the slow progress of reform in Latin America. But reform agencies—if they would use their admittedly limited mandate and budget more imaginatively—could spread the benefits much farther than they have to date by lowering per settler costs. Experience with colonization indicates that expenses can be reduced in a number of ways:

(1) In a fashion similar to the current Chilean situation, private land can be paid for over a longer period. Furthermore, reimbursements to landlords must not be made at market price especially if that land was not being used at its potential capacity.

(2) The colonists' own labor can be used to clear land, dig irrigation ditches, build houses and storage facilities, and lay roads. This method lowers original costs to the parcel holder, means less expense for the government agency, and gives colonists some sense of participation in their own future. If subcontracts for certain skilled labor are to be given, they should be let by the community of colonists and not by the government agency.

(3) Settlement should not initially be made in remote areas, where infrastructure expenses are high, if accessible, and poorly exploited areas can be made available. Frontier areas usually have the additional disadvantage of being located in tropical areas for which little research on the productive capacity and management of the soils exists. The following description for eastern Paraguay gives some perspective on the problem:

Typically, clearing is done by hand. First the trees and underbrush are cut, limbs are lopped off the trees, and the mass of vegetation is allowed to dry. Toward the end of the dry season it is burned, leaving the ground covered with a layer of ash. This adds to fertility and serves to correct the acidity of the forest soil. Consequently, the first two or three crops return a high yield from the accumulated or virgin fertility plus the ash. In addition, immediately after the land is burned over, the soil is in a very friable condition and requires no plowing or other work before planting.

In the second and third year, however, yields decline. Difficulty of operation develops also from the growth of grasses and weeds. These are soon beyond the control of the small settler or squatter, who usually has no implements but a machete and hoe. About the third or fourth year, therefore, he frequently decides that it will be easier to abandon his first clearing and start over by clearing another patch of land. [10, p. 56]

(4) Every effort should be made to cut down on administrative expenses. Carroll calculates the administrative costs in his estimates at 25 per cent of the total budget. [3, p. 40] Brannon has estimated that 80 per cent of the budget of Uruguay's colonization agency goes for administration. [2, p. 38] The land reform agency staff in Chile consisted of 537 persons before the Christian Democrat government took over. Only a small percentage of the staff members in the Chilean reform agency (15 per cent before the Frei term began) were technically trained in agriculture and worked in rural areas with colonists who had been granted land. Considering the few colonists settled (1,100 during the Alessandri Regime), it is difficult to imagine that so many administrators are necessary. Technicians, on the other hand, are probably

needed in greater numbers.

(5) A priority must be given to directly productive capital. Fertilizers and improved seeds are usually priority investments. Colonists can later improve their houses, storage facilities, and irrigation works when they have acquired sufficient capital to do so. Colonists and the general public can be prepared by the government agency for the rather difficult early years on the settlements. Fearful of protests from dissatisfied settlers in their pioneering years, many agencies have erected complete houses and outbuildings, engineered a complete irrigation renovation, and have even planted trees prior to moving the colonists to their new community. Given budgetary stringency, this policy utilizes public funds on a few without benefitting the remainder of the country's farm population.

(6) Alternative forms of post reform organization of the farm firm might also lower per settler cost. If the farm is not divided but farmed cooperatively, irrigation facilities need not be adapted to smaller fields, and fewer fences and fields are needed.

The Difficulties of Establishing a "Going Concern." One measure of the success of colonization projects is how quickly they can progress without government control. This, in turn depends on the expeditious development of a viable internal organization which requires that attention be given to (1) homogeneity of colonists' background; (2) developing the natural leadership capabilities of the colonists; (3) maintaining clear channels of communication between the colony and the colonization agency.

Patch suggests that settlers be family men over twenty-five who have some farming background. When miners and merchants were selected as parcel holders in Bolivia, he reports that they invariably failed. Furthermore, when more affluent nonfarmers are selected, they may simply lease their land to campesinos, who must return as much as 50 per cent of their net profits to the new landowner. Or the landowner may use it as a vacation plot. Or he may use it as his main source of livelihood, performing no physical labor himself but hiring resident farm labor to work it at a smaller salary than that paid by the owners of large haciendas. Such cases hardly alleviate the agricultural problems of the countryside—they merely reproduce, in miniature, the prevailing hacienda structure. [15]

Tinnermeier believes that the settlers' "experience in agriculture" is a crucial factor in colonization efforts. He argues that if inexperienced colonists are selected and if the government makes no effort to train them, their success will be doubtful even though they are provided enough land. [25]

In some cases foreigners from countries with a strong family farm tradition have been selected as land beneficiaries in hopes that they might provide a suitable model. When they are interspersed with native cultivators, however, there is little indication that their techniques actually "trickle down." On an Italian-Chilean colony there is little evidence that practices begun by the Italian families have been adapted by the Chileans living nearby. . . . Chileans who live on the colony seem to have respect for the Italians, . . . but are also convinced that they received better parcels and, because of that, are more successful. [21, p. 192]

In one Venezuelan colony, Canary Islanders were interspersed with native Venezuelans, and a study of this colony showed that "Canary Islanders earn significantly higher incomes on the average than Criollos. Indeed the Canary Islanders' mean net farm income was nearly ten times that of the Criollos. . . ." [23, p. 59] It was concluded that "recent immigrants from abroad have supplied an element of economic vitality to the community. But the kind of entrepreneurship they brought . . . has not, to date [after five years] diffused among the natives in the settlement." [23, p. 68]

Another danger is that the relationship between the more affluent foreigners and the native people may result in exploitation. "Sharecropping in reverse" was a fairly common practice in this same Venezuelan colony. In this dry season arrangement, a parcel holder who has land but neither irrigation pump nor the technical knowledge of profitable vegetable farming (climatologically possible in that season) contracts with someone who does have a pump and skills. The study maintains that

The land-borrowing *isleño* [Canary Islander] usually has the pump, capital, and knowhow, and he contracts with a *criollo* parcel holder to be his sharecropper *(medianero)* on the *criollo's* own land. The *isleño* entrepreneur supplies the inputs, mechanical services, and technical expertise. The *criollo* parcel owner supplies his land and half of the labor. The harvest is then divided 50-50. Unlike the usual *medianeria,* in which the cropper is not the landlord, this arrangement can be canceled whenever the owner of the parcel so desires. One effect of this system is that it teaches the *parcelero* certain farm management practices. While it could be assumed that, when parcel holders have learned the technology of summer farming, this curious tenure arrangement may cease and both parties may be better off for the experience, this had not yet occurred in any of the cases by the end of 1965. Yet, there are elements which make this situation more exploitive than it first appears. The tutelage of the entrepreneur does not extend to teaching the *asentado* how to enter the fruit and vegetable market in Caracas where all truck crop harvest must be sold. Rather, the entrepreneur transports the merchandise (in his truck) and sells it. The *criollo* peasant has no knowledge of the market mechanism and no check on the honesty of the entrepreneur once the marketing procedure is complete. Thus, many *medianero* arrangements are about as old as the settlement itself and there are no signs of termination. Without possibly encompassing a cooperative marketing system, it is doubtful that the nascent "extension" qualities of the relationship will ever mature into economic independence for the parcel holder. [23, pp. 23-24]

Colonies of local people interspersed with immigrants have, at times, been so unsatisfactory that some purely foreign colonies were established. Much has been written about the success of some recent Japanese colonies in Brazil and Bolivia and Mennonite colonies in Bolivia and Paraguay. But however successful, they hardly serve to alleviate the pressing local needs for land and employment in overpopulated rural areas. These successful communities do illustrate, however, that (1) the "colony" form of agricultural organization can be successful and (2) homogeneity of the backgrounds of the settlers, along with strong community cohesiveness, is likely to help make it so.

"Reformed situations" often tend to retain the paternalistic structure so engrained in the Latin Armerican society at large. On colonies founded by the Caja de Colonización Agrícola in Chile, several factors hampered the effectiveness of cooperatives from the very beginning. Little capital was supplied by the Caja. Heterogeneous backgrounds meant members had little in common. Leadership, when it developed at all, was mostly provided by the best educated and wealthiest colonists, who held a patronizing attitude toward their less favored neighbors. These more affluent settlers, frequently absentee operators themselves, often felt little need for a project-wide cooperative organization since they usually had personal access to government and private service agencies and at times had economic interests elsewhere to provide some of their livelihood. Scant attention was given to institution building.

In some cases an able person was promised two parcels if he would come to the colony to act as "manager." But since this request (and favored position) came not from the cooperative but from the Caja, the "manager" often had a rather strained relationship with the cooperative members. In most cases the "manager" regarded his co-op position as a sinecure; his major interest was in farming the land promised him.

Caja co-ops had no control over their own membership; the Caja chose the colonists and passed down the edict that all settlers would belong to the colony's "cooperative." A sense of loyalty to or faith in the cooperative seldom developed.

Cooperatives founded on privately sponsored INPROA colonies in Chile were more effective—colonists were, of course, more homogeneous in background, since settlers were largely former landless laborers. But on several farms the technical person, employed by INPROA early in the history of the project, was regarded as a patrón. On one farm paternalism took a slightly different form, and it was based upon the distribution of three size categories of plots. Conflicts developed between those receiving the largest plots and the others—the more favored colonists considered themselves patrones while those on smaller plots resented these new bosses. [21] (Similar cases have occurred on some CORA colonies. [11; 27]) On another, a campesino was elected to a co-op office and soon came to feel that his special position carried the privilege of avoiding most physical work and limited his activities to supervision. He was voted out of power partly because of the gulf that developed between him and other cooperators.

The problem is exemplified again in Venezuela where the secretary general of one *sindicato* also began to take on the role of a patrón:

He had a great deal of ideological motivation and personal capacity for union and party work, and was a "natural politician" to the extent that he was content with rewards in terms of his status with the peasants and with the delights of power itself. *Campesinos* appear dutifully in his office to ask advice on day-to-day matters—whether he would counsel cutting a tree on their property and what he would recommend for the solution of a neighborhood dispute, for example.

The *sindicato's* charismatic and paternalistic secretary general is supported by the community mostly because of his success in obtaining favors from the governmental agencies concerned with agrarian reform. While a strong and almost dictatorial leader may be useful—even essential—to a *sindicato* in its early stages, it matures as a viable institution only through shared power, developed responsibilities, and member participation. It is this process of "democratization" which has not occurred to any appreciable degree on this *asentamiento*. And the observer is led to the uncomfortable query, "What will happen to the local union if the secretary general achieves a higher political position to which he aspires and of which he is apparently capable?" [23, pp. 9-10]

Perhaps when formerly landless campesinos of fairly homogeneous backgrounds are chosen to occupy parcels, paternalism may develop because this institution serves a useful purpose where there are large numbers of laborers in agriculture seeking employment and relatively few jobs offered. One Brazilian study found that 62 per cent of a project's occupants employed sharecroppers or laborers, and that 40 per cent were absentees. [7] Another study concludes: "The *colono* who becomes an owner may seek others to do his work for him, if he can afford it, in order that he can assume the role of the patrão who does little physical work." [28, p. 7] Claiming that Brazilian society is characterized by the patrón-dependent relationship, this study concludes:

most people expect and depend upon the advice and instructions of someone superior to them in their family, work, or other affairs. This pattern is likely to be retained by the colonists even though they are set up to be independent farmers. [28, p. 7]

It may not be desirable to rid colonies at once of paternalism if it co-exists with the only kind of technical assistance available to the settlements. T. Lynn Smith calls the large settlement of Ceres in Goiás (Brazil) "by far the most noteworthy of all the colonization projects undertaken by the Federal Government." [16, p. 422] Yet its success is usually attributed to the work of one man, which prompts Warriner to conclude, "Such men are rare in all countries, and perhaps the solution of the problems of land settlement lies in their hands." [27, p. 301]

On the other hand, it apparently is possible at least to diminish the influence of paternalism in a social structure. Patch reports on an Aymara community of Pairumani in Bolivia almost a decade and a half after its agrarian reform and cites his experience at a local meeting called to discuss procedure for dealing with a fight which had erupted between two opposing factions of the community at a recent saint's day fiesta. Where previously the people had depended on a patrón to settle such matters, now they could reach a decision on their own. Patch says, "Numbers of persons spoke in turn, all to the point, and the consensus was reduced to a handwritten document. ... It was a healthy sign that we, the outsiders, were not consulted and did not speak." [14, p. 4]

Maintaining Clear Channels of Communication: Institutional Innovation and the Colony. Usually the patron-client relationship—if gradual replacement does not take place—seems ill-suited to the development of each colonist's ability and leads ultimately to dissatisfaction and open dissention. A closely related problem is that the government agencies administering the projects may regard themselves as the patrón, an assumption the campesinos seldom question immediately.

Colonization officials and technicians, often removed from the day-to-day problems of a colony's operation, may have little experience or ability in the elements of social organization and in transmitting the wishes of colonists through a complex bureaucratic structure. This lack of a two-way information flow may inhibit colonist initiative and foster continued campesino dependency on a far-off organization which, as a consequence, finds itself unable to be of real service.

Communications feedback between colonization agencies and campesino organizations must improve. As a government agency becomes more attuned to the necessities of the colony, it has a responsibility to modify some of its policies in accordance with the demands of campesino groups. On the other hand, it would seem as though the reform agency should deny some of these demands because of its obligations and restraints: (a) it has only limited funds; (b) it has obligations and limitations placed upon it by lenders and donors; (c) it has a number of organizations within its program, and demands of one may infringe upon the rights of others; (d) it represents a concentration of technical knowledge which gives staff members professional obligations to reject incorrect technical decisions by peasants while educating them in correct technique. Give-and-take between colonists and the government agency seems to be the essence of a pragmatic approach—one which can settle issues as they arise. In order to assist the cooperatives to develop into bargaining organizations, INPROA in Chile followed policies which:

(a) Allowed the land reform cooperative (in large part) to choose its own landholding members.

(b) Attempted to give all members more or less equal land rights.

(c) Placed on each project a person skilled in cooperative organization and management who worked only through elected campesino leaders.

(d) Split up the reformed fundo into parcels only after a number of years of centralized management during which members were dependent on the cooperative for many of their needs.

This last method is regarded by critics as a mere extension of the patronal system, but in fact it seems a rational step toward training campesinos for becoming entrepreneurs. Besides, in this intermediate period, they come to rely more on the cooperative—an institution which can provide an individual a voice in solving problems he could not cope with alone.

Writing on Colombia, Adams and Herrón suggest the possibility of using some communal work early in the reform period. They observed a club organized among underemployed day laborers near the ready market of Medellín. Members rented a plot on which vegetables could be planted and devoted one day a week to working it under the direction of an extensionist. Their efforts showed a healthy profit at the end of the club's first year (1964) although six of the nineteen dropped out of the project. [1]

Patch recommends that an orientation program be developed together with an adequately equipped reception center. Small groups within the colonies should be encouraged to cooperate in specific enterprises, thus leading to a better understanding of the functions of co-ops. Organizers well trained in sociology should be enticed to the colonies since they will, presumably, be better equipped to break the paternalistic patterns that do tend to develop. [15]

In the final analysis, of course, no local organization of this nature can succeed unless campesinos feel it helps them financially. Tinnermeier asserts that in Caquetá, Colombia, settlers distrust the poorly-organized co-op because they feel prices paid to them for their crops are too low and that prices they pay for consumption goods are higher than in neighborhood stores. [26, p. 41] Better organized co-ops, however, might bargain to obtain inputs more cheaply and sell production advantageously, thus demonstrating basic economic advantages to members.

Is Land Enough? If separate plots of land are distributed, the incomes of recipients will rise, but only a small group of the most innovative usually continue to make steady progress. The remainder often seem to plateau at an income level that is usually higher than formerly, being unable to advance further for lack of decent prices for output, technical knowledge, infrastructure, reasonably priced inputs, credit—sometimes even ambition. Income distribution may well become more skewed than before as some seize quickly upon new opportunities while others lag behind.

Little technical assistance accompanied land distribution on Ruíz Pineda, a colonization project in Venezuela, during the first five years of its existence. When surveyed in 1965,

disposable family income of settlers on Ruíz Pineda was at least 20 percent greater ... than before the reform ... [but] income distribution on the asentamiento is highly skewed. About 90 per cent of the net farm income generated on the asentamiento in 1965—and about 70 per cent of the disposable family income—accrued to the upper 25 per cent of the farmers. The top gross income quartile supplied about 86 per cent of the total marketings ...

The study goes on to explain,

Although in any agricultural community there is a range separating the best from the poorest farmers in terms of productivity and income, the problem on Ruíz Pineda is that this spectrum seems inordinately wide. Indeed, the results of this study seem to imply that with increasing technological progress and market involvement the productivity and income differences between families have become accentuated. On balance, the reform seems to have allowed the most innovative to progress and has increased employment, and probably the savings and investment potential, in the colony as a whole. To date, this project has not been particularly successful, however, in vesting those in the lower half of income receivers with the skills they need for economic advancement. [23, p. 67]

After the "lack of land" constraint has been overcome, other bottlenecks appear that hamper a colonist's progress. What they are will vary with the situation. Even if a government has analyzed the situation and discovers what these bottlenecks are, it will not always have the resources to solve completely the problems immediately even if it has the will. Priorities must be set. This is not to argue against "integral" reforms and colonization projects which embrace credit, extension, fertilizer, hybrid seeds, etc., although this does present the possibility of using integral reform as a euphemistic phrase for what is in fact "showcase colonization." Bureaucratic pressures within administrative agencies often favor the technical perfection of each project; if this view prevails, the distributional aspects of reform may be short changed or even forgotten. Input "packages" may differ from one situation to another. Administering agencies can cut costs by being flexible enough to vary their services accordingly.

The other side of the coin is the possibility that after land distribution little will be done in the second phase—a government may find it difficult to make the necessary shift in policy from land distribution to the establishment of the required service and marketing structures.

Research has pointed out some post land-distribution investment priorities in specific situations. Examining a group of government-directed and spontaneous settlers in the tropical lowlands of Colombia, Tinnermeier places primacy on supplying technical assistance to inexperienced colonists, implying that without it available credit will likely not be used well. He reports that spontaneous settlers received little government help, but because of their past entrepreneurial experience in agriculture (they often owned small plots of land before migrating to the lowlands), they were more successful than directed colonists. Although directed colonists were supposed to receive assistance from government technicians, it was largely ineffective. Extension workers knew little about general agriculture and less about tropical farming. There appeared to be no significant difference between government-directed and spontaneous settlement in terms of education, level of living, adoption of new practices, attitudes, labor efficiency, or material possessions. The government-directed settlers, however, had better access to credit, to the extension service, and to new agricultural techniques. Yet when compared to spontaneous settlers, these colonists had less livestock, sold less on the market, were less satisfied with their lot, and received less income.

Tinnermeier implies that once a colonist has possession of a reasonably sized farm, his knowledge of how to cope with the exigencies of farming becomes crucial. [26] And as Hill, Silva, and Hill have asserted, the limiting factor is often not the size of the unit, but the technical knowledge of cultivation and the lack of facilities for working the land. [9] T. Lynn Smith feels that the task of land distribution is "merely child's play in comparison with the one of developing the necessary managerial skills on the part of families whose only roles previously have been the limited ones of the agricultural laborer." [17, p. 11]

Management knowledge was likewise found to severely hamper development in Coto Brus, a trackless valley in Costa Rica in which an estimated 1,500 to 2,000 families live. [8] But farm-to-market roads were another major problem. Originally to be favored by the Pan-American Highway, which was to run through its heartland, plans were changed and the Carretera Pan-Americana bypasses the region entirely, so that it is still completely cut off from the rest of the country during the long rainy season. Largely because the zone lacks farm-to-market roads, its economy has remained relatively self-contained. Coffee, grown largely by Italian colonists, is the region's only link to the national market.

Costa Rican owner-operators in the zone have farms averaging about 61.2 hectares while those of squatters on state-owned land (ocupantes) average 34.8 hectares. But they cultivate only an average of 4.3 and 4.0 hectares of their farms, respectively. Italian colonists (whose farms average 30.5 hectares) cultivate about two and one-half times as much land as the ocupantes. Squatters on private lands in the area (called parásitos) claim an average 12.8 hectares and work only 2.4 hectares.

The Italian colonists who were favored by some early help in terms of capital from their government, now gross about twenty-eight times as much as parásitos and outproduce by almost three times their nearest competitors, the Costa Rican owners. Costa Rican proprietors, in turn, achieve a production about twice that of the average ocupante. Capital owned by the four tenure groups is positively correlated with production figures.

After paying only out-of-pocket operating expenses, the average Costa Rican owner and ocupante each came out with peon's wages, notwithstanding the risk and effort they went through to operate a farm. The Italian settler earned artisan's wages, nearly three times that of Costa Rican proprietors and occupants, while parásitos' wages are below those of peons.

The study concludes that in addition to improved farm-to-market roads, technical guidance is necessary to instill management principles. At least a modest supervised credit program based on five-year loans should be established since many come to the area with little or no operating capital, a prime limiting factor in the zone. This would allow a higher per cent of land on each farm to be brought into production.

Production and Employment Indicators. Production usually tends to rise after a colonization project is established, often because the land was all but idle previously. Likewise, more jobs per unit of land become available. Of course both of these favorable indicators may belie prohibitive costs. Few cost-benefit studies are available. When they are made, they are very arbitrary as to discount rates and the number of years over which initial investment is amortized. And subsidies are frequently not adequately specified.

It was quite obvious that with little investment, total production on four Church-land farms studied in Chile was greater after reform. Even so, by comparing per hectare production on each farm with production on a well-managed neighboring fundo with similar soil conditions and water availability, production on each—with the possible exception of one—was substantially lower than potential. And even in the exceptional case, where great reliance was placed on accumulated fertility of the soil, production may not remain high. This means that many colonists will not be able to pay their debts—land payments to the Church via INPROA and necessary capital. More intensive farming seems to be the most obvious remedy for production below potential. In order to raise productivity per hectare, more yield increasing inputs will have to be applied and the farms will have to be better managed. [21]

But more people were employed on the same land base after than before the reform.

In addition to supporting campesinos with a better standard of living than formerly, reform makes it possible for the fundos to support more families. When the reform on the four Church-land fundos studied [in Chile] has settled all families now planned for, the farms will be supporting 182 families or 23 per cent more than the number of families that lived there prior to the reform. [21, p. 202]

Likewise, production increases are often quite marked, as exemplified by a project in Venezuela.

Agricultural production on the land area now encompassed by the *asentamiento*—and marketings—rose substantially after reform. Considering double-cropping of irrigated land, nearly 90 per cent of the land is now farmed, compared with only 20 per cent prior to reform. [23, p. 67]

In the Chilean colonization program (Caja de Colonización Agrícola) 4,206 colonists were settled from 1929 to 1962. Of 544 colonists in the original universe studied, only 82 were former landless laborers. A study of thirty individual farms belonging to former landless workers revealed that land itself was not sufficient to bring about great production increases, although all families living on their own land—or relatives living with original owners—earned about three times the net income of the average resident farm laborer or sharecropper in Chile.

On the average, half of each farm was planted to annual crops and the other half was left to pasture which supported only a few animals. Improved pasture was found only on two parcels. Neither water for irrigation, the market system, nor input prices seemed to be the major bottlenecks accounting for the limited seeding of annual crops. Most colonists used either an inadequate amount of fertilizer or none at all.

While the tendency toward extensive land use (and frequently the hiring of labor which appears to be excessive) on the part of the colonists seems irrational, it probably is not in the institutional framework in which the peasant finds himself. For example, little or no credit was available to the colonists; few knew how to use productively the little that was available. The peasants had little or no management experience prior to receiving their parcels and little technical advice was offered from the government agency.

By law, title to parcels can be held only by the owner: in case of his death the heirs as a group may receive legal ownership. But even before the owner's death, de facto division of the farm is common. Only five of the thirty farms studied intensively were still supporting only the original family. The other twenty-five parcels, originally assigned to as many families, were supporting ninety-nine families who earned the major part of their income there. Twelve of these farms were physically divided. It is on parcels which have been colonized for the longest time that family income is usually smallest since, as the farm owners' children married, more and more people settled there. As this happens, profits are subdivided further. [21, p. 202]

Establishing a few isolated colonies does not spell economic success over the long run. If there is continued lack of dynamism in the economy, grown sons and heirs are either forced to remain on the parcel, thus dividing income among more and more families (and making the farm a haven for grown children and other relatives who cannot find work elsewhere), or they must leave for other areas where productive jobs are also in short supply.

References

[1]   Adams, Dale W., and Antonio Herrón O. "Como alcanzar nivel de proprietarios mediante esfuerzos cooperativos." Mimeografiado, no. 15. Bogotá: Centro Interamericano de Reforma Agraria, 1965.

[2]   Brannon, Russell H. "Agricultural Development and Policy in Uruguay." In *Latin American Agricultural Development and Policy,* edited by Lehman B. Fletcher and William C. Merrill. International Studies and Economics Mono. 8. Ames, Iowa: Iowa State University, 1968.

[3]   Carroll, Thomas F. "Issues of Financing Agrarian Reform: The Latin American Experience." Paper prepared for the World Land Reform Conference. WLR/66/5. Rome, Italy: United Nations, 1966.

[4]   Domike, Arthur L. *Colonization as an Alternative to Land Reform.* SR/LR/A-6. Washington, D.C.: Agency for International Development, 1970.

[5]   Dorner, Peter and William C. Thiesenhusen. "Relevant Research Programs to be Conducted in Developing Countries." *Journal Of Farm Economics* 46 (1964): 1095-1105.

[6] Felstehausen, Herman. "Agrarian Reform: Colombia." Chapter 8 of this book.

[7] Galjart, Benno. "Turnover of Farmers in a Land Settlement Scheme in Brazil." *América Latina* 8 (1965): 3-24.

[8] Hill, George W.; Manuel Gollas Quintero; Gregorio Alfaro. "Un área rural en desarrollo: sus problemas económicos y sociales–Costa Rica." San José, Costa Rica: Instituto Univerisitario Centroamericano de Investigaciones Sociales y Económicas, 1964.

[9] –––; Jose A. Silva; and Ruth O. Hill. *Vida rural en Venezuela.* Caracas: Ministerio de Sanidad y Asistencia, 1960.

[10] Hopkins, John. *The Latin American Farmer.* ERS–Foreign 257. Washington, D.C.: Department of Agriculture, 1969.

[11] Imable, Rogelio. "Asentamientos de Choapa: Cambios en la tenencia de la tierra y en los ingresos de los campesinos." *Economía* 25 (1967): 3-13.

[12] Inter-American Development Bank. *Socio-Economic Progress in Latin America.* Sixth Annual Report of the Social Progress Trust Fund, 1966.

[13] Parsons, Kenneth. "Research Evaluation of Land Reform and Land Settlement Programs." Paper No. 4, Development Center on Land Policy and Settlement for the Near East. Tripoli: Food and Agricultural Organization, 1965.

[14] Patch, Richard W. *Change on the Altiplano.* American Universities Field Staff Reports, West Coast South American Series 13. RWP-1-'66. New York, 1966.

[15] –––."Estudios de colonización en Bolivia." La Paz, 1962.

[16] Smith, T. Lynn. *Brazil, Peoples and Institutions.* Baton Rouge: Louisiana State University Press, 1963, rev. ed.

[17] –––, ed. *Agrarian Reform in Latin America.* New York: Alfred A. Knopf, 1965.

[18] –––. "Studies of Colonization and Settlement." *Latin American Research Review* 4 (1969): 93-123.

[19] Taylor, James Robert, Jr. *Agricultural Settlement and Development in Eastern Nicaragua.* Land Tenure Research Paper, no. 33. Madison, Wisconsin: Land Tenure Center, 1969.

[20] Thiesenhusen, William C. "Agrarian Reform: Chile." Chapter 6 of this book.

[21] –––. *Chile's Experiments in Agrarian Reform.* Madison, Wisconsin: University of Wisconsin Press, 1966.

[22] –––. "Latin American Land Reform: Enemies of Progress." *The Nation* 202 (1966): 90-94.

[23] –––; Ricardo Alezones; Ramon Pugh; and John Mathiason. *"Leonardo Ruíz Pineda: A Case Study of a Venezuelan Agrarian Reform Settlement."* Research Paper no. 7. Washington, D.C.: Inter-American Committee for Agricultural Development, 1968.

[24] Thome, Joseph R. "Title Problems in Rural Areas of Colombia: A Colonization Example." Mimeografiado no. 3. Bogotá: Centro Interamericano de Reforma Agraria, 1965.

[25] Tinnermeier, Ronald L. "New Land Settlement in the Eastern Lowlands of Colombia." Ph.D. dissertation, University of Wisconsin, 1964.

[26] –––. *New Land Settlement in the Eastern Lowlands of Colombia.* Land Tenure Paper no. 13. Madison, Wisconsin: Land Tenure Center, 1964.

[27] Warriner, Doreen. *Land Reform in Principle and Practice.* Oxford: Clarendon Press, 1969.

[28] Wilkening, Eugene A. and Sugiyama Iutaka. *Sociological Aspects of Colonization as Viewed from Brazil.* Land Tenure Paper no. 37. Madison, Wisconsin: Land Tenure Center, 1967.

[29] Wing, Harry E., Jr. *Land Reform in Venezuela.* SR/LR/C-3. Washington, D.C.: Agency for International Development, 1970.

CHAPTER 11

Improving Land Tenure Security

JOSEPH R. THOME

Professor of Law and the Land Tenure Center
at the University of Wisconsin–Madison

CHAPTER 11

Improving Land Tenure Security

JOSEPH R. THOME

The number of Latin American rural land holdings operated without a secure title of ownership runs into the hundreds of thousands, most of them in the small to medium size category. [4, pp. 162-163] The Chilean Ministry of Lands and Colonization, for instance, estimated that in 1967 approximately 150,000 small farms in Chile were operated without benefit of legal title. [7, p. 2] In Colombia, census data indicate that over 2 million hectares—8.6 per cent of all agricultural land—are occupied without any title. [3, p. 68] Approximately 65,000 farm parcels in Costa Rica do not have full legal titles. [13, p. 1] In the Dominican Republic, approximately 50 per cent of all land has yet to be registered under the Torrens system of title registration instituted there in 1920. [5, p. 41] And in Bolivia, thousands of peasant families are still waiting for clear titles to the land distributed to them under the post-1952 agrarian reform program. [14] Even in Mexico, the nation with the oldest agrarian reform process in Latin America, thousands of small farmers still have no tenure security. [10]

Nature and Dimension of Tenure Insecurity. Many small farms in Latin America operate near the subsistence level, with little surplus for sale to the market. As population grows at annual rates of around 3 per cent, peasants are increasingly migrating to the large cities, resulting in the transfer of rural underemployment to the urban areas, in the growth of slums, and in other familiar urban ills. [15]

Land reform—the distribution of large holdings among landless campesinos—is one measure for attacking these problems, but small land-holders and settlers already living in frontier areas should not be forgotten. This group too needs opportunities and incentives to change from subsistence to commercial farming, to increase their incomes, and to avoid fruitless migration.

An important incentive that can be provided to the small holder is tenure security, whether this particular tenure arrangement be individual holdings or some type of cooperative-collective farms. The lack of secure rights on the land is often a disincentive to increased production. In many countries, one reason why a small farmer finds it almost impossible to obtain institutional credit is his lack of collateral in the form of a valid land title.

Rights to the use of water are likewise often contingent on the possession of ownership documents. Moreover, a farmer without title may face eviction litigation, and may find it difficult to sell or otherwise transfer his property in the open market. The public sector too is economically affected by title insecurity, since it is very difficult to devise and enforce an effective system of land taxation under such conditions.

Tenure insecurity can also produce serious social repercussions—disputes and conflicts over land ownership and possession—which will in turn affect agricultural production. [2] Discord arises not only between squatters or homesteaders and the large landowners who claim legal ownership and try to evict the squatters, but also between the squatters themselves, or among other homogeneous communities and family groups. Disputes may involve competing claims to the lands of deceased peasants, or boundary conflicts between neighbors or between communities in the case of communally owned lands. Not only do such conflicts often disrupt the cohesiveness of a rural community, making cooperative ventures difficult, but they also take an inordinate amount of the affected peasants' time and limited financial resources, particularly when civil litigation of some kind occurs. Lawsuits in Latin America are usually slow and expensive, and unethical lawyers have been known to take advantage of peasants involved in such conflicts, exacting fees and retainers that may extend over several months and even years.

Tenure insecurity can result from a variety of factors ranging from traditional laws and practices to recent migratory movements. In many countries, part of the problem traces to the practice by the Spanish Crown—and after independence by national governments—of granting indeterminate and often overlapping titles to huge tracts of public land. Even when there was no question about the validity of these grants, the custom of describing boundaries by natural landmarks or by the names of adjoining farms made it very difficult in later years to fix accurately the boundaries of the lands involved. Frequently this problem was further complicated by conflicting and unrealistic land laws, and by judicial interpretations which not only made it difficult to prove the validity of titles but also failed to establish clear criteria for distinguishing public domain land from privately owned property. [8, p. 102; see also 12, p. 273]

In Colombia, for example, the combination of this legal heritage with more modern but poorly implemented procedures for granting titles to public domain lands has until recently failed to provide adequate institutional responses to the colonization movements into frontier areas or to invasions by impoverished campesinos. Such spontaneous actions

in a sense represent a sort of 'popular' land reform, carried out by an unfavored sector of society too impatient to wait for government projects or too dubious of their reach and effect. Usually only affecting public domain lands, these colonizations should not have created any conflicts with landowners. But sometimes the same lands had already been claimed as private property by other individuals, either through questionable titles or illicit extensions of their legally owned properties. In other cases, *colonos* have entered into idle and uncleared lands they thought to be in the public domain, but which were in effect privately owned property. At times, property known to be privately owned has been purposely invaded. As a consequence, serious title conflicts have developed involving the *colonos,* owners, supposed owners and the state: conflicts which in the past have often degenerated into physical fighting and created serious social and political problems for Colombia. [17, pp. 83-84]

Most countries in Latin America have long had legal procedures under which occupants on public lands can acquire full title to their lands. But as in the case of Costa Rica,

complicated legal requirements and high costs, however, have effectively denied most small and medium farmers the opportunity to title their lands through these procedures. The Ley de Informaciones Posesorias of 1941 epitomizes these procedures, which have primarily benefitted speculators and large landowners, who purchase the small farmer's 'right to title'. [13, p. 2]

Even rural areas settled during the earliest days of Spanish colonization are still plagued with tenure insecurity because implementation of laws and procedures regulating sale and registration of property, as well as inheritance transfers suffer from substantive legal defects, are poorly administered, expensive, and time consuming. Consequently, rural lands are often transferred through private agreements which are never recorded, and inherited properties are kept in the name of a deceased ancestor though they may have been subdivided several times. The formal legal system is abandoned in favor of informal or customary procedures, making the substantiation of property rights virtually impossible. [1]

Some countries experience tenure insecurity *as a result of* agrarian reform. In Bolivia, the rate of land redistribution to reform beneficiaries exceeded the capacity of the reform agency to legalize the new tenure patterns by distributing titles reflecting the new boundaries. As a result, many campesinos legally entitled to receive titles from the government

have grown weary of waiting, and have purchased 'titles' from their former landowners, who unscrupulously exploit their ignorance. These 'titles' have no legal validity whatsoever, and only serve to further complicate an already indefinite title situation, particularly as these transactions may result in the abandonment of their agrarian reform cases by the campesinos, who no longer feel the need for proceeding through the Agrarian Reform Agency.

Moreover, many changes take place during the nine or ten years that the proceedings last. Campesinos with rights over the land die, or abandon their holdings, and others without any legal rights take their place. As the families increase, the holdings are subdivided, or lands which legally pertain to the former landowner are occupied or invaded. And when the final legal determination is finally reached, it may have absolutely no relevance to the conditions now existing in the property, and more often than not, it will be impossible to enforce. [14, pp. 10-11]

The major cause of this confusion (now substantially modified with the introduction in 1968 of new titling methods) was the extremely legalistic, complicated, and bureaucratic procedure established both by law and practice for expropriating and distributing lands in the Bolivian reform. This quasi-judicial process was even more complex than the regular eminent domain procedures used for condemning lands needed for public uses such as roads and schools. Its only saving grace was that the most important stage—distributing lands to the campesinos under a temporary legal right—was achieved fairly rapidly. Thereafter, the number of required hearings, appeals, visual inspections, and presidential interventions afforded the process Kafkian proportions. In total, twenty-nine different steps had to be completed from the initial decision to expropriate to the final distribution of a registered title. These include five different hearings, all at different levels, at which new evidence could be introduced and the case remanded to lower administrative officers for further clarification. As of 1966, even the President of the Republic was involved in the process; he had to sign every expropriation decree as well as every single title distributed under the agrarian reform. Inadequate budgets further aggravated the problem. [14, pp. 59-66]

A very slow process of title distribution is also evident in the Dominican Republic. From 1962 through 1967, 24,214 hectares were distributed among 6,700 families by the Instituto Agrario Dominicano (IAD). Yet only 108 families received titles; the rest had only certificates of provisional assignment, which provide few if any substantive rights. Apparently, IAD has consciously decided to postpone the distribution of titles as long as possible, feeling that many of the benefitted settlers will prove unable or unwilling to meet the conditions and payments with which title recipients must comply. Furthermore, approximately 50 per cent of the land distributed by IAD did not at that time have the registered titles required by Dominican law. Accordingly, IAD cannot issue new titles for those lands until the necessary "quiet-title" actions are completed at the land courts. [5, pp. 36-37]

Unfortunately, there are only sixteen land judges for the entire nation and they are overburdened with work. The required cadastral surveys are slow and costly, and apparently constitute one of the main bottlenecks in the title registration process. Campesinos are frequently exploited by lawyers who may charge up to 20 or 30 per cent of the value of the land for their services, and sometimes exact fees for each appearance before the court while extending cases as long as possible. [5, pp. 13, 42]

Legal problems relating to tenure or title insecurity are not new; they date to the emergence of legal systems in which some sort of private property rights were recognized. In response, substantive and procedural rights, remedies, and processes began to emerge. Many of the present legal rights and actions concerning property ownership and tenure can be traced to Roman law, to the decrees and regulations issued by the Spanish Council of Indies regarding the colonization of the Americas, and to the very influential Napoleonic Code of 1804.

Latin America has long had some legal mechanisms through which an interested party could protect his property rights. These include notarial and registry systems, eviction or possessory actions against trespassers, and the like. At the same time, in order to encourage the settlement and cultivation of unoccupied lands, most legal systems of Latin America have provided certain rights to settlers or squatters on either public or private lands.

Under most legislation, for example, a legal eviction requires a judicial proceeding in which the claimant owner must prove his title and compensate the squatter for any improvements made on the land. Moreover, the owner or title holder must bring the eviction action within a specified number of years from the date of the initial squatting or lose his right through prescription. Since colonial times settlers could obtain titles to public domain lands they occupied, provided they lived on the land for a specified number of years and met other conditions stipulated in the various laws. [16, p. 3; 6, pp. 18-19]

The exercise of legal rights, however, has traditionally been left to the intiative of the interested party. He must take the trouble and expense to register the necessary documents, to initiate and carry through the relevant proceedings, and to compile evidentiary proofs (such as maps) before an administrative agency or a civil court. While this process may be satisfactory for those with the means to undertake the necessary actions, for campesinos or settlers these theoretical legal rights and actions often have little practical value.

Obtaining a secure title through prescription or adverse possession, for example, usually requires civil litigation, but few squatters have knowledge of their legal rights, most cannot afford the expenses involved, and many are simply too far away from the nearest court.

Even settlers or homesteaders on public lands must incur relatively large expenses to obtain their titles. Not understanding the procedure involved, they are often exploited by private tituladores, who charge a high fee for undertaking the transactions involved and at times pocket the money without supplying any services.

In Costa Rica, for instance, the applicable legislation from 1941 to 1967 for obtaining title to public domain lands required the claimant to file before a regular civil court. He had to show ten years of possession either by presenting notarized documents of ownership, or by bringing four witnesses from his neighborhood to testify to his length of possession. He also had to exhibit additional documentary evidence and meet other procedural require-ments, as is usual in most judicial actions. The result was a long and very expensive process, particularly for small farmers in remote areas. The average cost ranged from 20 to 100 colones (3 to 16 U.S. dollars) per hectare, depending on the parcel's size and distance from the capital. [13]

In many parts of Latin America, small farmers settling in frontier areas often do not bother to obtain a legal title to the lands they occupy. At times, latifundios can emerge on the frontier, even though the objective of most adverse-possession and titling-of-public-lands legislation is to strengthen the position of small holders. In the Llanos Orientales of Colombia, for example

a minifundia-latifundia pattern appears to be developing in the colonization areas. Due to the almost insuperable hardships they face, *colonos* often have to abandon their holdings, or sell them to a more prosperous neighbor, after only a few years of exploitation. They clear the land, but the benefits are reaped by those who can afford a long term investment. Many of the larger holdings in the Llanos have been formed through this process. [17; see also 6]

Obviously the mere existence of legal remedies is not sufficient. The conflicts and problems arising from tenure insecurity will continue unless all parties concerned have real access to judicial and administrative proceedings where such remedies will be fairly and efficiently enforced. Yet most Latin American campesinos cannot assert their legal rights individually, and they have traditionally lacked strong rural organizations which might through collective action provide the necessary support. They require the assistance of public entities for securing their legal rights.

Some Recent Efforts at Improving Land Tenure Security. Aware of these problems, several Latin American countries have in recent years adopted new legislation and services which try to simplify the legal procedures for titling smallholders' parcels, particularly those on the public lands.

The Costa Rican Ley de Informaciones Posesorias Administrativas of 1967 permitted small- and medium-sized farmers whose claims did not exceed 50 hectares to title public domain lands through a relatively informal procedure administered by the Instituto de Tierras y Colonización (ITCO). Unlike the 1941 statute, the 1967 administrative procedure did not require the settlers to show "good faith" through documentary evidence of ownership or possession; the necessary ten year possession by the claimants or their predecessors could now be proved through the written and notarized testimony of three witnesses. Other procedural requirements, however, remained unchanged. An applicant still had to present a survey map, a certification that he had not received other titles to public lands, and a certification that all lands taxes on the land had been paid. Moreover, the new procedure applied only to those settlers whose possessory acts or claims commenced before 1961, as the Ley de Tierras y Colonización of 1961 made illegal any possessory claims occurring in the national reserves subsequent to its enactment. (This 1961 legislation attempted to control the spontaneous colonization of public lands, and to reserve the remaining national lands for planned colonization programs administered by ITCO). [13, pp. 31-32, 42-43]

This new titling procedure produced no dramatic improvements. Costs to the settlers remained high, although ITCO in several instances provided financial assistance to small farmers lacking the necessary resources. Though much faster than the old process, the new measures did not prove as expeditious as they were supposed to be—the titles issued during this period had an average processing time of six months. Furthermore, the 1967 legislation benefitted only a small number of settlers; from 1967 through 1969, only 100 titling cases were filed by small- and medium-sized farmers.

Of these, only thirty-one received a final adjudication; moreover, the recording of the new title was left to the farmer's initiative, and many of these thirty-one failed to register their new title in the National Registry of Property Titles. [13]

Still, ITCO officials were at least able to limit the process to bona fide small farmers, and better records and administrative practices minimized the opportunities for evading the law. The six months' processing time for new titles was certainly an improvement over the average duration of four years under the old system. [13, pp. 38, 44-45][1]

In Colombia, Agrarian Reform Law No. 135 of 1961 created a new land reform agency—Instituto Colombiano de Reforma Agraria (INCORA)—and assigned to it the functions, among others, of clarifying the ownership of lands and facilitating the clearing of title defects. Law 135 delegated to INCORA the powers to administer public domain lands and to apply the unimplemented reversion of title provisions of Law 200 of 1936. Law 135 also stipulated new procedures for implementing these powers.[2]

While INCORA has made little progress in implementing its other agrarian reform powers—that is, expropriating privately owned rural properties in the populated areas of the country for their subsequent redistribution to landless peasants—it has nevertheless acted vigorously in the frontier areas, where many of Colombia's tenure insecurity problems exist. It has applied reversion of title actions and so obtained for the public domain over 2 million hectares formerly claimed as private property. As of July 1, 1969, INCORA had issued approximately 88,000 titles—many of them to squatters—covering some 2,800,000 hectares of public domain lands. [6]

Increased activity in the adjudication of public domain lands can probably be attributed to INCORA's efforts at improving titling procedures, particularly by bringing legal services to the settlers, rather than requiring them to seek such services in distant towns. Over thirty INCORA "title teams," each composed of a lawyer, topographer, and other personnel, have been stationed in areas of large scale colonization to provide free services to those settlers claiming less than 200 hectares. These teams perform all the technical tasks, such as surveying the land and drawing up the necessary documents. The small settler has merely to present a simple petition for adjudication, though he must still pay the costs of notarizing and recording his new title. From time to time INCORA has also contracted the services of private lawyers to undertake the necessary transactions in areas not covered

[1] Both the 1941 and 1967 statutes were replaced by the Ley de Informaciones Posesorias of 1970, under which all titling claims to public lands can now be made through a single administrative proceeding similar to the 1967 one. Mostly the new law follows prior patterns, yet some provisions were added to ease the burden of proving possession. [13, pp. 46-50] It is impossible at this time to judge its effectiveness though it seems to represent some progress.

[2] Article 6 of Law 200 gave the government the power to initiate proceedings under which all land not economically exploited for a continuous period of ten years would revert to the state, with *no* compensation being paid to the former landowners.

by the title teams. [6; 17]

While the services of INCORA do not yet meet the needs of all small settlers on public or potentially public land, and while the efficiency of some title teams is not optimal, the INCORA programs nevertheless constitute a distinct improvement over the titling procedures existing before 1961. Those old procedures are basically still in effect for settlers with claims exceeding the minimum sizes established by INCORA. [6]

Still neglected, however, or taken care of only sporadically, are those title conflicts occurring in regions where official INCORA projects or public domain lands are not involved, even though these problems affect thousands of small farmers. Most of these disputes concern properties over which one of the affected parties has a rightful claim but for which the legal situation is extremely confused due to factors already described. INCORA is aware of this situation and in 1965 it established a new department—the División de la Tenencia de la Tierra (Land Tenure Division), which is supposed to solve these title conflicts

by methodically investigating in areas of the country *not* falling within specific land reform projects, the legal aspects of the tenure and exploitation of the land in order to obtain the proper application of those laws which regulate the relations between occupiers, possessors, owners, and holders in the respective zones. [9, author's translation]

This division, however, has never been fully staffed or financed and has intervened in only a very few title conflicts, generally in response to complaints from small settlers or rural organizations.

INCORA, then, has recognized the seriousness of tenure insecurity in Colombia and has started comprehensive programs to resolve these difficulties. But the problems involved are very complex and many obstacles must still be removed before INCORA can achieve its goals. Some of these obstacles can be eliminated through more energetic action on the part of INCORA itself, such as providing more personnel and better financing to the proper divisions. Since the influx of settlers into frontier areas can be traced largely to the scarcity of land and opportunities in the more populated rural areas of the country, these migrations would be smaller and more manageable if INCORA were committed to an active program of expropriation and redistribution in the populated areas. But as Felstehausen and others have amply documented, the number of new titled parcels created through expropriation remains insignificant. [6]

Other problems exist over which INCORA has limited or no control—a lack of cadastral survey; inadequate law enforcement and judicial administration; inefficient probate, notarial, and registry procedures; and unethical practices by lawyers or those acting as lawyers. [17]

Efforts to improve slow and cumbersome title distribution procedures have also been made in Bolivia. Early in 1968, its agrarian reform agency initiated a program to simplify titling procedures by better selection and training of technical personnel, the use of computer data processing techniques, and the fielding of mobile agrarian title teams to resolve legal problems at the site of the controversy. These and other new techniques have markedly improved the rate of titling in recent years. In 1968 and 1969, some 117,000 new titles were processed for about 1,000,000 hectares and 58,000 families. This rate of titling is approximately double that of the pre-1968 period. [11]

Much of the improvement can be credited to the use of the mobile title teams, which consist of an agrarian judge, a secretary, topographers, and an inspector. These teams travel to the areas where title problems are more serious and resolve most problems and disputes at their source. Previously, campesinos either had to make long and costly trips to the provincial capitals—or even to La Paz—or had to pay the travel expenses of agrarian judges and other personnel.

There are still too few of these mobile teams and they cannot physically cover all parts of Bolivia in which title problems are common. Moreover, the Bolivian agrarian reform agency still suffers from inadequate financing and a lack of trained personnel. But at least the title insecurity problem has become a more manageable one. In fact, it has been estimated that with a few additional title teams, the legal phase of the agrarian reform process in Bolivia could be terminated by 1975. [11, p. 1]

In Chile, the Department of Titles of the Ministry of Lands and Colonization has for many years been entrusted with clearing up title defects on the thousands of small farms on which such tenure insecurity exists. For these purposes, a legal mechanism was created by Decreto con Fuerza de Ley (DFL) No. 6 of 1968, which established a simplified administrative procedure to accelerate the titling process by providing the Department with the necessary ex officio powers to act on its own initiative. Nevertheless, in 1968 the Department was able to secure title rights for only 300 farms—a miniscule proportion of the approximately 150,000 farms with insecure titles. [7] This is largely due to inadequate funding from the government which prevents the Department from obtaining the needed technical staff and equipment. The Title Department had only twenty-one lawyers, four administrative employees, and one vehicle to handle the title insecurity problems for the entire nation. [7, pp. 9-10]

The problem in Chile, however, is not as serious as it is in many other countries. Although the number of farms without legal title is large, there are few title conflicts because in many cases possession rights on these holdings have been established for several generations, and present claims are recognized by neighbors and authorities. Moreover, during the past decade a modern land survey using photogrammetric techniques has been carried out in Chile; identification of boundaries is consequently no longer a major problem.

Conclusions

Unfortunately very few data exist in Latin America on the relationship between tenure security and levels of farm investment and production. The few empirical studies on the subject suggest a positive correlation "between increasing levels of tenure security and increasing degrees of farm performance measured in terms of investment and gross income." [13, p. 22] Field studies in two rural areas of Costa Rica, one settled in the early 1900s and the other between 1940 and 1960, show that the "presence of tenure security, particularly a full title to land, substantially accounts for higher farm performance" and that "among all the different factors which provide a positive influence to increased agricultural performance, evidence shows that full, legal title to the land is one of the most important, if not the most important." [13, pp. 22-23] The conclusion held particularly true for the more recently settled areas, provided, however, that a rudimentary infrastructure—particularly roads and credit facilities—was also present.

It seems evident that many peasants in Latin America, whether for economic, social or psychological reasons, or because of their past experiences with large landowners, their neighbors, or the legal apparatus, actively seek to obtain some sort of security on the lands they hold. As noted, some of the still untitled beneficiaries of the Bolivian reform have resorted to purchasing titles from former landlords, though these titles have no legal validity, while others have increasingly relied on customary practices to define and enforce their rights to land. [2] Similarly, in Colombia the inefficiency or inaccessability of the formal institutional mechanisms has led to the development of informal or customary procedures for transferring properties. However, letters of sale, selling of possession rights, private inheritance subdivisions, and other such methods have value only insofar as the parties act in good faith. "The anomalous ownership in these cases can result in legal, economic and social conflicts after the original contractors are no longer available for consultation." [1, p. 164]

Obviously, efficient and flexible legal mechanisms and institutions are needed to clear title defects, transfer ownership rights, and determine the tenure rights of settlers on public domain lands or in agrarian reform programs. Whenever possible, such services should be administered ex officio by administrative government agencies, particularly as regards small holders. Relying on adversary proceedings before either a court or an administrative agency, as has been traditional, limits their use to those of certain economic means. Services should be made more readily accessible to the affected campesinos, preferably through use of mobile units as in Colombia and Bolivia. These units could provide all the technical and legal services required, including representation before the courts and property registries.

Notarial, registry, and cadastral services, which legally regulate and control most private property transactions and will likely continue to do so, especially in the more populated areas, are in need of substantive and procedural reforms. Most notarial functions, for example, could probably be eliminated altogether without reducing the legal security of property transactions. Cadastral (surveying) practices still depend too much on ancient chain and stick techniques. In certain cases, the necessary surveying could be achieved by faster and sometimes cheaper aerial-photogrammetric techniques, as has been done in Chile. More efficient administrative practices, better trained personnel, and the use of new devices, such as computers, could yield dramatic improvements in registry systems. Some authors suggest it may be necessary to nationalize the property registries, since reliance on what is in many cases essentially a private service—perhaps justified in the large cities—has left most rural areas without adequate services. [1]

Providing tenure security does not necessarily demand distribution of *individual* titles. In many instances some kind of cooperative or communal title makes more sense, as in consolidation projects for minifundios and on land reform projects involving production patterns more efficiently carried out on large units. For a variety of social and economic reasons, this approach is receiving increasing support in various countries, particularly Chile and Peru. Consequently, it is important to devise new types of tenure rights which will provide the necessary security and incentives to the operating farmers.

Yet attaining tenure security, particularly in the more remote frontier areas, requires much more than the mere issuance of legally valid titles of ownership. Unless adequate credit facilities, access to markets, and other forms of assistance are provided to the small holders, they may be forced after a few years to sell their holdings or even to abandon them, often to the benefit of the financially stronger landowners who can afford a long term investment.

Finally, even a massive title distribution program together with credit and other infrastructural facilities may not resolve all the problems associated with tenure insecurity. Large uncontrollable migrations into frontier areas, for example, are frequently a symptom of the inaccessibility of either land or alternate sources of employment in the populated areas from which the migrations derive. In these cases, there will always be some tenure insecurity until such time as the root causes of this problem are tackled and eliminated.

References

[1] Arévalo, Luis. "The Legal Insecurity of Rural Property in Colombia: A Case Study of the Notarial and Registry Systems." Ph.D. dissertation, University of Wisconsin, 1970.

[2] Clark, Ronald J. "Problems and Conflicts over Land Ownership in Bolivia." *Inter-American Economic Affairs* 22, no. 4 (1969): 3-18.

[3] Comité Interamericano de Desarrollo Agrícola (CIDA). *Colombia: Tenencia de la tierra y desarrollo socioeconómico del sector agrícola.* Washington, D.C.: Organization of American States, 1966.

[4] de Debuyst, Federico. "Tipología socioeconómica de los países latinoamericanos: El variable social." *Revista interamericana de ciencias sociales, segunda Epoca 2,* special issue (1963): 162-163.

[5] Dorner, Peter; Raymond Penn; C. W. Loomer; and Joseph Thome. "Agrarian Reform in the Dominican Republic: The Views of Four Consultants." Land Tenure Center Paper, no. 42, University of Wisconsin, December 1967.

[6] Felstehausen, Herman. "Agrarian Reform: Colombia." Chapter 8 of this book.

[7] Fuenzalida, Hernán. *Estudio sobre el problema de saneamiento de títulos de dominio en áreas de minifundio.* Proyecto de Investigación. Valparaíso: Centro de Investigaciones de Recursos Naturales (CIREN), 1968.

[8] Hirschman, Albert O. *Journeys toward Progress: Studies of Economic Policy Making in Latin America.* New York: Twentieth Century Fund, 1963.

[9] Instituto Colombiano de Reforma Agraria (INCORA). Resolution No. 02075 of March 25, 1965.

[10] Karst, Kenneth, and Norris C. Clement. "Legal Institutions and Development: Lessons from the Mexican Ejido." *UCLA Law Review* 16 (1969): 281-303.

[11] Oficina de Promoción y Divulgación, Consejo Nacional de Reforma Agraria. *Reforma agraria boliviana* 1, no. 1 (1970), La Paz.

[12] Orozco Ochoa, Germán. *Jurisprudencia de la Corte Suprema de Justicia de 1887 a 1944.* Vol. 3. Medellín: Editorial Gran América, 1945.

[13] Salas, Oscar; Foster Knight; and Carlos Saénz. *Land Titling in Costa Rica: A Legal and Economic Survey.* San José: University of Costa Rica, 1970.

[14] Thome, Joseph R. "Problems Which Obstruct the Process of Title Distribution under the Bolivian Agrarian Reform." Unpublished report. Land Tenure Center, University of Wisconsin, 1967.

[15] ———. "The Process of Land Reform in Latin America." *Wisconsin Law Review,* no. 1 (1968): 11-25.

[16] ———. "Title Insecurity in Colombia." Mimeographed. Madison, Wis.: Land Tenure Center, 1964.

[17] ———. "Title Problems in Rural Areas of Colombia: A Colonization Example." *Inter-American Economic Affairs* 19, No. 3 (1965): 83-100.

240

CHAPTER 12

Private Efforts at Reform

MARION BROWN

Associate Professor of Agricultural Journalism
and the Land Tenure Center
at the University of Wisconsin-Madison

CHAPTER 12

Private Efforts at Reform

MARION BROWN

Hardly anyone in Latin America now opposes land reform outright. Its advocates include conservative politicians and even members of the landed aristocracy. Still the debate over "effective means" continues at a lively pace. Among the various measures proposed, and occasionally tried on a small scale, are several private schemes which involve little direct government action. Our purpose in the present chapter is to evaluate the success of such private efforts and spontaneous changes in achieving "acceptable" land reform objectives. This is admittedly a risky undertaking. Like any discussion of alternative means, it runs the risk of overlooking the basic discrepancy on the question of ends.

Controversy over "tactics" often obscures disagreement on more fundamental issues, and one must be wary of taking apparent consensus at face value; when people are at odds about the best way to reach a goal, they usually disagree as well (sometimes knowingly) about what they really want as a final outcome. Thus when the hacendado advocates land reform, he often attaches some adjective such as "rational," and his criticism of particular reform measures may signal little more than his preference for the status quo.

The debate over means is really part of the process of formulating objectives, and both means and objectives must be decided within a particular historical context. Still, in a manner of speaking one can compare alternative means to the "same" goal, provided the goal is not taken as fixed and final. In the present discussion we will use generally accepted land reform objectives as a guide to analysis, but in no sense are these intended as final or incontrovertible. We are well aware that there is no real concensus on these issues. In any case, regardless of how we define it here, the meaning of land reform will continue to change with time and place. The specific goals as well as the tactics of any particular reform are defined not so much by theory as by circumstance.

With these reservations in the background, we will proceed in succeeding sections to establish our point of view on reform objectives, and then to discuss in turn three possible alternatives to public reform: (1) subdivision by inheritance, (2) private land sale, and (3) profit sharing plans.

The Meaning of Land Reform

To most people land reform means giving land to the landless. It means giving underprivileged rural people access, not only to unused lands, but also to the fertile lands of the big estates. It also means "an increase in the economic and political power and the social status of the 'campesinos' in relation to that of the traditional landed elites." [4, p. 1]

What Latin American governments accept as the meaning of land reform was spelled out as one of the objectives of the Charter of Punta del Este:

To encourage, in accordance with the characteristics of each country, programs of comprehensive agrarian reform leading to the effective transformation, where required, of unjust structures and systems of land tenure and use, with a view to replacing latifundia and dwarf holdings by an equitable system of land tenure so that, with the help of timely and adequate credit, technical assistance and facilities for the marketing and distribution of products, the land will become for the man who works it the basis of his economic stability, the foundation of his increasing welfare, the guarantee of his freedom and dignity. [quoted in 4, p. 2]

In reviewing the literature on land reform, including other parts of this volume, one notes several recurring themes consistent with the above definitions; taken together, these provide a more detailed conceptualization of the term. Dorner has brought these ideas together in his article, "Land Tenure Institutions." [11] We have borrowed freely from this work to develop a summary statement of generalized goals of reform. These objectives, or issues as Dorner calls them, are: (1) more equitable income distribution and a greater effective demand; (2) a broader distribution of economic and political power; (3) more intensive investment in agriculture and rising farm productivity; (4) increasing contribution to public investments in other sectors; and (5) greater labor absorption in rural areas. Each of these is discussed briefly on the following several pages.

Income Distribution and Demand. There is, of course, a direct relationship between the land tenure system, income distribution, and effective demand. Campesinos with no secure rights to land have claim to only a meager income, and a very insecure claim at that. And poor people are poor customers.

Some have argued that wider distribution of income will necessarily depress rates of saving and investment, but this problem may be more apparent than real. For example, Kaldor's analysis of the Chilean situation led him to conclude that "if luxury consumption could be reduced to a more modest proportion of the income of property owners, the proportion of savings in the national income could be considerably raised without lowering the standard of living of the mass of the population." [16; 5]

Many countries face the dual problem of a highly skewed income distribution (which provides little demand expansion for industrial growth) and conspicuous consumption by high income groups (which suppresses saving and investment).

Of course, land reform will not make peasants rich over night. But it can give them a *little* more income now and secure expectations of greater income in the future. This can have a significant impact on demand and investment.

Economic and Political Power. The rich quite obviously have more power than the poor. In most of Latin America those who control the large estates are able to influence the political processes to a degree that is greatly disproportionate to their numbers. Redistribution of lands and related resources will almost certainly change the political power structure and the goals and policies that are formulated through the political process. [5; 6; 8; 25]

Concentration of power in a relatively small group has many implications for development. For one thing, powerful people at the central state level are likely to be closely related to and connected with powerful people at the regional and local level. That is, the same people, the same interests, are involved. Under these circumstances the prospect of pragmatic compromise and evolutionary change is largely foreclosed as is the possibility that the economy can grow in a way that will provide new opportunities for other interest groups.

Farm Investment and Productivity. Raup has argued that "capital formation in farming is rarely concentrated either in space or in time. It accumulates by an incremental process that is best described as accretionary." He also points out that tenure security can contribute to this "by making the use of productive assets the preclusive right of an individual or group. This security of expectation is crucial for biological forms of capital, for slow-maturing enterprises, and for undertakings involving numerous incremental additions made successively over many production cycles." [26]

The tenure form that provided the necessary security and incentive conditions in the United States is the owner-operated family farm. However, there are cases of progressive agriculture outside the family farm pattern. [23] Local circumstances, climate, and cultural factors are all extremely significant in determining the performance of a particular tenure arrangement. [7] However, it is clear that one key variable is control of investment decisions. Where investment decisions are dispersed, with many small investors reaping the benefit of the increased output, the demand generated will more nearly match the supply and thus be less likely to depress prices. On the other hand, if most investment decisions are left to large landowners, many of whom may view investments only in the monetary sense (not in the accretionary, labor-time sense) and whose business and family connections provide alternative investment opportunities, they may well decide to shift their investments out of agriculture. [10] This may be the economically rational decision, given the limited demand and the resulting price structure.

But a wider sharing of the investment decision could, under these circumstances, have two advantages. First, it could provide a more equal distribution of income and thus generate more demand. Second, it could stimulate the kind of investment which includes capital creation on the farm through use of the investors' labor. [26, pp. 267-314]

Investments in Other Sectors. All developing countries need large public investment programs, and governments must control a substantial pool of investment funds. In those countries where the agricultural sector is large relative to the total economy, agriculture must provide a major share of these funds. In simple physical terms, agriculture must feed the people who are building roads, schools, factories, canals, and other capital structures. Since these investments do not have a quick payoff, farmers must, so to speak, "donate" part of this food without an equivalent short-term return.

This process Owen has termed the "production squeeze" on agriculture, and it is a feature of all developing societies, whether socialist or capitalist. [22] The concept presents an apparent dilemma. Agricultural investment must increase, and at the same time the terms of trade must be kept somewhat unfavorable to agriculture. [21] This tactic seems inconsistent with the recommendation of many economists for increasing farm prices to encourage investment. However, land reform can play a significant role here by dispersing control over investment decisions, thus stimulating increased agricultural investments.

It is important to note that the squeeze on agriculture cannot be applied without *some* return-flow of public investments in transportation systems, agriculture schools and experiment stations, extension services, credit institutions, and the like. In many countries the peasants have been squeezed for generations—indeed for centuries. But it has been a one-way exploitive process. There has been no return flow of public investment and redress, and the surpluses squeezed out of agriculture have sometimes been badly invested.

Tenure institutions are important here because it is usually the landlord who extracts the surplus from the peasants. And since landowners are also very influential in government, there is no public mechanism for taking it from them. The decision for investing the surplus rests with the landowning class, and investments guided by their private interests do not always, or even usually, serve the most critical needs of the nation's development.

Labor Absorption in Rural Areas. The most spectacular failure of traditional land tenure institutions in most Latin American countries is their inability to provide even subsistence opportunities for their growing farm populations. The result is massive migration to the cities, most of which is premature since there are not enough jobs being created in the nonfarm sector. Schumacher cites a World Health Organization release which states that "shantytowns of more than 100,000 inhabitants at the fringes of our modern cities concentrate 12 per cent of the world's population, more than one-third of the world's city population." [27] Reforms are required to hold and absorb more of this labor in productive work in agriculture.

With this brief discussion of land tenure and reform concepts in mind, we turn to an analysis of private reform efforts and other spontaneous adjustments taking place in rural Latin America. We will refer to the preceding discussion from time to time in evaluating these changes as potential substitutes for more direct reform measures.

Subdivision by Inheritance

Perhaps the most "natural" process by which large estates become small farms is through inheritance. It could be argued that, given time, this process would do away with the large estates and many of the problems that go with them. The fact is, however, that several centuries of subdivision by inheritance have had remarkably little impact on the agrarian structure. Most of the arable land in Latin America is still held in large estates: nearly 80 per cent is in farms larger than 100 hectares, and 51 per cent is held in estates that are larger than 1,000 hectares or that employ more than twelve man-years of hired labor. [28, p. 50]

One study of subdivision in a relatively modern area on the Argentine Pampas concluded that it would take 130 years for "natural" subdivision to convert the sample area into family-size farms. [6] To my knowledge, no one has made an exhaustive study of subdivision by inheritance in Latin America as a whole. However, there have been a number of excellent case studies, and these suggest that: (1) subdivision is often more apparent than real; (2) small farms are being divided much more rapidly than large ones; (3) the process is more rapid in families that are for one reason or another experiencing downward mobility; and (4) the net consequence is not a more equitable distribution of land, but rather a relative increase in concentration of land ownership. [3; 24]

Paper Subdivision. Cadastral data, tax rolls and even recent census data are notoriously inaccurate and inconsistent when it comes to documenting land ownership in Latin America. In Chile, for example, official tax data underestimate or disguise both the extent of concentration of ownership of large properties and the extent of fragmentation of smaller ones. Large landowners frequently own or control several large farms, though this may not be apparent in public records. And de facto subdivision of small properties is the rule rather than the exception, since official subdivision entails red tape, fees, and taxes which can be avoided by informal agreements.

The Inter-American Committee on Agricultural Development (ICAD) studies of land tenure in seven Latin American countries have also found that concentration is greater than is indicated by the size of the farm units; in general, Latin American census data show many more large farms than large farm owners. [6] In some regions they found the amount of land held by large owners to average about twice the amount reported in census data. It is increasingly common for heirs to subdivide land on paper, but to continue to operate it as a single unit. Also, to evade possible expropriation, many large landowners have put their land in the names of their children, relatives, and business associates, even though they continue to operate it as before. [14]

Subdivision and Farm Size. In one of very few available studies of subdivision, Baraona, Aranda, and Santana traced the history of land ownership in Chile's Putaendo Valley from the colonial period through the late 1950s. [3] By the middle of the seventeenth century, the flat lands of the valley (about 12,240 hectares) had been ceded by the Spanish Crown to owners of eight large properties ranging in size from 880 to 6,400 hectares. The next half century saw much of this land consolidated into even larger estates, one of which included 40 per cent of the irrigable land in the valley plus more than 80,000 hectares of mountain pasture. This hacienda remained intact through the next two centuries and had been divided only once (into equal parts) by the time of Baraona's study in 1958. [3, p. 148] Two other large estates formed at about the same time also survived virtually intact.

At the same time that the large haciendas were becoming larger, the number of smaller properties in the valley was increasing geometrically. This discovery is consistent with the findings of the ICAD studies, which showed that medium and small farms are being divided much more rapidly than large farms in the seven Latin American countries studied. [6]

Subdivision and Downward Mobility. Aranda's data on the Putaendo Valley in Chile suggest that rapid subdivision has occurred principally on farms owned by families that never quite achieved—or were unable to maintain—a "critical mass" of wealth and influence. Families that did accumulate great wealth during the eighteenth and nineteenth centuries have tended not to subdivide their lands. They take care of heirs by expanding rather than dividing their resource base. Because of the influence and educational advantages that go along with great wealth, they have been able to place their sons in government, in industry, in professional careers, in the clergy, or on newly purchased land. After careful analysis of subdivision and consolidation since the seventeenth century, Aranda concludes that in Putaendo, "properties of a certain type—generally those of less than 800 hectares—disintegrated after a few years because of the pressure of family growth. . . ." [3, p. 166] She notes that the initial subdivision was almost always attended by acute financial difficulties and debts, and that the heirs often lost their new holdings to creditors. In these cases subsequent subdivision was rapid and severe, since the land was the principal family resource and there was little else to pass on to the next generation.

Relative Concentration of Ownership. The net result of the uneven pace of subdivision on small and large holdings is that average farm size is dropping while the relative concentration of land ownership is increasing. The large estates are not only slow to divide; some are actually growing. The ICAD research teams documented many cases of large landowners purchasing adjoining or nearby small farms in all of the countries studied. Martin also found some reconsolidation in his study of the Maipo Valley near Santiago, Chile. While the dominant trend was toward smaller units, he reports that fourteen relatively large landowners increased their holdings in the valley between 1928 and 1954.[20] Others who acquired holdings in Maipo during this period already owned land in other parts of Chile. Martin also found that farms larger than 250 hectares in 1928 had not been divided by 1954, whereas rapid subdivision had occurred on smaller farms. His data clearly demonstrate the increase in relative concentration, in that the number of small farms doubled several times between 1896 and 1954, while the area they occupied increased at a much slower pace. Figure 1, taken from the ICAD report on land tenure in Chile, shows Martin's data in graphic form.

FIGURE I

ESTIMATED CHANGES IN RELATIVE CONCENTRATION OF LAND OWNERSHIP IN CHILE'S MAIPO VALLEY

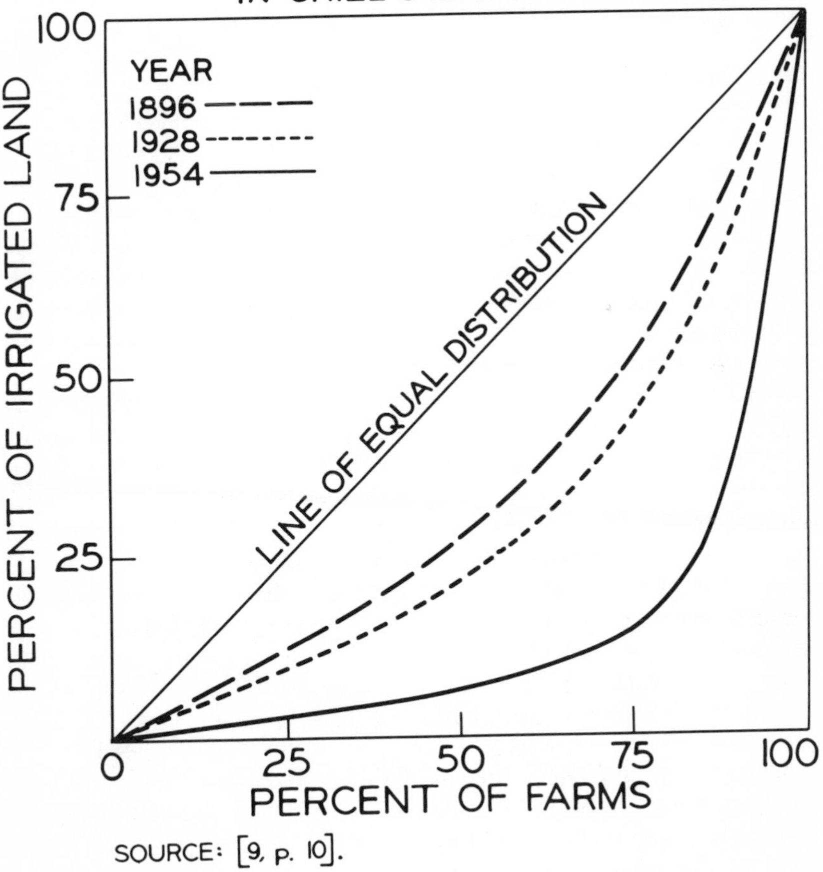

SOURCE: [9, p. 10].

In summary, it seems fair to say that subdivision by inheritance has done little to alleviate the need for more direct reform measures. Its pace on the large estates is very slow indeed, and because of the unavailability of land to accommodate population growth in the small farm sector, its impact on medium and small properties is all too strong. It does not have a significant redistributive effect on income, and consequently, little effect on demand. If the large properties were in fact being divided, inheritance subdivision might have a long range impact on the distribution of power, since large landholdings constitute a power base.

On the positive side, if the large estates were to be subdivided by inheritance over the next several generations, they would likely become more intensively managed and more productive. Likewise, there might be greater dispersion of investment decisions and increased investment, effects which might make it easier for government to extract surpluses for public investment. However, on the crucial matter of labor absorption, this kind of slow subdivision can make very little contribution. At best it provides increased employment opportunities for a very restricted segment of the future population, but it does very little to relieve the urgent need for more rural jobs, a need already acutely felt in most Latin American countries.

Private Land Sale

According to some observers, most of the essential objectives of land reform could be accomplished by massive private real estate transactions. Typically, land markets are relatively inactive in Latin America. Some land is bought and sold, of course, but the volume of sales is not sufficient to even establish a "going market price" in many areas, much less to significantly restructure ownership patterns. Land reform by private sale, whatever its potential impact, must await the creation of some mechanism or contrivance capable of greatly stimulating the land market.

Realizing this, proponents of private reform have come forward with several schemes which would presumably facilitate the sale of private land. [13, pp. 183-185; 29; 2; 18; 19; 1] One such plan has been suggested by Harberger and modified and elaborated by John Strasma. [13; 29] Although primarily addressed to the question of reassessment of agricultural lands for tax purposes, this proposal would, if it worked as planned, almost certainly stimulate the land market. Basically the idea is to "encourage" landowners to assess their own property at or near its real value by forcing them to either sell the land at its assessed value or to raise their assessment and pay more taxes. This would stimulate greater productivity by encouraging present owners to use their land more intensively, or by getting more land into the hands of more active managers.

Another plan for facilitating private land transfers has been put forward by the United States Agency for International Development (USAID) mission in Ecuador. [2] In the words of the proposal, "The philosophy underlying the program is that appropriately assisted, free market private enterprise activities can be the basis for reform of the land tenure structure thus eliminating politically traumatic recourse to expropriation or other nonconsentual forms of land title transfer." The idea is to establish long term loans from the government (backed by USAID) to campesino cooperatives. These loans would enable campesinos to buy land and obtain inputs and technical assistance.

The plan is novel among private parcelization schemes in that it contemplates (though does not require) cooperative ownership and is concerned not only with land, but also with a broad package of resources and services and with social as well as economic issues.

The plan presumes a willingness on the part of present owners to sell their land. While this assumption is certainly not safe for many parts of Latin America, the proponents of the plan present some evidence that conditions are "right" in parts of Ecuador because of the growing number of land invasions by organized campesino groups. Owners threatened with either expropriation or invasion are, apparently, quite willing to sell, provided they can have reasonable expectations of payment. Presumably, those whose lands have already been invaded are even more anxious to strike a bargain. So instead of "market-enforced self-assessment," this plan depends on "campesino enforced self-divestment," which could have a significant effect on both the availability of the land and the price that present owners are willing to accept.

Given these conditions, the Ecuador plan has intriguing possibilities. There seems to be no previous experience in Latin America which provides a basis for predicting the outcome if the plan is ever tried.

If, however, the campesinos are unable to gain sufficient bargaining power to negotiate land purchases from a position of some considerable strength, this plan and others like it including the above self-assessment scheme, will at best produce a proliferation of conventional real estate transactions. There has been enough experience with such sales in recent years to portend their effects in terms of land reform objectives.

Chile, for example, experienced a mild flurry of sales when the present agrarian reform law was being debated in Congress in 1965 and 1966. During this time Idiáquez studied nine large farms that had been recently divided into 118 parcels.[14; 15] Idiáquez, who interviewed several actual and prospective sellers, reports that they were motivated at least in part by fear of the proposed government reform, which they saw as imminent and threatening. Their idea, says Idiáquez, was to "confront the government with a fait accompli—'When they come to do their land reform they will find that it has already been done.' "[14]

Idiáquez' findings can be briefly summarized as follows: [14; 15]

(1) The costs of parcelization—changing roads, fences, ditches, etc.— averaged about 20 per cent of the cost of the land. This portion is comparable to the costs encountered by INPROA, the Chilean private agency which conducted reform experiments on several large properties belonging to the Catholic Church.[see also 31, p. 118]

(2) Seven of the nine farms were in rundown condition. Two of the owners had been unable to find renters because of weed problems and poorly maintained fences, buildings, and irrigation canals.

(3) The nine farms averaged about 350 hectares apiece of irrigated land before subdivision. The new units—including de facto subdivision of the parcels as sold—averaged approximately 24 hectares, ranging from less than 2 to more than 200 irrigated hectares.

(4) Nearly two-thirds of the buyers had not been previously connected with agriculture and earned most of their income from business or professional sources. Another 14 per cent already owned land in the area. Only about 17 of the 86 buyers were campesinos who depended on the parcel as their primary source of income. Of the 118 original parcels, only 6 were purchased by farm workers. In each of those cases, two or more workers went together to buy a parcel and then divided it among themselves. Thus seventeen campesino buyers were crowded onto 6 parcels totaling only about eighty-four irrigated hectares. In addition twenty-six workers bought sitios (building sites) at the time of the parcelization. These averaged about half a hectare and were not included in the 118 parcels.

On the other end of the scale were buyers who bought several parcels. Eight such cases accounted for forty-four of the original parcels.

(5) Proximity to urban areas is closely related to the size and quality of the parcels and to the occupation of the buyers. Four of the nine farms were within fifty miles of Santiago or Valparaíso. On these the buyers were predominantly professional and business people. On three other farms, somewhat more removed from the cities, but still quite accessible, the principal buyers were medium and large farmers in the zone. Almost all the campesino purchases were on the two remaining farms, both of which were more isolated.

(6) The usual payment contract called for a down payment of between 10 and 25 per cent and the remainder within four years. Each year the balance was readjusted according to the price of wheat to compensate for inflation. Interest rates varied from 7 to 12 per cent, going as high as 18 per cent in case of default. In no case was a parcel yielding enough income to keep up with annual payments. The only buyers who were up to date with payments were those who had income from other investments or occupations. Those who depended on the parcel for most of their income (about 20 per cent of the sample) were behind in payments and were charged penalty interest rates of 15 to 18 per cent. There had been no foreclosures, but several of the smaller buyers said they were considering turning back their parcels.

(7) Parcels employed more labor per hectare than the undivided farms had. The increase in the use of labor ran between 30 and 50 per cent; however, there tended to be large seasonal fluctuations, and while there were more jobs available at certain times of the year on the small farms, they were not as secure as they typically are on large, traditional farms. Martin found much the same pattern in the Maipo Valley near Santiago.[20, p. 108]

(8) Absentee ownership and passive or indirect management was the rule among the larger parcel holders. Eighteen buyers lived in Santiago or Valparaíso, and their holdings were, on the average, larger than those of other buyers. Only thirteen lived on their parcels. The other fifty-six for whom Idiáquez obtained residence data lived in towns near their land or on other farm properties in the area. Again Martin's findings in Maipo are very similar.[20, p. 93]

(9) On the positive side, intensity of land use has increased with parcelization. For example, irrigated natural pastures are not as common on the parcels as they were on the undivided farms. Here again, however, there is variation within the sample according to residence and primary occupation of the owner. Thirteen of the urban-based buyers produce almost nothing on their land other than what hired caretakers grow for their own subsistence. In these cases the land has been converted essentially to recreational use for the owner's family.

Lyon studied three parcelization projects near Pichidegua, Chile and found results substantially similar to those on the isolated cases analyzed by Idiáquez.[17] Of the nineteen buyers he interviewed, seven were ex-inquilinos (permanent resident laborers), and two of these had purchased half a parcel each. Four buyers had no previous connection with agriculture, and three of these bought more than one parcel. The twelve remaining buyers were independent small farmers and farm administrators. Income data on these parceleros (parcel holders) show that the ex-farm workers are, in general, doing well as or better than the other buyers.

Adams and Montero reported on a commercial parcelization project at Bocore, Colombia in which the Colombian Tobacco Development Institute bought and subdivided some 600 hectares.[1] This project, which the authors judged very successful in terms of increased productivity and employment, was characterized by rigorous selection of parceleros and strong control by the Tobacco Institute. The 98 parceleros, chosen from more than 500 applicants, had to pass through a test period of several years before they could qualify to buy a parcel.

This Colombian case is quite different from private land sales on the open market; in many ways it is more similar to the projects of government reform and colonization agencies. It does show that these projects can be successfully carried out by private or semi-private concerns.[1] However with so much emphasis on selection and supervision, this kind of program hardly seems to hold the promise of widespread benefit to campesinos, or to be appropriate for reforms involving masses of peasants, many of whom do not have all the characteristics on which selection was based in these test projects.

A common feature of all the private land transfers discussed so far is that they are initiated and controlled by the sellers. Yet there have also been a few case studies in which most of the initiative has come instead from the

---

[1] Thiesenhusen presents a thorough analysis of a somewhat similar private reform experiment in Chile.[31]

campesinos. For example, Whyte documents six cases in Peru where organized campesinos have succeeded in buying out their patrones.[32] On one farm a dispute over the expulsion of forty-four families ended, after a three year struggle, in the campesinos purchasing the property outright. At another spot an organization originally set up to build a school eventually was able to establish claim to the land. When the syndicate's lawyers discovered that the apparent owner did not have a clear title, the campesinos bought out the challenger's claim and took over the property. Four other conflicts between organized campesino groups and their patrones have also ended in campesino land purchases. In all of these cases the land was purchased by communities rather than individuals, with evident implications for employment security, which was a prime issue in most of the disputes leading up to the purchases. Unfortunately, very few production, land use or investment data are available on these farms. However, all are apparently producing enough to keep up with sizeable debt obligations.

This form of private transaction is far different from the kind of sales reported by Idiáquez, Martin, and Adams and Montero. In a sense the AID/Ecuador proposal is a combination of these two types—it depends to a considerable extent on campesino initiative and campesino bargaining power, but it also includes technical assistance and institutional support from above.

In sum, private sale of land in Latin America seems to do very little to alter the traditional structure. Where it occurs on a strictly private basis, with existing wealth as the primary mechanism for selecting new owners, it seems to lack even the potential of contributing meaningfully to broad reform objectives. This failing is partly attributable to the very low volume of sales, but it would likely persist even if the sales process accelerated considerably, since such sales involve very little redistribution of wealth and income. Investment and productivity consequences are also very uneven, but the tendency seems to be toward passive management and low productivity on the larger, better located lands at the same time that smaller parcels are used more intensively. The employment impact of purely private sales is apparently positive, but also somewhat mixed. In general the number of jobs tends to increase (again however, this does not always hold for the larger parcels near large cities), but job security tends to decline.

Land transfers initiated by campesinos who have managed to achieve enough bargaining strength to affect the terms of sale seem to produce more significant changes in the local power structure and in job security. Other consequences are not known, but in any event these cases are very few. To have a broad impact, their number would have to increase many times over. The possibility of accelerating, supporting, and institutionalizing a similar kind of change, as suggested by the AID/Ecuador proposal for land sale guaranties, is an intriguing one.

Profit-Sharing

A third type of private reform activity which can be found in Latin America involves worker participation in management and profit-sharing plans. This effort is being made mostly by large landowners, usually on well operated farms, in an attempt to demonstrate that labor conditions can be improved and other reform objectives met without recourse to expropriation.

Dorner and Collarte estimated that perhaps as many as 70 large farms in Chile's central zone had such plans in operation in 1965.[12] On these farms, a large part of the traditional administrative staff—supervisors, foremen, and overseers—had been replaced by delegates elected by the workers. Committees were also elected to rate each worker's performance. This rating determined his share of the profits. On the average these plans increased the incomes of participating workers by about 30 per cent, which is not a great deal considering that, at the time of the study, the average rural wage in Chile, including perquisites, was approximately seventy cents per day. At the same time that the incomes of some workers have risen on profit-sharing farms, the number of workers has often been reduced. Consequently, at least a part of any redistribution of income which occurs goes not from rich to poor, but rather from poor to poor, leaving some campesinos worse off than before. In none of the cases studied by Dorner and Collarte had there been a transfer of ownership rights. Furthermore, the profit-sharing itself is a form of "welfare capitalism" which can be annulled at any time by the owner. Thus workers still depend on his good will, without any reliable recourse to public authority.

It would be easy—perhaps too easy—to conclude that such schemes as these have nothing to offer in the way of meaningful reform. They do stimulate some organization among the campesinos and increase their managerial experience. It would be instructive to restudy these farms after five years to see how these incipient campesino groups have evolved. They seem to have the potential—especially under Chile's current rural labor laws—of becoming increasingly active, both as pressure groups and as participants in the affairs of the farm. They may also play a significant role in government reform efforts when these are carried out on farms with profit-sharing plans. Dorner and Collarte proposed a public land reform process which included profit-sharing as a transitional stage during which campesinos would use their share to buy out much of the present owner's claim. The idea was to place more of the weight of government on the side of the campesinos in "bargaining" for land, and at the same time to salvage and make use of the managerial skills of those large farmers who were active and successful in running their farms. Absentee owners who were not actively managing their lands were to be expropriated outright. The proposal has not been tried—at least not all of it. However, the three to five year asentamiento period in Chile's current reform program is not unlike a profit-sharing plan, with the government taking over some of the activities that Dorner and Collarte envisaged for the large landowner.[30]

In short, profit-sharing has contributed very little to the aims of land reform in Chile. However, the general idea seems to have merit as part of direct, publicly controlled reform.

Summary

Subdivision by inheritance, private land sales, and profit-sharing schemes, all considered by some to be viable substitutes for more direct reform measures, appear to have had remarkably little impact on the existing structure of rural Latin America. The "natural" inheritance process is too slow on the large farms and too fast on the small ones, and in any case does not directly benefit campesinos who are not born into landed families. Private land sales are few and far between, and where they have occurred, especially on the open market, they have accomplished practically nothing in the way of redistribution of income, and have had very mixed consequences for investment, productivity, and employment. Campesino-initiated sales probably produce more profound structural change where they occur, but their number is extremely restricted. Private profit-sharing plans seem to hold the least promise of all when it comes to direct reform benefits, although the idea may have potential as part of government reform efforts.

References

[1]   Adams, Dale W. and L. Eduardo Montero. "Land Parcelization in Agrarian Reform: A Colombian Example." *Inter-American Economic Affairs* 19 (1965): 67-71.

[2]   Agency for International Development. *Ecuador: Land Sale Guaranty.* AID-DLC/P-854. Washington, D. C.: Department of State, 1969.

[3]   Baraona, Rafael; Ximena Aranda; and Roberto Santana. *Valle de Putaendo: Estudio de estructura agraria.* Santiago: Departmento de Geografía y Instituto de Geografía, Universidad de Chile, 1961.

[4]   Barraclough, Solon. "Agrarian Reform in Latin America: Actual Situation and Problems." In *Land Reform, Land Settlement and Cooperatives.* Rome: Food and Agricultural Organization, 1969.

[5]   ———. "Agricultural Policy and Land Reform." Unpublished paper prepared for Conference on Key Problems of Economic Policy in Latin America, University of Chicago, November 1966.

[6]   ——— and Arthur L. Domike. "Agrarian Structure in Seven Latin American Countries." *Land Economics* 42 (1966): 391-424.

[7]   Brewster, John M. "Traditional Social Structures as Barriers to Change." In *Agricultural Development and Economic Growth,* edited by Herman M. Southworth and Bruce F. Johnston. Ithaca: Cornell University Press, 1967.

[8]   Carroll, Thomas F. "Land Reform as an Explosive Force in Latin America." In *Explosive Forces in Latin America,* edited by John J. Tepaske and Sydney Nettleton Fisher. Columbus, Ohio: Ohio State University Press, 1964.

[9]   Comité Interamericana de Desarrollo Agrícola. *Chile: Tenecia de la tierra y desarrollo socio-económico del sector agrícola.* Washington, D. C.: Unión Pan Americana, 1966.

[10]   Dorner, Peter. "Open Letter to Chilean Landowners." Published in Spanish in *La Nación* (Santiago), June 21, 1965 and in English in Land Tenure Center *Newsletter,* no. 21. University of Wisconsin (1965): 1-14.

[11]   ———. "Land Tenure Institutions." In *Institutions in Agricultural Development,* edited by Melvin G. Blase. Ames: Iowa State University Press, 1971.

[12]   ——— and Juan Carlos Collarte. "Land Reform in Chile: Proposal for an Institutional Innovation." *Inter-American Economic Affairs* 19 (1965): 3-22.

[13]   Harberger, Arnold. *Aspectos de una reforma tributaria para América Latina.* Documentos y Actas. Washington, D. C.: Pan American Union, 1964.

[14]   Idiáquez, Antonio. "Private Subdivision of Land." Land Tenure Center *Newsletter,* no. 22. University of Wisconsin (1965-1966): 15-20.

[15]   ———. Unpublished data.

[16]   Kaldor, Nicholas. "Economic Problems of Chile." Santiago, Chile: United Nations Economic Commission for Latin America, 1959. Published in Spanish in *El Trimestre Económico* 26 (1959): 170-221.

[17]   Lyon, Juan. "La parcelación particular: Una alternativa dentro del proceso de reforma agraria." Santiago, Chile: Universidad Católica de Valparaíso and Land Tenure Center, University of Wisconsin, 1967.

[18]   Mamalakis, Marcos and Clark Winton Reynolds, eds. *Essays on the Chilean Economy.* Homewood, Ill.: Irwin, 1965.

[19]   Mann, Fred; Melvin G. Blase; and Luis Paz. "A Potential Institution and Procedure for Financing Agrarian Reform and Stimulating Industrialization in Peru." Lima: Iowa Universities-AID Contract Group, 1964.

[20]   Martin, Gene Ellis. *La división de la tierra en Chile Central.* Santiago: Departamento de Geografía y Instituto de Geografía, Universidad de Chile, 1960.

[21]   Mellor, John W. "Toward a Theory of Agricultural Development." In *Agricultural Development and Economic Growth,* edited by Herman M. Southworth and Bruce F. Johnston. Ithaca: Cornell University Press, 1967.

[22]   Owen, Wyn F. "The Double Developmental Squeeze on Agriculture." *American Economics Review* 56 (1966): 43-70.

[23]   Parsons, Kenneth H. "Land Reform in the United Arab Republic." *Land Economics* 35 (1959): 319-326.

[24]   Pascal, Andres. *Relaciones de poder en una localidad rural: Estudio de caso en el Valle Hurtado, Coquimbo.* Santiago: Instituto de Capacitación e Investigación en Reforma Agraria, 1968.

[25]   Penn, Raymond J. "Public Interest in Private Property (Land)." *Land Economics* 37 (1961): 101-104.

[26]   Raup, Philip M. "Land Reform and Agricultural Development." In *Agricultural Development and Economic Growth,* edited by Herman M. Southworth and Bruce F. Johnston. Ithaca: Cornell University Press, 1967.

[27]   Schumacher, E. F. "Economic Development and Poverty." *Intermediate Technology Development Group Limited,* no. 1 (1966): 3-9.

[28]   Sternberg, Marvin. "The Latifundista." Mimeographed. Albany: State University of New York, 1970.

[29]   Strasma, John. "Market Enforced Self-Assessment for Real Estate Taxes." *Bulletin for International Fiscal Documentation* 9 and 10 (1956).

[30]   Thiesenhusen, William C. "Agrarian Reform: Chile." Chapter 6 of this book.

[31]   ———. *Chile's Experiments in Land Reform.* Madison: University of Wisconsin Press, 1966.

[32]   Whyte, William F. "El mito del campesino pasivo: la dinámica del cambio en el Perú rural." *Estudios Andinos* 1 (1970): 7-15.

PART V

CONCLUSIONS

CHAPTER 13

Policy Implications

PETER DORNER

Professor of Agricultural Economics,
Director of the Land Tenure Center
at the University of Wisconsin-Madison

CHAPTER 13

Policy Implications

PETER DORNER

Major distributive land reforms, still awaiting implementation in most Latin American countries, could have an important positive impact on both the agricultural and the industrial sectors. It is difficult to foresee, under present agrarian structures, the needed achievements in increased total farm output, increased productivity and higher incomes for the large mass of rural poor people, increased employment opportunities for a rapidly growing labor force, and the incorporation of the peasant into the mainstream of the economic and political life of the nation.

Agrarian Reform and Development

As economic development proceeds, a progressively larger production surplus from agriculture is required to feed the growing urban populations. The industrialized nations have used a variety of devices to enlarge this surplus and to siphon some of it from agriculture. At times there were substantial net capital flows from agriculture to other sectors. Yet such a squeeze on agriculture cannot continue indefinitely; it must be accompanied by public investments designed to improve the conditions of life and to increase production in the farm sector. All countries must face the issue of extracting a surplus from agriculture while at the same time providing for public investments in the agricultural sector. In the United States this return flow of investments included government loans and subsidies for constructing transportation and communication networks, federal land grants to the states for establishing agricultural colleges, financial support for agricultural experiment stations and extension services, a system of rural credit institutions, direct payments for soil conservation practices, and price support programs. All these were aspects of government policy aimed at influencing the supply of agricultural products *and* redressing the distortions in the distribution of income and opportunity that accompany technological change and economic growth. Despite these efforts, substantial numbers of rural as well as urban people have been left in poverty, and this would certainly have been the fate of millions more had it not been for the jobs provided by a rapidly expanding industrial sector.[19]

In Latin America this process of public investment and redress works even less well than in the United States; sometimes it is ignored entirely. With land ownership and political power concentrated in the hands of relatively few people, a production squeeze on agriculture has its major impact not on the resource owners but on the landless uneducated peasants who have little voice in economic and political affairs. These peasants are not stupid and lazy—they are often unschooled, poor, unorganized, and neglected.

In past years Latin American agrarian systems offered a measure of economic participation at low levels of living to the majority of the people. Such participation was based not so much on objective opportunities as on the personal judgment and good will of the benefactor. But conditions in rural sectors are deteriorating and many cannot be provided with even this meagre participation. Larger populations, higher rates of population increase, and aspirations for a better life on the part of these increasing numbers are major new conditions for which the traditional system has no adequate response.

Without strong rural organizations pressuring for change, there is little incentive for redistribution and widening of opportunities. People in power do not, without compelling reasons, initiate action which deprives them of special privileges. The basic dilemma is that a major investment program in human and material resources creating an opportunity-oriented system reduces the short-run advantage and privilege of the favored group, whereas a system built on inequality and privilege is inconsistent with economic development.

Private property, freedom of contract, and competition frequently accentuate these inequalities. The result is laissez faire with a vengeance. Not surprisingly, many of the underprivileged respond to the suggestion that the root evil is capitalism, frequently equated with foreign investment and monopoly. While there is nothing inherently evil in foreign investments or oligopolistic market structures, national political institutions must be strong enough to exercise effective control over their performance and to make them responsible and responsive to public needs.[7]

Reform of the land tenure system may appear destructive of such institutions as private property and freedom of enterprise, but distributive reforms are not inconsistent with these institutions. The fact of the matter is that these institutions in Latin America cannot perform in the public interest unless there is a more equal distribution of power and opportunity. On the other hand, there is no reason to assume that the Latin American nations will all choose a system based on private property. More than likely, major reforms will lead to mixed systems with very substantial state participation in the economy. These are questions that must be worked out and agreed upon by the people of each country.

Under conditions of rapid industrial growth with employers searching for laborers, the economic condition of agricultural workers would soon improve. They would have new alternatives, greater opportunities for education and development of new skills, more bargaining power, etc. The response of rural employers to their workers would then have to be quite different from what it is today, and the terms and conditions of tenure would be altered. In the absence of rapidly increasing economic alternatives, however, tenure systems are characterized by personal dominance of the landlord over those in an inferior tenure status.

Development theory and planning are often based on the implicit assumption that the energizing force in the development process is provided primarily by the top echelons of administrators and entrepreneurs through the investment plans and projects they direct. However, systems based solely upon authority without enlisting the informed self-interest of farmers and urban workers are not likely to perform well. Where wealth and power are monopolized by a small minority of the population, the masses are separated from all incentives to improvement.

Releasing and fostering the creative human energies of the mass of the people is strategic to any development effort. While exploitive measures can carry development to a certain stage, eventually the common men and women must provide the energy, the markets, and the creative drive to keep the process going. This requires widely shared economic and political citizenship, which can only be realized by basic reforms and the reallocation of power.

There are, of course, certain dangers in distributive reforms, accompanied as they almost inevitably are by some confiscatory measures. Confidence and security of expectations among potential investors, especially expropriated landowners, may be shaken. But there are no risk-free solutions. And proposals for indirect measures to accomplish the same results as land distribution—tax and tenancy reforms and minimum wage legislation—have been advocated and some legislation has been passed, but the results have been inconsequential.

Theoretically, progressive income taxation can redistribute income just as progressive land taxes (increasing with size of holding) can lead to land redistribution. Progressive taxation as an effective vehicle for income redistribution has been used successfully mainly in the highly industrialized countries having the facilities to handle the administrative problems inherent in progressive income taxation. The public imagination is not usually captured by tax reforms. Although agrarian reforms generally are supported by the peasants, tax reforms invariably produce intense opposition without garnering offsetting support. Politically, taxes are never popular, even among the potential beneficiaries.[4]

In addition to problems of enforcement and lack of support, increased land taxes, although obviously required, have many other weaknesses insofar as realizing distributive land reform objectives are concerned. Landowners may require more work from their laborers without more pay and release workers to meet the increased tax bill. Some advocates of increased land taxes anticipate the sale of many extensively operated large farms to entrepreneurs who would use the land more intensively. There is, however, no active buyers' market for these huge estates. Moreover, paper subdivisions can be employed to circumvent the intent of the law. Even if actual subdivision does take place, very few (if any) farm laborers will have the financial capacity to obtain a farm.

Some of the same weaknesses inhere in improved wage legislation and tenancy reforms. Without strong rural labor organizations, enforcement is difficult. Indeed, such regulations have at times induced landowners to withdraw land from commercial use or to substitute machines for men. Rural work opportunities may thus be reduced and the economic status of the peasant worsened. Tax, wage, and tenancy legislation must be viewed as supplementary to but not as substitutes for distributive land reforms.

Distributive Reforms and Industrial Growth[1]

Some argue that a more equitable distribution of income accompanying land reform will reduce the private savings rate and consequently constrain investment. The United Nations' Economic Commission for Latin America (ECLA) has provided evidence that in Latin America no close statistical correlation exists between high degrees of income concentration and development.[24, p. 50] Kuznets has suggested that policy makers must weigh the savings contribution of the top groups in the income pyramid against the potential increase in the contribution of groups below the top that might result from narrower inequality in the income distribution." [17, p. 42]

Income in Latin America is concentrated in fewer hands than in currently developed countries. In 1964 ECLA compared the top 5 per cent of earners with the bottom 50 per cent and concluded that "in Latin America the high average is twenty times the low average, whereas in the economically developed countries of Europe this difference is only half as great, and in the United States it is even less." For 1968 it reported that the top 20 per cent received an average income twelve times that of the bottom half in Latin America; in the U.S. the average income of the top fifth was only five times that of the poorer half.[22, p. 53; 23, pp. 1-25][2]

One important economic consequence accompanying land reform is the increased purchasing power that the expected redistribution of income would provide to current low income groups. This higher purchasing power could serve to stimulate both the mass consumption and some of the agricultural input industries. Land reform could help to invigorate the industrial sector.[21] Several interdependencies and linkages between the agricultural and the industrial sector should be noted:

(1) If peasant farmers were brought into the market at some expense to those with higher incomes, the structure of demand would be altered

---

[1] This section draws freely from a paper by Thiesenhusen, "A Suggested Policy for Industrial Reinvigoration in Latin America."[21]

[2] Kuznets elaborates the general argument from which he concludes, " . . . the size distribution of income among family units, adjusted for the number of persons per unit and for other effects, is distinctly more unequal in underdeveloped than in developed countries."[18, p. 63]

considerably in the short run to favor simple consumer goods or even consumer durables such as radios and bicycles. Overall, a lower import requirement per unit of output could be expected for these items than for current import substitution industries in most Latin American countries. Hence the export constraint on economic growth would be somewhat relieved.

(2) The current tendency for import substitution to move into wasteful luxury lines to satisfy demands of the well-to-do would be restricted. These manufactures often have a high import content, demand exhorbitant protection, and squander scarce resources.

(3) Many other more complex goods with a substantial potential for economies of scale in production but requiring high protection could be bypassed for the time being as resources are redirected to the production of consumer goods and strategic production inputs. This does not preclude government investment in those manufactures which seem uneconomic by current cost accounting but prove promising when shadow pricing criteria are applied, and in those intermediate products which have strong linkage effects. As the market expands and if this is deemed desirable national policy, privately sponsored production of more complex goods could resume; as light consumer goods develop, backward linkages to the sectors that supply inputs to them will be strengthened.

(4) At least some types of fertilizer processing and manufacture should be stimulated, given proper government policy, since income elasticity of demand for fertilizers can be high at low income levels in the farm sector.[3] This was one major effect of the Japanese reform, according to Kazushi Ohkawa, who "believes that these changes have not only strengthened the incentive to increase output, but in addition have created a mentality more receptive to innovations and have left farmers with sufficient cash incomes to substantially increase their use of purchased inputs."[14, p. 251]

(5) The serious unemployment problem that exists in Latin America would be somewhat alleviated. Not only should land reform itself provide more jobs in agriculture [3; 5; 20], but the manufacture of simple consumer goods is typically more labor-intensive than the manufacture of the more complex intermediate products and consumer durables.

A recent study shows that small scale industrial establishments in Latin America (those employing from five to forty-nine persons) hired 31 per cent of all factory workers and produced 21 per cent of the regional factory

---

[3] It is of course possible that this development might merely lead to increased imports of inputs. It should be emphasized that "rural demand will obviously give a greater stimulus to industrialization if a country pursues an agricultural development path relying to a substantial extent on increased use of farm inputs that are within the capacity of a developing country's industrial sector at successive stages of technical maturity."[15, p. 284] A large country such as Brazil has certain advantages over the smaller nations in undertakings such as fertilizer manufacture. In these and similar areas, common market arranements can be extremely important for helping smaller nations overcome their present small market disadvantage.

product. For this reason it concluded that

every industrialization policy should take into account the important social function of small-scale industry, namely the drawing of large labor contingents into the production process. It has a particularly effective contribution to make in such activities as food processing, the production of certain types of textiles and wearing apparel and the manufacture of furniture, in which it can achieve a satisfactory level of efficiency with little capital. For instance, in the textile industry in Latin America small mills of low technological levels exist side by side and in competition with large scale modern establishments.[25, pp. 63, 66]

(6) More locational decentralization would become possible since simple consumer goods manufacture usually requires fewer external economies than more complex products do. Small-scale establishments spread throughout a country also provide opportunities for a more widespread development of entrepreneurial talent. These combined effects could alleviate some population pressure on the primate city and favor a more balanced regional growth pattern.[4]

Thus major distributive reforms have the potential for positive impacts on the industrial sector as well as on the agricultural sector. There are, of course, powerful interests opposing land reform. But at the same time, pressures for reform are growing, and governments everywhere represent a variety of interests—there is no homogeneous, monolithic view on such fundamental policy issues. There is diversity and conflict. The situation is relatively fluid and major shifts in policy can come rather quickly. Mexico, Bolivia, and Cuba have had major reforms. Substantial redistributions have occurred and are in process in Venezuela and Chile. The military government in Peru seems likely, as of this writing, to carry forward its promised measures for a major land reform. Therefore, even though present political forces may not in all cases be favorable to land redistribution, new alignments of power sometimes emerge rapidly.

Strengthening the Small Farm and Reformed Subsectors of Agriculture[5]

Still, as the analysis in preceding chapters has shown, land redistribution is not a sufficient condition for development. Even in countries that have had basic land reforms, such as Mexico and Bolivia, there is a pronounced tendency in agricultural policy to favor the larger, commercial producers. The

---

[4] Hauser feels that the present rapid rate of growth of urban areas—and especially primate cities—compounds the difficulties of development.[12; for an opposing view, see 1]

[5] This section draws freely from a paper by Dorner and Felstehausen, "Agrarian Reform and Employment: The Colombian Case."[8] The small farm subsector is emphasized since it now exists in all Latin American countries and will likely continue to exist even after basic reforms. This is not to ignore the prospect of combining these small units into larger cooperative type farms. This, however, is a more difficult task than the conversion of some of the expropriated large farms into cooperative production organizations.

special needs of small farmers in Latin America—reform beneficiaries as well as others, including those organized in communal and cooperative types of farming arrangements—have often been ignored. Changes in national agricultural policies are required to strengthen this small farm subsector. With appropriate modifications in the lending policies and programs of international agencies, such shifts in agricultural policies might be achieved even in countries with strong internal opposition to reform. Strengthening the small farm subsector not only will create new and more secure income earning opportunities in rural areas, but could also speed the required structural transformation of the traditional agricultural system. Without special programs many peasant farmers are either driven out of agriculture or back to the margins of subsistence. Summarized below are several key areas in which policy changes could strengthen the economic, and subsequently the political position of the small farm subsector.[8] Some are especially relevant in countries where major land redistributions have already occurred; others are of particular significance to those nations which have as yet achieved little redistribution.

(1) *Allocation of land on the basis of its ability to employ labor.* A land redistribution program as well as a land settlement policy for remaining public lands must be an integral part of a small farm assistance policy. The small farm subsector needs additional land in order to employ the growing number of new workers without further dividing existing small holdings. Some of this land *must* come from existing large private holdings if peasant farmers are to be accommodated within farming regions similar to the ones they now occupy.

In addition to expropriation and reallocation of land from the private sector, new policy guidelines are often required for the settlement of remaining state lands. Several Latin American countries still possess frontier territories. Although much of this land is poorly suited to agriculture and can be brought under cultivation only after making large public investments in land improvements and local infrastructure, some possibilities do exist. In those cases where frontier lands have been made accessible, persons with greater access to transportation, legal services, and capital often dominate these new regions. Strictly enforced limits could be placed on the amount of land any individual can own in these new areas. Programs are needed for guiding the pattern of future settlement and land use along with such complementary services as land measurement, titling, and registration.[2] International lending agencies could play a direct and important role by providing technical personnel to assist in designing rural infrastructure and in improving land measurement and registration systems, and by providing funds for implementing such programs.

(2) *Development and introduction of new technology to increase employment and production.* There is nothing new or unique about having the public sector finance the development of new technology for agriculture. Most agriculture research and extension throughout the world is carried on at

public expense. However, strengthening the small farm and reformed subsectors often requires the development of some separate technologies. Agricultural research generally has been most beneficial to large farm agriculture. Research and demonstrations are usually geared to mechanized field cropping or large scale ranching as opposed to small farm agriculture.

Some argue that it would be impractical to develop modern technology for small farms, but the opposite argument is equally convincing. One need only examine the record of agricultural performance in countries with small farm systems, such as Japan, Taiwan, Holland and Denmark. Land saving technologies—fertilizers, improved seeds, and pest controls—can be applied just as effectively on small farms as on large. Mechanization, by contrast, is mainly labor saving and consequently its advantages accure only if labor can be displaced and/or the farm's land area enlarged.

Primary emphasis must fall on land saving technologies if both increased production and employment objectives are to be served. This emphasis does not preclude the introduction of some types of mechanization into the small farm subsector provided they are specifically designed with small farms in mind. For example, a well adapted garden tractor with complementary implements may be labor saving, but it is also land saving inasmuch as it permits working the land more intensively, often improving yields as well as utilizing more land for cultivation—land which would otherwise be unused or pastured.

Even more important than improved cultivation practices is another relationship that sometimes exists between land saving and labor saving technologies. Peasant farmers in the Puebla region of Mexico, for example, find that even with the cultivation of a traditional crop like corn, it becomes more critical to plant and to apply fertilizers within very limited time spans as they change from native corn varieties to hybrids. In other words, weather patterns often severely restrict the number of days available for field work—especially with double cropping. If the package of more productive technology is to be applied at all, some form of mechanization may be required in order to complete the work within the seasonal schedule.[13]

A reallocation of agricultural research efforts is needed to develop new technologies appropriate to the type of farming practiced on small farms. Mechanical technology is mentioned only to illustrate the principle, but the same reasoning applies to new crop varieties and related practices as well as to livestock production. Much research is concentrated on industrial, often export, crops. The small farm subsector has realized little benefit from these efforts.

Besides the development of technology, its introduction and distribution will require additional investments in information and other farm services. The very large number of small farms and their greater isolation from transportation and communication facilities makes them difficult to reach. Here again the Puebla project in Mexico offers some interesting experience. Special extension techniques were developed and a major effort undertaken to educate the government bureaucracy and commercial firms to the needs of small farmers.

(3) *Modification of rural service structures to assure access to small farmers.* Families on farms large or small require a variety of human as well as production and marketing services. Improved procedures for the registration of property documents and the rapid consideration and resolution of conflicts would benefit all. Yet the small farm subsector, with respect to most services, has needs that differ from those of the larger, commercial farms.[10]

For example, many of the present large farmers send their children to urban schools, own their own transportation and storage facilities (and have better access to those provided publicly), bypass local market channels, and depend less on village service and supply agencies. The small farm subsector, on the other hand, is the main client for rural schooling and health facilities, collective forms of transportation and communication, and local product handling and marketing facilities. Improved average incomes for the large number of small farmers will provide them with more economic and political leverage with which to influence decision making bodies on the questions of improved rural services. Improved income, as noted earlier, would also strengthen the demand for nonfarm inputs and consumer goods in the small farm subsector, pulling additional commercial services into the countryside and creating some additional jobs.

With increased production and income to lift the average peasant somewhat above the margin of subsistence, one would expect rising demands for education and training. Adequate accommodation of these demands will obviously mean that certain government expenditures will increase. Part of the new revenue needed could be raised by improved tax measures on agricultural lands, but a large transfer might initially have to come from the nonagricultural sector. International lending agencies could greatly aid in the transition period if loans were made specifically for service structures to serve the small farm and reformed subsectors of agriculture.

(4) *Provision for dual systems of capital and credit.* In most Latin American countries there are separate credit programs for small and large farm borrowers, and a number of them have introduced supervised credit programs. While these approaches recognize that small farms need credit too, the amounts allocated to the small farm sector fail to meet the needs. Most small farmers must rely on noninstitutional sources, often at exorbitant interest rates. In the credit market, the small farmer remains in an insecure and vulnerable position. Credit programs for the small farm subsector must expand, and they should likewise have special terms and conditions for borrowing. Subsidized lending to small farmers should not be ruled out if it assists in making agricultural adjustments, increases employment, and generally aids in improving income distribution.

Shifts in national investment allocations are called for. In some cases these shifts could be made within existing agricultural budgets and investment programs. There may also be need for a net reduction in at least the short run availability of capital for industrialization. However, the overall effect would probably not be serious compared to the advantages accruing from increased employment and incomes in agriculture.

A Possible Realignment of Power

Agrarian reform remains essentially a political problem internal to each country. The optimist will, however, be able to see the seeds of a realignment of power implied in the former arguments. While industrialists have traditionally found common cause with the large landowners in opposing land reform, it is conceivable that with the increased incomes and purchasing power of the small farm subsector, the manufacturers of simple consumer goods may add their weight to the existing loose coalition of intellectuals, students, landless peasants, an increasingly liberal church and (in a few countries) left-of-center military factions. The motivation of an expanded market might conceivably join some industrialists with those who desire reform on the basis of land hunger or social justice. As John H. Kautsky has remarked, " . . . where industry produces consumer goods for the domestic market, rather than raw materials for export, it is in the interest of the capitalists to raise the standard of living and the buying power of the peasantry, possibly even to advocate land reform." [16, p. 23]

Perhaps simple consumer goods and farm input manufacturers may be joined by a broader cross section of the urban middle class who see rapid migration to cities and its concomitants—increasing unemployment, political malaise, overcrowding, and higher city budgets—as a collective threat. This array of forces might swing the balance of power from the landlords allied with other conservative elements, among which are the protected "advanced" industrialists. The power of this latter group should not be underestimated. Its interests are interlocked with landlords in a variety of ways. In some cases, it depends on them for foreign exchange. It may be bound to agriculture by family ties. This sector tends also to include powerful foreign elements. Because of their current privileged and protected position these groups will doubtless fear a weakening in their economic status unless they are already vertically integrated in the production of simple consumer goods. There will be a lag between admission of the peasant to the consumer goods market and the more complex demands that would—in time—result from rising incomes. In fact, because of the needs of the economy for long-term investment and because of the extremely rapid population growth over the past several decades, peasant incomes may have to remain at a level where they can buy only simple goods for a fairly long time.

Reform and Development within the International Context

But in the present world, domestic policies of the Latin American nations will not be wholly effective in bringing about a more rapid and balanced development. Changes in the policies of international agencies and those of the industrial nations are required.

International agencies, of course, cannot carry out a land reform. This is a decision that must be made by national governments. In any case, it would be wrong to assume that there is widespread support and enthusiasm for land reform among those agencies. Rather, the prevailing position is one of either outright hostility or a vague hope that programs designed to increase production will result in agricultural development without the need for reform. And international lending for agricultural development has benefitted primarily the large farm sector. In part at least this is a result of the underlying economic analysis which evaluates investment alternatives *within a given* institutional structure whereas land reform concerns changing this very structure.

Writing on the Green Revolution in Asia, Falcon notes that incomes of some large farmers have risen dramatically, that land prices are increasing as these farmers seek to expand farm size and to find new investment outlets for their larger incomes, and that in the process tenants and other small farmers are frequently displaced. He also calls attention to the

powerful forces that are pressing for mechanization of all kinds. Large farmers, foreign and domestic industrialists, politicians and even aid agencies have vested interests in promoting various implements, including tractors. . . . The I.B.R.D., for example, is currently proposing a $25 million loan to finance tractors in India, and has several other similar loans pending. In Pakistan, an I.B.R.D. mechanization loan also provided for the special importation of tractors at the official exchange rate and, in addition, provided special credit arrangements.[9, p. 706]

The emphasis given by international agencies to loans which aid primarily the large farm sector is a rather common phenomenon. These agencies could have a powerful influence if they would change the nature of their lending policies and place special emphasis on loans for the small farm sector and reformed agricultural subsectors and on those which would aid in restructuring the land tenure system.

An analysis of the U. S. aid program to Latin American agriculture discusses the many difficulties in trying to identify the beneficiaries of various loans and grants. However, using the Agency for International Development's (AID) own classification and carefully studying the official documents and reports, the author concludes that only about 10 per cent of all U. S. assistance in the period 1962-1968 was specifically earmarked for agriculture. Of this total, over 50 per cent was classified as benefitting primarily commercial farmers. Only 15 per cent was aimed directly at agrarian reform or the beneficiaries of reform programs. The remaining 35 per cent was for general improvements likely to benefit both large and small farms.[6]

Increased domestic policy emphasis on agrarian reforms and greater support for these by international lending agencies are needed. A decreased emphasis on military expenditures is long overdue. And yet, even assuming that these difficult matters can be accomplished, there are several additional problems in the international sphere which, if not altered, may impede more rapid development in Latin America and elsewhere.

One of the issues concerns the general position of the industrial world vis-à-vis the less developed world in matters of trade and markets. Policies of the industrial nations frequently prevent developing economies from taking full advantage either of static or dynamic comparative advantage. There are many problems in the international economic sphere that have been attacked and more or less successfully resolved, but these have been the problems affecting primarily the industrial countries—not the less developed ones—e.g., the massive credits for preventing monetary instability, but the inability to raise much needed funds for soft loan money for the World Bank's International Development Association (IDA); the substantial progress in achieving international monetary reforms but the lack of progress in devising ways and means of halting the erosion of the terms of trade for primary goods exports; the creation of restrictive textile agreements but the lack of sanctions on dumping farm surpluses; etc.[11]

The resolution of these issues has benefitted the industrial economies (with some secondary gains for the less developed nations), but the obligations and costs have been placed on all, with the major burden often borne by the less developed countries. Solution of the unresolved international economic issues would favor the less developed countries with costs bearing more heavily on the industrial economies. "The basis for problem selection and resolution could hardly be more glaringly biased were it designed to impede development." [11, p. 8]

One need not seek explanations for these phenomena in a "devil theory of causation." These outcomes are much too complex to be explained by a theory of conspiracy and too well managed to be attributed to blind market forces. "The problems of central concern to the metropolitan economies are the ones they [those who manage the world economic system, including the European socialist subsystem] readily see and understand as affecting them and for which they are trained and attuned to finding solutions." [11, p. 8]

The intellectual paradigm of the international economic order influences their thinking. The record of the International Monetary Fund in Latin America and the World Bank's export development advice "can only be explained rationally in this context—it does not stem either from malevolence or stupidity." [11, p. 8]

An even more fundamental issue related to international economic planning, one certainly more ominous in its implications, is the destructive and ever spiraling arms race. Resources of the major industrial powers are drawn into this in a ratio of about $25 in armaments to every $1 of public aid expenditure. It is rather meaningless to speak of a "decade of development" with such a misuse of capital and human resources. And not only are resources of the industrial powers dissipated in this buildup of destructive weapons, but the resources of the developing countries too are misallocated in the process.

References

[1] Alonso, William. "Urban and Regional Imbalances in Economic Development." *Economic Development and Cultural Change* 17 (1968): 1-14.

[2] Arévalo, Luis. "The Legal Insecurity of Rural Property in Colombia: A Case Study of the Notarial and Registry Systems." Ph.D. dissertation, University of Wisconsin, 1970.

[3] Barraclough, Solon. "Rural Development and Employment Prospects in Latin America." Paper presented at Second Conference on Urbanization and Work in Modernizing Areas, St. Thomas, Virgin Islands, November 2-4, 1967.

[4] Barraclough, Solon and Arthur Domike. "Agrarian Structure in Seven Latin American Countries." *Land Economics* 42 (1966): 391-424.

[5] Domike, Arthur. "Industrial and Agricultural Employment Prospects in Latin America." Paper presented at Second Conference on Urbanization and Work in Modernizing Areas, St. Thomas, Virgin Islands, November 2-4, 1967.

[6] Davis, L. Harlan. *United States Assistance to Agriculture in Latin America through the Agency for International Development.* Land Tenure Center Paper, no. 71. Madison, Wis.: University of Wisconsin, 1970.

[7] Dorner, Peter. "Land Tenure Reform and Agricultural Development in Latin America." Presented to Subcommittee on International Finance of the Committee on Banking and Currency, U.S. House of Representatives, 89th U.S. Congress, 2d sess., August 29, 1966.

[8] —— and Herman Felstehausen. "Agrarian Reform and Employment: The Colombian Case." *International Labour Review* 102 (1970): 221-240.

[9] Falcon, Walter P. "The Green Revolution: Generations of Problems." *American Journal of Agricultural Economics* 52 (1970): 698-710.

[10] Felstehausen, Herman. "Local Government and Rural Service Barriers to Economic Development in Colombia." Mimeographed. Bogotá, June 1968. Published in Spanish by the Secretary of Agriculture of Antioquia, Medellín as Special Publication, no. 85, September 1968.

[11] Green, Reginald Herbold. "The International Economic System and Development: Some Limitations of a Special Case." Mimeographed. Dar es Salaam: Economic Research Bureau, University College. This paper was delivered to the Columbia University Conference on International Economic Development, Williamsburg, Virginia and New York, February 15-21, 1970.

[12] Hauser, Philip M. "The Social, Economic, and Technological Problems of Rapid Urbanization." In *Industrialization and Society,* edited by Bert F. Hoselitz and Wilbert E. Moore. UNESCO, 1963.

[13] International Maize and Wheat Improvement Center. *The Puebla Project, 1967-69.* Mexico City, 1969.

[14] Johnston, Bruce F. "Agricultural Development and Economic Transformation: A Comparative Study of the Japanese Experience." *Food Research Studies* 3 (1962): 223-276.

[15] ——— and Soren T. Nielson. "Agricultural Structural Transformation in a Developing Economy." *Economic Development and Cultural Change* 14 (1966): 279-301.

[16] Kautsky, John H., ed. *Political Change in Underdeveloped Countries: Nationalism and Communism.* New York: John Wiley and Sons, 1962.

[17] Kuznets, Simon. *Modern Economic Growth: Rate, Structure, and Spread.* New Haven: Yale University Press, 1966.

[18] ———. "Quantitative Aspects of the Economic Growth of Nations: Distribution of Income by Size." *Economic Development and Cultural Change* 11, no. 2, Part 2 (1963): 1-80.

[19] *The People Left Behind: Report by the President's National Advisory Commission on Rural Poverty.* Washington, D.C.: U.S. Government Printing Office, 1967.

[20] Thiesenhusen, William C. "Population Growth and Agricultural Employment in Latin America with Some U.S. Comparisons." *American Journal of Agricultural Economics* 51 (1969): 735-752.

[21] ———. *A Suggested Policy for Industrial Reinvigoration in Latin America.* Land Tenure Center Paper, no. 72. Madison, Wis.: University of Wisconsin, 1970.

[22] United Nations, Economic Commission for Latin America. *The Economic Development of Latin America in the Post-War Period.* E/Cn.12/659, Rev. 1. New York: United Nations, 1964.

[23] ———. *Economic Survey of Latin America, 1968.* E/Cn.12/825. Lima, 1969.

[24] ———. "Income Distribution in Latin America." *Economic Bulletin for Latin America* 12, no. 2 (1968): 38-60.

[25] ———. "Small Scale Industry in the Development of Latin America." *Economic Bulletin for Latin America* 12, no. 1 (1967): 63-103.